GW01219226

# SAMUEL JOHNSON

# Samuel Johnson

## *The Arc of the Pendulum*

FREYA JOHNSTON AND
LYNDA MUGGLESTONE

OXFORD
UNIVERSITY PRESS

# OXFORD
**UNIVERSITY PRESS**

Great Clarendon Street, Oxford, OX2 6DP,
United Kingdom

Oxford University Press is a department of the University of Oxford.
It furthers the University's objective of excellence in research, scholarship,
and education by publishing worldwide. Oxford is a registered trade mark of
Oxford University Press in the UK and in certain other countries

© Oxford University Press 2012

The moral rights of the authors have been asserted

First Edition published in 2012

Impression: 2

British Library Cataloguing in Publication Data

Data available

Library of Congress Cataloging in Publication Data

Data available

ISBN 978–0–19–965434–5

Printed and bound by CPI Group (UK) Ltd, Croydon, CR0 4YY

# *Acknowledgments*

Thanks are due to the John Fell Oxford University Press Fund for supporting the tercentenary conference 'Johnson at 300', held at Pembroke College, Oxford, in 2009, at which some of these chapters originated. We would also like to thank the News International Fund of the Faculty of English, University of Oxford, for additional assistance with research costs; the readers of Oxford University Press for their helpful comments and suggestions on the original proposal for the volume; and our copy-editor, Richard Mason. We are grateful to The Bodleian Libraries, The University of Oxford, for permission to use the image from Renati Descartes, *Opera Philosophica*, 2 vols. (1650). Shelfmark: F1. 51 Line, Fol. 93', and to The Lewis Walpole Library, Yale University, for permission to reproduce William Walker's engraving of *A Literary Party at Sir Joshua Reynolds's* by James Doyle (1848).

# Contents

# Note on Texts and Short Titles

The following short titles are used throughout the volume:

| | |
|---|---|
| *Dictionary* | Citations from Johnson's *Dictionary*, unless otherwise specified, are from the first edition: *A Dictionary of the English Language; in which the words are deduced from their originals and illustrated in their different significations by examples from the best writers. To which are prefixed, a history of the language, and an English grammar* by Samuel Johnson (London: for J. and P. Knapton, T. and T. Longman, C. Hitch and L. Hawes, A. Millar, and R. and J. Dodsley, 1755) |
| *Hawkins* | Sir John Hawkins, *The Life of Samuel Johnson, LL.D.*, ed. O M Brack, Jr. (Athens: University of Georgia Press, 2009) |
| *Hazlitt* | *The Complete Works of William Hazlitt in Twenty-One Volumes: Centenary Edition*, ed. P. P. Howe (London: J. M. Dent, 1930–4) |
| *Johnsonian Miscellanies* | *Johnsonian Miscellanies*, ed. George Birkbeck Hill, 2 vols. (Oxford: Clarendon Press, 1897) |
| *Letters* | *The Letters of Samuel Johnson: The Hyde Edition*, ed. Bruce Redford, 5 vols. (Princeton: Princeton University Press, 1992–4) |
| *Life* | *Boswell's Life of Johnson; Together with Boswell's Journal of a Tour to the Hebrides and Johnson's Diary of a Journey into North Wales*, ed. George Birkbeck Hill, revised and enlarged by L. F. Powell, 6 vols., 2nd edn (Oxford: Clarendon Press, 1971) |
| *Life of Savage* | Samuel Johnson, *Life of Savage* (1744), ed. Clarence Tracy (Oxford: Clarendon Press, 1971) |
| *Lives* | Samuel Johnson, *The Lives of the Most Eminent English Poets; with Critical Observations on their Works*, ed. Roger Lonsdale, 4 vols. (Oxford: Clarendon Press, 2006) |
| *Pope* | *The Twickenham Edition of the Poems of Alexander Pope*, ed. John Butt, 11 vols. (London: Methuen, 1939–69): <br> I: *Pastoral Poetry and An Essay on Criticism*, eds. E. Audra and Aubrey Williams (1961) <br> III.i: *An Essay on Man*, ed. Maynard Mack (1950) <br> VII: *The Iliad of Homer*, ed. Maynard Mack (1967) |

*Shaw-Piozzi*   William Shaw, *Memoirs of the Life and Writings of the Late Dr Samuel Johnson; Hester Lynch Piozzi, Anecdotes of the Late Samuel Johnson, LL.D.*, ed. Arthur Sherbo (London: Oxford University Press, 1974)

*Thraliana*   *Thraliana: The Diary of Mrs Hester Lynch Thrale, Later Mrs Piozzi, 1776–1809*, ed. Katherine C. Balderston, 2 vols., 2nd edn (Oxford: Clarendon Press, 1951)

*Yale*   *The Yale Edition of the Works of Samuel Johnson*, eds. John Middendorf et al. (New Haven and London: Yale University Press, 1958–):

I: *Diaries, Prayers, and Annals*, ed. E. L. McAdam, Jr., with Donald and Mary Hyde (1958)

II: *The Idler and The Adventurer*, eds. W. J. Bate, John M. Bullit, and L. F. Powell, 2nd edn (1970)

III–V: *The Rambler*, eds. W. J. Bate and Albrecht B. Strauss (1969)

VI: *Poems*, ed. E. L. McAdam, Jr., with George Milne (1964; repr. 1975)

VII–VIII: *Johnson on Shakespeare*, ed. Arthur Sherbo (1969)

IX: *A Journey to the Western Islands of Scotland*, ed. Mary Lascelles (1971)

X: *Political Writings*, ed. Donald J. Greene (1977)

XIV: *Sermons*, eds. Jean Hagstrum and James Gray (1978)

XVI: *Rasselas and Other Tales*, ed. Gwin J. Kolb (1990)

XVII: *A Commentary on Mr Pope's Principles of Morality, or Essay on Man (A Translation from the French)*, ed. O M Brack, Jr. (2004)

XVIII: *Johnson on the English Language*, eds. Gwin J. Kolb and Robert DeMaria, Jr. (2005)

XXI–III: *The Lives of the Poets*, ed. John H. Middendorf (2010)

# List of Contributors

**Charlotte Brewer** is Professor of English Language and Literature at Hertford College, University of Oxford. She has written extensively on the *OED* and on dictionaries more widely. Her book *Treasure-House of the Language: The Living OED* was published by Yale University Press in 2007 and she is now working on *OED*'s treatment of 'great writers' (e.g. Shakespeare, Jane Austen, and others). Previous publications include *Editing Piers Plowman: The Evolution of the Text* (Cambridge University Press, 1996).

**Philip Davis** is Professor of English Literature at the University of Liverpool. His books include *In Mind of Johnson* (Athlone, 1983), *The Experience of Reading* (Routledge, 1992), *Sudden Shakespeare* (Athlone, 1996), *Real Voices: On Reading* (Macmillan, 1997), *The Victorians* (Oxford University Press, 2002), *Shakespeare Thinking* (Continuum, 2007), and *Bernard Malamud: A Writer's Life* (Oxford University Press, 2010). He is general editor of a forthcoming series for Oxford University Press, The Literary Agenda, on the study of literature in the twenty-first century.

**Robert DeMaria, Jr.** is the Henry Noble MacCracken Professor of English at Vassar College, Poughkeepsie, NY. He is the author of *Johnson's Dictionary and the Language of Learning* (Clarendon Press, 1986), *The Life of Samuel Johnson* (Blackwell, 1993), and *Samuel Johnson and the Life of Reading* (Johns Hopkins University Press, 1997). With Gwin Kolb he edited *Johnson on the English Language*, volume 18 in the *Yale Edition of the Works of Samuel Johnson* (Yale University Press, 2005), and he is now the general editor of the Edition. He is also the editor of the *Johnsonian News Letter*. Outside the Johnsonian world, DeMaria has edited several anthologies and the Penguin edition of *Gulliver's Travels* (2001). He is currently editing, with two colleagues, the *Blackwell Companion to British Literature* and, with another two colleagues, *The Yale Anthology of the Works of Samuel Johnson*.

**David Fairer** is Professor of Eighteenth-Century English Literature at the University of Leeds. His most recent book, *Organising Poetry: The Coleridge Circle 1790–1798* (Oxford University Press, 2009), traces the development of English poetry during the 1790s, building on the concerns of his previous study, *English Poetry of the Eighteenth Century, 1700–1789* (Longman, 2003). He has edited *The Correspondence of Thomas Warton* (University of Georgia Press, 1995) and the first complete printing of Warton's *History of English Poetry* (Routledge, 1998), and has edited with Christine Gerrard *Eighteenth-Century Poetry: An Annotated Anthology* (Blackwell, 2nd edn, 2003).

**Isobel Grundy** is a Fellow of the Royal Society of Canada and a Professor Emeritus at the University of Alberta. Her publications include *Samuel Johnson: New*

*Critical Essays* (edited for Vision Press and Barnes and Noble, 1984), *Samuel Johnson and the Scale of Greatness* (Leicester University Press and Georgia University Press, 1986), *The Feminist Companion to Literature in English: Women Writers from the Middle Ages to the Present* (with Virginia Blain and Patricia Clements; Batsford and Yale University Press, 1990), and *Lady Mary Wortley Montagu* (Clarendon Press, 1999). Most recent is *Orlando: Women's Writing in the British Isles from the Beginnings to the Present* (edited with Susan Brown and Patricia Clements), an electronic work of literary history published online by Cambridge University Press in 2006—http://www.cambridge.org/online/orlandoonline/—and revised and expanded at six-monthly intervals.

**Freya Johnston** is a University Lecturer and Tutorial Fellow in English Language and Literature at St Anne's College, Oxford. She is the author of *Samuel Johnson and the Art of Sinking, 1709–1791* (Oxford University Press, 2005), and of various essays and chapters on Johnson, Austen, and their contemporaries. She is general co-editor, with Matthew Bevis, of *The Cambridge Edition of the Novels of Thomas Love Peacock* (Cambridge University Press, forthcoming 2015).

**Lawrence Lipking** is Emeritus Professor at Northwestern University, where he was Chester D. Tripp Professor of Humanities from 1979 to 2007. His books include *The Ordering of the Arts in Eighteenth-Century England* (Princeton University Press, 1970), *The Life of the Poet* (Chicago University Press, 1981; Christian Gauss Award), *Abandoned Women and Poetic Tradition* (Chicago University Press, 1988), and *Samuel Johnson: The Life of an Author* (Harvard University Press, 1998). He has edited *Modern Literary Criticism 1900–1970* (Atheneum, 1972; with A. Walton Litz), the section on the Restoration and the Eighteenth Century in *The Norton Anthology of English Literature* (Norton, 1974–2006), and *High Romantic Argument: Essays for M. H. Abrams* (Cornell University Press, 1981). His current project, 'What Galileo Saw: Imagining the Scientific Revolution,' analyzes relations between the arts and sciences in the early seventeenth century.

**James McLaverty** is Emeritus Professor of Textual Criticism at Keele University. In 2000 he saw the late David Fleeman's *A Bibliography of Samuel Johnson* (Oxford University Press) through the press and currently serves as textual adviser to *The Cambridge Edition of the Works of Jonathan Swift*.

**Lynda Mugglestone** is Professor of the History of English at Oxford University, and Fellow and Tutor in English at Pembroke College. She has published widely on language (including the history and social and cultural roles of dictionaries), with a particular focus on the eighteenth and nineteenth centuries. Recent work includes: *Lexicography and the OED: Pioneers in the Untrodden Forest* (Oxford University Press, 2000); *Lost for Words: The Hidden History of the Oxford English Dictionary* (Yale University Press, 2005); *'Talking Proper': The Rise of Accent as Social Symbol* (Oxford University Press, 2nd edn, 2003; revised paperback edn, 2007); and *Dictionaries: A Very Short Introduction* (Oxford University Press, 2011). She is editor of *The Oxford History of English* (Oxford University Press, 2006, 2007, 2012).

**John Mullan** is Professor of English at University College London. His books include *Sentiment and Sociability: The Language of Feeling in the Eighteenth Century* (Oxford University Press, 1990), *How Novels Work* (Oxford University Press, 2006), and *Anonymity: A Secret History of English Literature* (Faber and Faber, 2007). His World's Classics edition of Samuel Johnson's *Lives of the Poets* was published in 2010.

**Adam Phillips** is a psychoanalyst and writer, and a Visiting Professor in the English Department at the University of York.

**John Richetti** is A.M. Rosenthal Professor (Emeritus) of English at the University of Pennsylvania. He has lately edited and contributed to *The Cambridge Companion to Daniel Defoe* (Cambridge University Press, 2008) and in 2005 published *The Life of Daniel Defoe: A Critical Biography* (Blackwell). He has also edited *The Cambridge History of English Literature: 1660–1780* (Cambridge University Press, 2005). In 2011 he received a Mellon Emeritus Fellowship to work on his new project, Performance in 18th-Century English Verse.

**Philip Smallwood** is Emeritus Professor of English at Birmingham City University and Visiting Fellow in the School of Humanities at Bristol University. He is the author of books and essays on the history and theory of modern and eighteenth-century criticism including *Reconstructing Criticism: Pope's 'Essay on Criticism' and the Logic of Definition* (Bucknell University Press, 2003), *Johnson's Critical Presence: Image, History, Judgment* (Ashgate, 2004), *Critical Occasions: Dryden, Pope, Johnson, and the History of Criticism* (AMS Press, 2011), and is co-editor of the unpublished cultural and critical manuscripts of the British philosopher R. G. Collingwood (Oxford University Press, 2005). He co-edited, with Greg Clingham, the volume of tercentenary essays *Samuel Johnson after 300 Years* (Cambridge University Press, 2009).

**Jane Steen** undertook graduate research at Cambridge on Johnson's Anglicanism. She was subsequently ordained in the Church of England and is now the Canon Chancellor of Southwark Cathedral and the Canon Theologian of the Diocese of Southwark. She has spoken on Johnson at academic conferences and published articles on his faith and his *Dictionary*.

**Howard D. Weinbrot** is a Reader at the Huntington Library, and is Ricardo Quintana Professor of English Emeritus, and William Freeman Vilas Research Professor Emeritus in the College of Letters and Science at the University of Wisconsin, Madison. His latest book is *Literature, Religion, and the Evolution of Culture 1660–1780* (Johns Hopkins University Press, 2012). He is co-editor of the forthcoming *Yale Anthology of the Works of Samuel Johnson*.

# 1

# Johnson's Pendulum: Introduction

*Freya Johnston and Lynda Mugglestone*

In William Hazlitt's lecture 'On the Periodical Essayists' (1819), Samuel Johnson stands as the epitome of bad writing. Convicted as both formal and formulaic, artificially elevated and unnatural, Johnson is an author 'upon stilts,' his 'pomp of diction' fixed at a level above the commonplace and spontaneous. Such 'monotony of style,' Hazlitt argues, 'produces an apparent monotony of ideas. What is really striking and valuable, is lost in the vain ostentation and circumlocution of the expression' (*Hazlitt* VI.101).

Hazlitt's embodiment of 'true eloquence' was instead found in Edmund Burke (*Hazlitt* XII.228). Whereas Johnson is the 'elephant,' heavy-footed and monotonous, Burke is agile and adventurous, a 'chamois' (or mountain antelope) whose prose ascends in unpredictable directions, immediately responsive to the terrain on which it moves (*Hazlitt* VI.101, XII.10). Other metaphorical identities strengthen the opposition Hazlitt forges between them. Burke is 'forked and playful as the lightning,' he notes in 'On Reading Old Books' (1821); Burke is 'crested like the serpent,' able to strike and move, to challenge and surprise (*Hazlitt* XII.228).

Such metaphors point towards a sharply divided aesthetic. As Tom Paulin observes, both motion and nature describe critical values that are central to Hazlitt's writing.[1] The elephant, unlike the serpent, cannot dart, nor does its characteristic pattern of movement evoke the flexible sinuosity of Burke. Still less is the elephant able to dazzle with lightning's abrupt brilliance. For the writer 'upon stilts,' movement is constrained and restricted, opposed to the 'airy, flighty, adventurous' and the 'increased or varying impulse' for which Burke's prose is cherished (*Hazlitt* XII.10).

In a further elision of nature in favor of the artificial and mechanical, Hazlitt turns to the pendulum as a means of depicting Johnson's prose style: 'the close of the period follows as mechanically as the oscillation of a pendulum, the sense is balanced with the sound; each sentence, revolving round its centre of gravity, is contained within itself like a couplet, and each paragraph forms itself into a stanza' (*Hazlitt* VI.102). Incapable of the kinetic abruptness Hazlitt prizes in the work of Burke, Marlowe, and Swift,[2] Johnson's pendulum is self-evidently negative. Its emblematic properties suggest the restrictive and confined; oscillating with predictable regularity, its movement is circumscribed within a particular and narrow axis. As it is denied flexibility or creative response, so it is rendered constitutionally incapable of latitude and compromise. Johnson is duly configured as an automaton who merely rebounds from one position to its opposite extreme: 'he never encourages hope, but he counteracts it by fear; he never elicits a truth, but he suggests some objection in answer to it.' Still worse, 'he seizes and alternately quits the clue of reason' (*Hazlitt* VI.102).

Johnson is, Hazlitt asserts, the 'complete balance-master,' a writer who moves between established patterns of opposition and contrast, as well as fatally enclosing himself within antitheses that, by their nature, preclude advance. If Johnson as a speaker remains largely exempt from such charges ('when he threw aside his pen...he became not only learned and thoughtful, but acute, witty, humorous, natural,' *Hazlitt* VI.103), Johnson the writer is lambasted for his 'monotonous and balanced mode of composition' and for the 'mechanical recurrence of the same rise and fall in the clauses of his sentences' (*Hazlitt* XII.6).[3]

Hazlitt's metaphorical censure illustrates what was, at that point, a relatively new figurative sense of *pendulum* (the *Oxford English Dictionary*'s first example dates from 1765).[4] In other ways, however, Hazlitt merely consolidates—albeit in memorable form—what was already a popular critical response to Johnson. James Boswell noted that the Scottish critic Hugh Blair had 'animadverted on the Johnsonian style as too pompous' in his lectures on rhetoric at Edinburgh in 1777 (*Life* III.172). Blair had seized, too, on Johnson's fondness for antithesis, for the predictable patterns of opposition and contrast that seemed to define the true Johnsonese. Where Addison's *Spectator* 411 (1712) had asserted that, for those who do not know 'how to be idle and innocent...their very first Step out of Business is into Vice or Folly,' Blair conjectured that Johnson would write: 'Their very first step out of the regions of business is into the perturbations of vice, or the vacuity of folly' (*Life* III.172). In this imagined Johnsonian version of Addison, both syntax and sense move in established forms of contrast, the appositional genitive being one of Johnson's stylistic hallmarks: not only is vice weighed against folly, but perturbation against vacuity.

Jane Austen toys with similar Johnsonian patterns in her teenage skit 'Jack and Alice' (*c.*1790). Her character, Lady Williams, in whom 'every virtue met,' is said to be 'Tho' Benevolent and Candid,' also 'Generous and sincere; Tho' Pious and Good, she was Religious and amiable, and Tho' Elegant and Agreable, she was Polished and Entertaining.'[5] Lady Williams's uniformly praiseworthy qualities are elaborated in a series of false oppositions, as if to say 'on the one hand this, on the other hand this.' Whereas the syntactic structures promise meaningful comparisons and oppositions—perhaps even the emergence of psychological contradictions—the wholly conventional content is too much of a piece. Rather than demonstrate the speaker's nicety of distinction, the balancing pairs ('Benevolent'/'Generous,' 'Candid'/'sincere,' 'Pious'/'Religious,' 'Good'/'amiable,' 'Elegant'/'Polished,' 'Agreeable'/'Entertaining'), coupled with the adversative 'Tho,' create first bafflement, then nothingness. Behind the plethora of stock literary compliments, is there anything to this character at all? Why would anyone try to adjudicate between qualities so close to one another?

Johnson praised John Dryden's criticism for being 'so artfully variegated with successive representations of opposite probabilities...the criticism of Dryden is the criticism of a poet' (*Lives* I.412). But it is those 'successive representations of opposite probabilities' in Johnson himself to which Hazlitt repeatedly objects, and which Austen seizes as ripe for parody. In the description of Lady Williams, a cluster of synonyms masquerades as oppositions; conversely, later in the tale, a cluster of oppositions masquerade as synonyms: 'I shall be miserable without you—t'will be a most pleasant tour to you—I hope you'll go; if you do I'm sure t'will be the Death of me,' Lady Williams declares upon the threatened departure of her friend to Bath.[6] A picture that comically aspires to wholeness disintegrates into one of confusion and then vacuity.

Within as well as after Johnson's lifetime, his perceived 'adherence to contradictions' amounted to a critical commonplace, picked out for negative comment in James Thomson Callender's *Deformities of Dr Johnson* (1782),[7] and in Robert Anderson's *Life of Samuel Johnson* (1795), where 'frequent paradox' and 'irreconcilable contradictions' are specified as features of Johnson's style.[8] 'No man who writes naturally, could shape his sentences with such uniformity,' argued Arthur Browne in 1798, outlining 'a prescription for composing in the Johnsonian manner.' Johnson, he added, seemed 'ready at any time to submit to his love of contradiction and affectation of superiority.'[9] For John Ruskin, writing in the 1880s, 'Johnsonian symmetry and balance in sentences intended...to cleave an enemy's chest, or drive down the oaken pile of a principle' seemed overwhelmingly hostile, amounting to a form of stylistic imprisonment that Ruskin himself spent years trying to escape.[10]

Hazlitt's image of the Johnsonian pendulum, bound in an apparently infinite series of oppositions, can therefore seem wholly apt. In the

'Preface' to the *Dictionary*, 'praise' is set against 'reproach' and the 'budding' of language against its inevitable 'falling away' (*Yale* XVIII.73, 110). In *Rambler* 158, the writer 'that reveals too much' is juxtaposed with the writer 'that promises too little'; 'he that never irritates the intellectual appetite' is countered by one 'that immediately satiates it' (*Yale* V.80). Each, Johnson adds, 'equally defeats his own purpose.' For Clarence Tracy, antithesis likewise 'rings through' Johnson's *Life of Savage* (1744): 'he scarcely ever mentioned one of Savage's merits without afterwards balancing it with a weakness, or mentioned a weakness without balancing it with a merit' (*Life of Savage*, xviii). Tracy's oppositional patterning here paraphrases Johnson's own chiastic summary of Savage's character, in a sentence that rebounds on itself in order to express the trials of befriending such a man: 'It was his peculiar Happiness, that he scarcely ever found a Stranger, whom he did not leave a Friend; but it must likewise be added, that he had not often a Friend long, without obliging him to become a Stranger' (*Life of Savage*, 60). The oppositional relationship of one thing to another is clear. Yet the experience of reading such a sentence, at once resolute and inconclusive, is also disorientating. 'Friend' and 'Stranger' coexist uncomfortably; the contrast they enforce is neither neat nor balanced. The 'Stranger' can become a 'Friend,' and then perhaps resume, in some sense, the status of the 'Stranger,' but more is at stake than the simple movement from one to the other and back again. What has been known cannot, in reality, become unknown; to be no longer a 'Friend' invites new thoughts about what it means to be a 'Stranger.' In this light, Hazlitt's readings of Johnson's prose can seem disconcertingly inadequate. As Sir John Hawkins had earlier stressed, in 1787: 'In all Johnson's disquisitions, whether argumentative or critical, there is a certain even-handed justice that leaves the mind in a strange perplexity' (*Hawkins*, 290).

Both Johnson and the image of the pendulum by which he was condemned by Hazlitt can therefore invite and reward further scrutiny. Hazlitt may have construed the pendulum in terms of its balanced certainties and recursive oppositions; conversely, for earlier writers, it could be made to challenge received opinion, revealing the ambiguities and cross-currents of knowledge. As the *Dictionary* confirms, Johnson did not always identify the pendulum with monotony, precision, uniformity, or rigidity. Take, for instance, Johnson's citation from John Locke, which he included in his entry for *swing*: 'Men use a pendulum, as a more steady and regular motion than that of the earth; yet if any one should ask how he certainly knows that the two successive *swings* of a pendulum are equal, it would be very hard to satisfy him.' These words, for Johnson, illustrate not certainty but flexibility, providing authoritative evidence for the definition of *swing* as 'Motion of any thing hanging loosely.' Johnson's choice of quotation under *swing* in the sense 'To wave to and fro hanging loosely' is similar. Here, too, the pendulum figures prominently: 'I tried if a pendulum would *swing* faster, or continue *swinging* longer in our receiver, in case of exsuction of the air, than otherwise,' states Robert Boyle.

Johnson's definition of *pendulum* itself centres on the characteristic pattern of movement by which the mechanism 'may easily swing backwards and forwards.' While this may suggest uniformity ('Upon the bench I will so handle 'em,/That the vibration of this pendulum/Shall make all taylors yards of one/Unanimous opinion,' as the accompanying citation from Samuel Butler's *Hudibras* [1663–78] affirms), Johnson's related conception of *balance* incorporates marked freedom of movement, involving the act of comparison as well as a degree of hesitation between two opposing positions: 'To hesitate; to fluctuate between equal motives, as a balance plays when charged with equal weights' (definition of *balance, v. n.*). Even within Johnson's working methods for the *Dictionary*, if balance is specified as an ideal, it cannot be assumed to be either regular or predictable in its realization: 'The rigour of interpretative lexicography requires that *the explanation, and the thing explained, should always be reciprocal.*' And yet, Johnson adds, 'this I have endeavoured, but could not always attain' (*Yale* XVIII.91).

Critical developments in the eighteenth-century investigation of time and longitude shared this recognition that the pendulum's mechanism, however regular it might seem, was not tantamount to enslavement.[11] 'The Hope of an accurate Clock or Time-keeper is...specious,' as Johnson wrote in *An Account of An Attempt to Ascertain the Longitude at Sea* (1755);[12] the pendulum was too flexible, too responsive to movement, to resolve the problem of longitude. Rather than indicating the enclosed and rigidly calibrated, the pendulum, across a range of contexts, is employed to suggest not only the capacity for movement but also the potential for human mutability and variation. To Byron, writing a year before Hazlitt's 'On the Periodical Essayists,' it seemed a wholly appropriate image in which to sum up the contrarieties and caprice inherent in all human beings: 'Man!/Thou pendulum betwixt a smile and tear.'[13] For Burke himself, the pendulum stood for change and a wide responsiveness to external conditions: 'if after first putting it in motion in one direction, you push it into another, it can never reassume the first direction; because it can never move itself, and consequently it can have but the effect of that last motion; whereas, if in the same direction you act upon it several times, it will describe a greater arch, and move a longer time.'[14] As here, the pendulum could vary, articulating wide or narrow movements, depending on what had impelled each individual trajectory.

If the pendulum is not always what it might seem, neither is Johnson's writing. The sense of a double movement within his prose can, as some critics have observed, be liberating rather than constraining, energizing rather than flattening. Thomas Tyers drew attention as early as 1784 to Johnson's ability to say 'common things in the newest manner' (*Johnsonian Miscellanies* II.366), indicating a 'process of mind' that Walter Jackson Bate glosses as 'the original shuffling of perspectives...surprising us with elements we had overlooked or forgotten.'[15] Tyers's pre-emptive challenge to the predictabilities of movement by which Hazlitt later characterized Johnson was echoed in twentieth-century criticism. Antithesis, for Lawrence Lipking, confirms the presence of a 'double register,' as well as the potential for a 'double voice' in Johnson's work, freighted with unresolved oppositions and critical tension.[16] Bate likewise attends to what he terms Johnson's 'bisociative' ability to bring together 'two different frames of experience,' in ways that do not simply oscillate to and fro, backwards and forwards, in a predetermined pattern of style, meaning, or ideas.[17] As Tracy writes of the *Life of Savage*, Johnson's habitual alternations operate in complex ways, partly because they are true to the experience of life. Johnson's syntax exhibits 'the real state of sublunary nature, which partakes of good and evil, joy and sorrow...expressing the course of the world, in which the loss of one is the gain of another' ('Preface' to Shakespeare, *Yale* VII.66).

Critical opinion, in this respect, can seem to manifest a pendulum-like shift of perspective, informing what both Bertrand Bronson[18] and Donald Greene have described as a 'double tradition' of Johnson. As Greene comments, one of the striking characteristics of Johnson's prose seems to be its capacity to generate 'two quite contradictory ways of reading the words on a Johnsonian page'; what for some readers is 'inflated, pompous verbosity' is, for others, testimony to 'exuberant...concrete and vivid imagery.'[19] Readings of the Johnsonian pendulum operate within a similar divide. Johnson's potential to embrace rival impulses—a salient feature of his life, work, and reception—begins to seem a matter for celebration rather than complaint.

As the following chapters demonstrate, Hazlitt's brilliantly flawed account of Johnson's pendulum remains open to dispute and revision. The individual contributors to this volume focus on the uses and enjoyments of inconsistency—and the varieties of instability, irresolution, and active change—which are revealed by and within Johnson, as well as in writing about him and his work. Philip Davis in Chapter 5 and Adam Phillips in Chapter 6 engage with the double readings that Johnson's prose contains and encourages, revealing how his syntactic and semantic antitheses are structured not only on opposition but on forms of connection between people, thoughts, and feelings. If Johnsonian antithesis highlights the disparity between two points of view or attitudes to the world, it also acknowledges that such contrasts and oppositions, such rival impulses, are common to us all as individuals. Antithesis is in this context not formulaic, but a faithful likeness of the self-divided human mind, of the contradictions and mutability of daily experience.

Other chapters examine how the stylistic and narrative journeys on which Johnson embarks can be surprising and unpredictable. As Philip Smallwood argues in Chapter 2, Johnson's imaging of time offers a productive way of exploring the 'pleasure in contradiction' presented by his work. Johnson challenges perceptions of time, so that time recalled and computed are often markedly discrepant. Johnson's combative and resigned engagements with time and change, often revealing the kind of 'advance' that Hazlitt denied (*Hazlitt* VI.102), inform Chapter 3, in which Robert DeMaria maps out patterns of stylistic development in Johnson's later prose. Johnson's fundamental openness to opposing positions—and his compelling attraction to what he rejects—occupies John Richetti in Chapter 4. Richetti's Johnson is both dialogic and responsive, practicing a form of rigorous moral examination in which the dyads of antithesis are made to yield patterns of irresolution and a lack of conclusiveness.

Johnson's oppositional tendencies, like Hazlitt's, are most in evidence in his work as critic. John Mullan's Chapter 7 addresses 'fault-finding' in the *Lives of the Poets*. Against a popular culture of 'beauties,' Johnson stresses Dryden's 'pedantick ostentation' and the 'injudicious' selection evident in William Collins's diction (*Lives* II.151, IV.122). Such critical antitheses often place Johnson in the role of *faultfinder*: 'a censurer; an objector,' as he explains in his *Dictionary*. And yet, although faults may be construed in terms of 'deficit' and 'absence,' they can (as Johnson's *Dictionary* confirms), act as 'puzzles' and challenges to a reader—as forms that may, in turn, provoke a critical response.[20] Fault-finding, as Mullan suggests, thereby participates in ideas about the generative interplay of meaning rather than in the diametric opposition of one thing to another. For Johnson, the identification of 'faults' can be positive and negative, located within the appreciative duty of the critic—and removed from the uncritical (and therefore undemanding) apprehension of 'beauty.' Lawrence Lipking's Chapter 8, on genius, offers compatible insights into the value of Johnson's critical apprehension, moving away from the categorical excess of 'panegyrick' (and the empty certainties that this may seem to offer in terms of how genius is conceived). Here, too, the rigidity assumed by Hazlitt fails to be realized in the creative patterning of Johnson's pendulum. Instead, as Lipking argues, '*genius* swings round with a pliancy that might be construed as oscillation or, more positively, as flexibility and balance.' Rather than enact patterns of simple recurrence, of presence and of absence, Johnson's conception of genius is complex and plural.

The unpredictable treatments of character and agency in Johnson's allegorical *Vision of Theodore* and in his life-writing are the subjects of Freya Johnston's Chapter 9 and Jane Steen's Chapter 10. Both chapters stress the force, mobility, and vigilance of Johnson's sympathy, as well as the doubleness of his authorial motivations. Similar potential for doubleness attends Johnson's work on language and lexicography. Charlotte Brewer in Chapter 11 considers gender and balance in the *Dictionary*, examining the pull of evidence from male and female writers. Chapter 12 by Lynda Mugglestone explores the complexity of eighteenth-century responses to Johnson as a lexicographer, and the oppositional discourses that often framed the *Dictionary* (not least when voiced by competing lexicographers). Here, the swing of opinion can be marked, counterbalancing popular assumptions about Johnson's immediate and unquestioned pre-eminence as lexicographer,[21] as well as enabling other narratives of the *Dictionary* and its reception to be explored. Critical renegotiations of texts, readings, and authority inform James McLaverty's Chapter 13. Against Hazlitt's sense of the mechanical foreclosure of Johnson's writing, McLaverty instead stresses Johnson's challenges to stability and certainty. Textual history brings out what is not known and elicits the presence of other forms of 'doubleness' that continue to underpin our sense of Johnson's works.

In Chapter 14, Isobel Grundy tackles the essential unpredictability of the critical pendulum. As she demonstrates, Johnson is a writer unusual in his tendency to attract divergent responses (as well as in his capacity to generate dispute among modern readers). Conversely, readings of Johnson's life, as Howard Weinbrot observes in Chapter 16, often serve to ignore complexity or uncertainty. In another challenge to the trajectories by which Johnson is repeatedly characterized as melancholy and miserable, depressive and depressed ('a most miserable being,' as John Hawkesworth early declared),[22] Weinbrot underlines the need for continued and active rebalancing, here by a renewed emphasis on happiness and solace, on family, and on faith. Other mixed and ambiguous biographical narratives are negotiated by David Fairer in Chapter 15. In this symbiotic account of Johnson's relationship with the Warton brothers, 'elements of mutual stimulus and fruitful provocation, both critical and creative' come to the fore. Familiar images of entrenched opposition are occluded; Johnson appears instead as creative, alert, responsive, and playful.

Metaphors, as Johnson noted, embody doubleness, giving 'two ideas for one' (*Life* III.174). Yet, as he knew only too well, the 'exuberance of signification' to which language is heir rarely submits to rules or confinement (*Yale* XVIII.92). Revealing an uncanny ability to enact their own surprises, metaphors share in such 'exuberance.' Hazlitt may have alighted on the elephant as an apt representation of Johnson's plodding, mono-lithic nature; Hester Lynch Piozzi and her circle, however, had already 'pitched upon the elephant for [Johnson's] resemblance,' arguing that 'the proboscis of that creature was like his mind most exactly, strong to buffet even the tyger, and pliable to pick up even the pin' (*Shaw-Piozzi*, 129). Johnson's sense of the elephant was different again; the *Dictionary*, in an extensive quotation from William Camden's *Remaines concerning Britain* (1605), stresses the elephant's 'sagacity, faithfulness, prudence, and un-derstanding,' of which 'many surprising relations are given.'

That the pendulum is open to new readings and alternative views is part of this same process. 'Whatever else a metaphor may be, it is a rela-tion,' as Christopher Ricks has pointed out.[23] The relation posited by Hazlitt, between the literal pendulum and the apparent rigidities of John-son's style, clearly occupies one kind of trajectory. As the chapters of this volume reveal, however, Johnson's pendulum occupies another, one in which assumed regularity is countered by unexpected directions, and antithesis can serve both to dissolve and unite.

## NOTES

1. See Tom Paulin, *The Day-Star of Liberty: William Hazlitt's Radical Style* (London: Faber and Faber, 1998), 26.
2. See e.g. Hazlitt's praise of Swift's 'honest abruptness' in his essay 'On Swift, Young, Gray, Collins etc' (*Hazlitt* V.112). Johnson 'did not like Swift,' as Hazlitt points out (*Hazlitt* V.110).
3. For Further discussion of Hazlitt and Johnson, see Chapter 5.
4. See *OED pendulum* (n.), sense 3: 'a. *fig.* A person who or thing which oscil-lates between different or opposite positions, as public opinion, personal feeling, a fashion, etc.; an imagined register or measure of such oscillation.' The earliest evidence of its use is taken from James Otis, *A Vindication of the British Colonies against the Aspersions of the Halifax Gentleman [M. Howard] in his Letter to a Rhode-island Friend*, published in 1765: 'To atone for this indelicacy, the next moment the pendulum vibrates as far the other way.'
5. *The Cambridge Edition of the Works of Jane Austen*, ed. Janet Todd, 9 vols. (Cambridge: Cambridge University Press, 2005–9), *Juvenilia*, ed. Peter Sabor (2006), 14.
6. Austen, *Juvenilia*, 27.
7. James Thomson Callender, *Deformities of Dr Samuel Johnson. Selected from his Works* (Edinburgh: W. Creech, T. Longman, 1782), 62.
8. Robert Anderson, *The Life of Samuel Johnson. L.L. D. with Critical Observa-tions on his Works* (London: J. and A. Arch; Edinburgh: Bell & Bradfute, J. Mundell, 1795), 302.
9. Arthur Browne, *Miscellaneous Sketches: or, Hints for Essays* (London: G. G. and J. Robinson, J. Johnson, and R. Faulder, 1798), I.37, 69.

10. John Ruskin, *Præterita: The Autobiography of John Ruskin* [1885–9] (Oxford: Oxford University Press, 1978), 210–11.

11. See Dava Sobel, *Longitude: The True Story of a Lone Genius who Solved the Greatest Scientific Problem of his Time* (London: Fourth Estate, 1995), and Stuart Sherman, *Telling Time: Clocks, Diaries, and English Diurnal Form 1660–1785* (London and Chicago: The University of Chicago Press, 1996); Lynda Mugglestone, 'The Dictionary as Watch,' *The New Rambler* (2007–8) [2010], 70–7.

12. Samuel Johnson, *An Account of an Attempt to Ascertain the Longitude at Sea...* (London: R. Dodsley, 1755), 2.

13. George Gordon, Lord Byron, *Childe Harold's Pilgrimage*, Canto the Fourth (1818), CIX.974–5, in *Selected Poetry of Lord Byron*, ed. Leslie A. Marchand (New York: Modern Library, 2001), 141.

14. Edmund Burke, *A Philosophical Enquiry into the Origin of our Ideas of the Sublime and Beautiful* [2nd edn, 1759], ed. James T. Boulton, rev. edn (Oxford: Basil Blackwell, 1987), 140–1.

15. Walter Jackson Bate, *Samuel Johnson* (London: Chatto & Windus, 1978), 497.

16. Lawrence Lipking, *Samuel Johnson: The Life of an Author* (Cambridge, MA: Harvard University Press, 1998), 243.

17. Bate, *Samuel Johnson*, 497.

18. See Bertrand Bronson, 'The Double Tradition of Johnson,' *English Literary History* 18 (1951), 90–106.

19. Donald Greene, '"Pictures to the Mind": Johnson and Imagery,' in *Johnson, Boswell, and their Circle: Essays Presented to Lawrence Fitzroy Powell, in Honour of his Eighty-Fourth Birthday* (Oxford: Clarendon Press, 1965), 156.

20. See Johnson's *Dictionary*, in which *fault* is anatomized in sense 1 as 'Offence; slight crime; somewhat liable to censure or objection' and in sense 2 as 'Defect; want; absence,' but also as 'Puzzle; difficulty' in Johnson's third, final sense.

21. See e.g. Patrick Hanks's conviction (in 'Johnson and Modern Lexicography,' *International Journal of Lexicography* 18 [2005], 253) that 'Johnson's expectation of malignity was, of course, to be disappointed'; 'His explanations gained universal acceptance, virtually from the outset, as the "correct" meanings or the "true definition" of almost all the words which they define.'

22. See *Johnsonian Miscellanies* II.359: 'Hawkesworth, one of the Johnsonian school, upon being asked, whether Johnson was a happy man...confessed that he looked upon him as a most miserable being.'

23. Christopher Ricks, *Allusion to the Poets* (Oxford: Oxford University Press, 2002), 245.

# 2

## Johnson and Time

*Philip Smallwood*

'Tis with our *Judgments* as our *Watches* ...
Alexander Pope, *An Essay on Criticism*
(1711), l.9 (*Pope* I.239)

Everyone admires the amazing speed and productivity of Samuel Johnson in the matter of publication. We need think only of the papers he so efficiently turned out for the *Rambler* or the *Idler* and the grind of the parliamentary reporting for the *Gentleman's Magazine*. A quick competitive wit and a ready creative intelligence mark poetical compositions that suggest a talent for the extempore.[1] Similar qualities infuse Johnson's conversations with all who engaged in intellectual exchange with him; but he is also, in many ways, a genius in slow motion. 'SLOW RISES WORTH, BY POVERTY DEPRESS'D,' as Johnson laments in l.177 of *London* (1738) (*Yale* VI.56).

Not only did Johnson's professional elevation prove slow, but we also remember him for his succession of busted deadlines—the *Dictionary* that took so much longer than projected; the delays dogging the Shakespeare edition; the spurts and flurries of compositional energy that punctuate periods of lassitude and procrastination, combined with a good deal of traveling about, distracted by other tasks, that characterize the tardy completion of the *Prefaces* to the English poets. Detailing the composition of these late productions, Roger Lonsdale notes that, on a visit to Lichfield in 1777, 'There is no sign that [Johnson] tried, or wished, to start work on his biographies while visiting his birthplace: as he told Mrs Thrale, he loitered, "and what is worse, loitered with very little pleasure. The time has run away, as most time runs, without account, without use, and without memorial"' (*Lives* I.19).[2] Johnson's reckoning with time, and his running the race of the writing life against it, are profoundly connected to life's possibilities and limits, to his religion, to the pleasures of literature, and to his reading experience of writers whose work seemed so much longer than it was. How time is connected to mind is a constant source of imagery and analogy in Johnson's writings, and his comments on all manner of things, persons, and poets are haunted by a sense of the temporal.

Some of Johnson's most famous passages and celebrated sayings (on the prospect of being 'hanged in a fortnight,' for example, *Life* III.167) entail a sense of time and its expiration. Amongst Johnson's various forms of alertness to time, less often recalled, is his commendation of chronology to the teachers of young minds in the *Preface to the Preceptor* (1748). His advice deserves to be better known in circles where courses in English Literature are devised:

> it should be diligently inculcated to the Scholar, that unless he fixes in his Mind some Idea of the Time in which each Man of Eminence lived, and each Action was performed, with some Part of the contemporary History of the rest of the World, he will consume his Life in useless reading, and darken his Mind with a Croud of unconnected Events, his Memory will be perplexed with distant Transactions resembling one another, and his Reflections be like a Dream in a Fever, busy and turbulent, but confused and indistinct.[3]

There is much on the measuring out of time in the work of Johnson, who is reputed to have bought his first watch at the age of fifty-nine.[4] His adjudication between Henry Fielding and Samuel Richardson in 1768, according to the difference between the face of a timepiece and its complex inner workings, is the substance of one oft-quoted critical remark, and this is the more important because relatively little of Johnson's published critical output is devoted to the novel. 'In comparing those two writers,' Boswell records, 'he used this expression: "that there was as great a difference between them as between a man who knew how a watch was made, and a man who could tell the hour by looking on the dial-plate"' (*Life* II.48–9).

Less prominent, perhaps, is the sense in which Johnson grasps the imponderables of time at the level of its philosophy. With this he seems to have been rarely credited—arguably because philosophers and their historians have largely ignored his achievement, though also, as Fred Parker has shown, because the categories made available by historians of philosophy are ones that Johnson does not easily fit.[5] In this chapter I will suggest that Johnson offers nevertheless a conduit to the conceptually elusive nature of time and that its mental experience is a factor in his judgments of literary value. Johnson resists an explanatory formula in order to explain time as such, while one dimension of his sense of time is made available to us through records of the painful, untheorized intimacies of daily experience. But Johnson also brings a high degree of personal detachment to a problem central to philosophy. His concepts lead into later theories and make him party to metaphysical debate. Time remains a central theme of Johnson's work, and the unresolved contradictions entailed in his engagements with time reveal his own nature and that of his subject matter.

A philosophically conscious parallel between on the one hand the material and measurable universe, and on the other the time-inhabited universe of mind, is brought out very eloquently in *Rambler* 8. In a manner directly pertinent to his literary, lexicographical, and editorial labors, Johnson draws attention to the vast discrepancies between the mental time taken to conceive a project and the time needed to carry it out:

> It is said by modern philosophers, that not only the great globes of matter are thinly scattered thro' the universe, but the hardest bodies are so porous, that, if all matter were compressed to perfect solidity, it might be contained in a cube of a few feet. In like manner, if all the employment of life were crowded into the time which it really occupied, perhaps a few weeks, days, or hours, would be sufficient for its accomplishment, so far as the mind was engaged in the performance. (*Yale* III.41)

With, perhaps, something of his own Pembroke College undergraduate swagger in mind, Johnson wrote in his biography of Richard Savage that he admired 'the extent of his knowledge compared with the small time which [Savage] spent in visible endeavours to acquire it' (*Lives* III.186). And the movement of time, as Greg Clingham has shown, is a determinant in Johnson's eloquent memorials of human lives, which found durable meaning in poetry.[6] Time and its tendency to expire, to drag, to betray, to be wasted, to pass, or (as we shall see) to destroy, create the existential structure of Johnson's last great critical work and reflect back on the endurance of a literary life that was not long from its end as composition of the *Lives* was concluded.

Johnson's regret for time's dreadful subtractions and extinctions is painfully felt, and as his diaries and annals show, the metaphorical life of these records gives voice to a personal experience of hard times, and expresses a will to 'endure' that combines difficulty with duration. The 'Annals,' a fragment of autobiography composed in the 1760s, commences with a combination of memorized and reported glimpses of Johnson's precarious birth and boyhood. This includes the recollection of what he must have been told of his early self and even of his pre-natal struggle. The entry is written in the past tense from an advanced adult perspective: '7 SEPTEMBER 1709, I was born at Lichfield. My mother had a very difficult and dangerous labour' ('Annals,' *Yale* I.3). In the course of this record, Johnson reflects on his yet-to-be-born and infant self from the position of middle age, and he relays the common experience that in one's childhood world time passes more slowly, and is more drawn out, than in grown-up life: 'I was with Hawkins but two years, and perhaps four months. The time, till I had computed it, appeared much longer by the multitude of novelties which it supplied, and of incidents, then in my thoughts important, it produced' (*Yale* I.17).

For the young Johnson the crowding of life with new experience elongates time, so that time recalled and computed (or remembered to have been computed) are discrepant. But in the entries dating from 1734 Johnson begins to take temporal stock of experience and the annals reflect the pain of self-examination we find in his diaries, prayers, and occasional letters. For an entry in 1736 under 'Friday, 27th August, 10 at Night,' he writes: 'This day I have trifled away, except that I have attended the school in the morning. I read to night in Rogers's sermons. To night I began the breakfast law anew' (*Yale* I.35).

In this habit of self-accounting, not only the day but the hour of the day bears the burden of emotion. It matters that it is '10 at Night.'[7] Johnson's privacies of self-exposure develop from the conventional way time is divided up and from the names given to the divisions. The 'hours' and the 'days' in the calculus of Johnson's time-awareness are often dogged with anxiety or regret, or an unbearable self-reproach. 'Forgive me,' Johnson prays on 19 November 1752, that 'I have this day neglected the duty which thou hast assigned to it.' And on 1 January 1753 he prays to Almighty God 'who hast continued my life' to 'this day' (*Yale* I.49). The phrases 'the hour of death' and 'the day of judgment' movingly evoke the nomenclature of time that accompanies Johnson's religious observance, his spiritual vulnerability, and the regular tending of his Christian soul. Johnson habitually (as on 1 January 1745) offers a prayer on New Year's Day, and his language captures his characteristic sense of the relation of being to time:

> Grant, O merciful Lord, that thy Call may not be in vain, that my Life may not be continued to encrease my Guilt, and that thy gracious Forbearance may not harden my heart in wickedness. Let me remember, O my God that as Days and Years pass over me, I approach nearer to the Grave where there is no repentance.   (*Yale* I.40–1)

The ratio of an expired past to an unexperienced future changes with time and the suggestion that days and years 'pass over' us offers likewise a literary metaphor of time that Johnson repeats. The essential nature of being is first conceived as static in relation to time's dynamic movement. As we stand still, time moves anyway, and leaves us trailing in its wake. But then, in a characteristically Johnsonian about-turn of perspective, the approach to the grave orientates the shifting nature of being toward an immoveable datum corresponding with the individual's death. For this interval between present time and the moment of one's extinction no language is available—as Johnson suggested in his 'Observations on the Tragedy of Macbeth' (1745), in an editorial note to Shakespeare's 'last syllable of recorded time':

> 'Recorded time' seems to signify the time fixed in the decrees of Heaven for the period of life. The 'record' of 'futurity' is indeed no accurate expression, but as we only know transactions past or present, the language of men affords no term for the volumes of prescience, in which future events may be supposed to be written.   (*Yale* VII.42)

Johnson does not approach death as melodramatically as King Lear, by 'crawling' towards it, but the vital powers are given up bit by bit: 'Days and months pass in a dream,' writes Johnson on 6 April 1777, 'and I am afraid that my memory grows less tenacious, and my observation less attentive' (*Yale* I.267). When time is passing, as Henri Bergson was later to observe, it is we who pass.[8]

Some of the most moving expressions of this temporal self-accounting, including the time of eternity, occur in the period immediately after the death of Johnson's wife on 17 March 1752. On 24 April, Johnson prayed to God that 'by the assistance of thy Holy Spirit I may repent, and be comforted,' and 'obtain that peace which the world cannot give,' and 'pass the residue of my life in humble resignation and cheerful obedience' (*Yale* I.45). That phrase, the 'residue of my life' (the smaller part of the whole of life that is left, the computed remainder, the probable, then the certain minority), is repeated by Johnson in his 1 January prayer of 1753:

> Almighty God, who hast continued my life to this day grant that by the assistance of thy holy spirit I may improve the time which thou shalt grant me to my eternal salvation. Make me to remember to thy glory thy judgements & thy mercies. Make [me] so to consider the loss of my wife whom thou hast taken from me that it may dispose me by thy grace to lead the residue of my life in thy fear.   (*Yale* I.49–50)

Such revelations of Johnson's time-conscious and time-penetrated inner life, and especially his communings with his creator, suggest the consolations available whenever he is read. His imaginative and rhetorical engagement with his emotional nature makes available to philosophical thought insights that are not presented in formal terms as a philosophy. But there is also an impersonal quality to some of his expressions of time that brings Johnson within range of philosophical tradition and suggests a remoteness from the unprocessed and undistanced pain expressed in the annals, diaries, and prayers.

One such moment might be Johnson's tribute to Shakespeare's undimmed durability as a writer in the 'Preface' (1765), where he describes the unusually lasting appeal of the dramatist's comic scenes, beyond, he seems to be saying, that of the celebrated tragic material: 'The sand heaped by one flood is scattered by another, but the rock always continues in its place. The stream of time, which is continually washing the dissoluble fabricks of other poets, passes without injury by the adamant of Shakespeare' (*Yale* VII.70).[9]

Alexander Pope had used the metaphor of 'the stream of time' in his *Essay on Man* (*Pope* III.i.165), while Shakespeare had anticipated this image in lines attributed to the Duke of York from *Henry IV, Part 2*:

> Hear me more plainly.
> I have in equal balance justly weigh'd
> What wrongs our arms may do, what wrongs we suffer;
> And find our griefs heavier than our offences.
> We see, which way the stream of time doth run,
> And are inforc'd from our most Quiet sphere,
> By the rough torrent of occasion.[10]

Sometimes the passage of time's stream transforms into the 'torrent' of Fate, which we are doomed (in l.346) to roll darkling down in *The Vanity of Human Wishes* (1749). Sometimes events in time divert the stream, and disrupt its smooth flow by the turbulence of a conflicted present and the urgent call to action. The metaphor of 'the stream of time' also appears from time to time in other Johnsonian writings. The epigraph of *Rambler* 102 (1751) is quoted (in Latin) from the XVth book of Ovid's *Metamorphoses*. In rendering these lines for English readers, Johnson cites the translation of James Elphinston (*Yale* IV.179), though the passage may also be interpreted for the modern world through John Dryden's elegant version of Ovid from the *Fables Ancient and Modern* (1700):

> For Time no more than Streams, is at a stay:
> The flying Hour is ever on her way;
> And as the Fountain still supplies her store,
> The Wave behind impels the Wave before;
> Thus in successive Course the Minutes run,
> And urge their Predecessor Minutes on,
> Still moving, ever new.   (ll.268–74)[11]

In this gathering of sources the temporal metaphor shifts its terms of comparison, while in the body of the essay Johnson adds the complementary sense of advancing life as an oceanic meander:

> 'Life,' says Seneca, 'is a voyage, in the progress of which, we are perpetually changing our scenes; we first leave childhood behind us, then youth, then the years of ripened manhood, then the better and more pleasing part of old age.' The perusal of this passage, having excited in me a train of reflections

on the state of man, the incessant fluctuation of his wishes, the gradual change of his disposition to all external objects, and the thoughtlessness with which he floats along the stream of time, I sunk into a slumber amidst my meditations, and, on a sudden, found my ears filled with the tumult of labour, the shouts of alacrity, the shrieks of alarm, the whistle of winds, and the dash of waters.   (*Yale* IV.179)

Fluidity, process, interminability, uncertainty of prediction, are all called up by this image of the stream of time, and time assumes at this point an elemental identity, unfixed by calendar or clock.

These are striking expressions, and they engage the enduring perplexity of how, curiously and at once, we can exist in time and yet seem to observe time as it flows 'over' our heads, or 'before us' as a stream viewed from a point high and dry on the adjacent banks. Johnson is drawn to such problems and shares with the philosophy of time an ambition to disentangle them. But he is also a literary artist writing about time, and while his words have philosophical value and effect (without direct influence on philosophers), Johnson's treatment recalls the metaphorical temper of those for whom thought about time is a central theme, as it is for Ovid or Dryden, for example, or for Shakespeare or Proust. Like them, Johnson allows us access to a consciousness of time that has subsequently been partitioned off by the specialized investigations of cosmology, philosophy, or quantum physics. Other literary artists also suggest a contrast with Johnson on the subject of time. 'Time's winged chariot' is a formulation that leaves us in awe of Marvell's glorious conceit.[12] But when confronted with the irony of time by the poetical image, we are onlookers, like the Epicurean deities of Johnson's 'Life of Cowley' who 'never enquired what, on any occasion, they should have said or done; but wrote rather as beholders than partakers of human nature; as Beings looking upon good and evil, impassive and at leisure' (*Lives* I.201). By uniting observer and object, Johnson's writing about time folds us back into our own consciousness. He gives us first hand, as it were, an experience of what it means to be in time and out of time as an intimately shared condition. This condition is no less real for being elusive, ironic, comic, and tragic; it is one and indivisible, as a function of General Nature, indefinable because universal.

More urgent and emotional is the time recalled in Johnson's own poetry as the uncompromising enemy of mental content. Johnson's compulsive marking of the calendar in the annals and diaries of his middle age and late middle age registers a restless and active mind for whom, nevertheless, despair was criminal. For Martin Heidegger, writing in less combative terms than Johnson, the concept of 'Dasein' '"reckons with time" and regulates itself *according to it*.'[13] But for the Johnson of *The Vanity of*

*Human Wishes*, we have not only to reckon but more actively to contend with Time as a destructive agent (the 'antagonist not subject to casualties' of 'He that runs against Time' in the 'Life of Pope' [*Lives* IV.16]). Toward the end of life: 'Time hovers o'er, impatient to destroy/And shuts up all the passages of joy' (ll.259–60, *Yale* VI.104). Time's superintending presence in these lines does not fly as an arrow might in a line from point A to point B, or flow as a stream, but keeps perpetual station. Time is here in suspension above the humanity on which it preys. The second line of the couplet is dominated by its seven monosyllables, and seems exceptionally compacted. Joy has its 'passages' or avenues or channels of expression and reception, but Time's impatience to 'shut' them 'up' suggests how the ledger of life's opportunities falls closed with unnegotiable finality. Time devours its victim in the end, but not without a contest. Johnson's flux of time is restrained by a pessimistic scorn that holds fatalism at bay.

From Time externalized as the hovering agent of annihilation, we can move to the experience of time that pervades Johnson's literary criticism. Here, Johnson's philosophical understanding appears historically akin to the imaginatively produced 'Concept of Time' of the 'Metaphysical Exposition' from Immanuel Kant's *Critique of Pure Reason* (2nd edn, 1787): 'Time is nothing but the form of inner sense,' writes Kant, 'that is, of the intuition of ourselves and of our inner state.' Kant denies that time is something that exists of itself, 'or which inheres in things as an objective determination,' and he goes on to characterize time as 'nothing but the form of our inner intuition.'[14] In Johnson's phrase from the 1765 'Preface' to Shakespeare, time is the 'mode of existence' that is 'most obsequious to the imagination' (*Yale* VII.78). Johnson is using the word 'imagination' here as we might use the word 'consciousness,'[15] and, in adopting the phrase, he is famously defending Shakespeare's ditching of the Renaissance pseudo-classicizing unity of time without damage to the continuity of his plays. Adopting a logic that philosophers would recognize as consistent with their own discipline, Johnson explains why the passage of years is as easily accepted as the passage of minutes or days:

> The time required by the fable elapses for the most part between the acts; for, of so much of the action as is represented, the real and poetical duration is the same.... The drama exhibits successive imitations of successive actions, and why may not the second imitation represent an action that happened years after the first; if it be so connected with it, that nothing but time can be supposed to intervene... a lapse of years is as easily conceived as a passage of hours. (*Yale* VII.77–8)

When carried along by the pace and passion of the action, we do not 'count the clock' (*Yale* VII.77). Here Johnson does not mean to consult the dial-plate on one's watch, but to 'count' the number of tolls of the bell or the chiming of the hour, where the recording of time is audible and takes time, suspending the experience. In that time is 'obsequious to the imagination,' the mind takes causal priority over time's unfixities and perceptual warps:

> A play read, affects the mind like a play acted. It is therefore evident, that the action is not supposed to be real, and it follows that between the acts a longer or shorter time may be allowed to pass, and that no more account of space or duration is to be taken by the auditor of a drama, than by the reader of a narrative, before whom may pass in an hour the life of a hero, or the revolutions of an empire.   (*Yale* VII.79)

The unity of the play is experienced as a coherence without gaps because we keep the past action in our heads as a memory.

Samuel Taylor Coleridge later echoes this famous Johnsonian passage when he claims in 1810 that, so far as Shakespeare has the power of exciting our internal emotions 'as to make us present to the scene in imagination chiefly, he acquires the right and privilege of using time and space as they exist in the imagination, obedient only to the laws which the imagination acts by.'[16] But later enquiry on time's relation to space confirms Johnson's philosophical prescience. In reacting against Kant's sharp line of separation between time and space,[17] for example, Bergson distinguishes between the spatial, in which the elements are mutually exclusive and externally related, and the temporal, in which the quantitative is replaced by the qualitative. 'Space contains only parts of space,' writes Bergson:

> and at whatever point of space we consider the moving body, we shall only get a position...But in time we are compelled to admit that we have...to do with a synthesis which is, so to speak, qualitative, a gradual organization of our successive sensations, a unity resembling that of a phrase in a melody.[18]

This different experience of the 'unity' of time involves a gradual synthetic organization of our successive sensations as not external one to another. Conceived in philosophical terms, Bergson's formulation pinpoints the irrelevance of the Renaissance, pseudo-classical unity of time that Johnson rejects as a critic. Johnson brings a philosophical psychology to a category error in contemporary critical thought, and suggests how Shakespeare's willed or ignorant abandonment of the clock-counting unity of time weaves the seamless fabric of artistic experience. For Johnson, as for W. B. Yeats in 'Sailing to Byzantium' (1927), the markings off of 'what is past, or passing, or to come' collapse within consciousness.[19]

When enjoying Shakespeare, as with other pleasures, time speeds up: 'others please us by particular speeches,' Johnson writes in his 'Preface,' 'but he always makes us anxious for the event, and has perhaps excelled all but Homer in securing the first purpose of a writer, by exciting restless and unquenchable curiosity' (*Yale* VII.83). Yet Johnson's thought on time often speaks of its slowness. This burdensome dragging out of time is ironic, because there is no desire that life should arrive with abnormal swiftness at its terminus, and, in the finite life of the critic, a part of the available whole is used up by the reading of poetry and plays. This time can be measured (as if it were space), and a spatial metaphor of time in fact appears prominently in Johnson's criticism when the time-compressing excitements of Shakespeare are replaced by a more tedious eighteenth-century poetry. Thus Johnson writes in his 'Life of Prior' that the author of *Solomon* (1708) did not discover 'that [the poem] wanted that without which all other [qualities] are of small avail, the power of engaging attention and alluring curiosity.' The passage exhibits the impatient consciousness of wasted time that Johnson brought to negative literary judgments:

> Tediousness is the most fatal of all faults; negligences or errors are single and local, but tediousness pervades the whole; other faults are censured and forgotten, but the power of tediousness propagates itself. He that is weary the first hour, is more weary the second; as bodies forced into motion, contrary to their tendency, pass more and more slowly through every successive interval of space.    (*Lives* III.61)

The experience of empty time is not here made replete by literary pleasure, and Johnson remarks in *Rambler* 41 that 'So few of the hours of life are filled up with objects adequate to the mind of man, and so frequently are we in want of present pleasure or employment, that we are forced to have recourse every moment to the past and the future for supplemental satisfactions, and relieve the vacuities of our being, by recollections of former passages, or anticipation of events to come' (*Yale* III.221). Because its slowness seems to extend unwanted experience, time is oppressive; and when the measurements of time impose themselves too heavily on the conscious mind they contaminate what is left of our lives, recalling the lines from Lucretius where Man is revealed 'Unsatisfy'd with all that Nature brings;/Loathing the present, liking absent things.'[20] Rudyard Kipling wrote of the urgency of the 'unforgiving minute' as the inspiration to pack life full with the immediate living of it;[21] but for Johnson the 'hours of life' are subdivided by 'the weary minutes flagging wings' (*The Vanity of Human Wishes*, l.300; *Yale* VI.105). Whether the time is long or short, linear as an arrow or a stream, or volumetric (and able to be 'filled'), the duplicity of time is at the heart of Johnson's experience.

Stuart Sherman has suggested that time's void for Johnson is 'transformed into a plenum by text.' By this he is referring to the sense of fulfilled purpose, by which Johnson keeps boredom at bay, and that comes from writing down daily experiences of the Western Isles tour in his journal (1775) and in letters to friends. Sherman observes that time, for Johnson, 'is left vacuous,' or is inclined to drag, when no writing is done.[22] But from the evidence of Johnson's criticism, salvation from empty time also depends on the quality of the literary experience available to the reader and this is registered in the capacity of works to compress time, as Shakespeare does, or to slow it down, as does Prior. Johnson's critical imagery suggests that this time, while immeasurable as simply time, symbolizes or analogizes duration by the external, measurable, non-imaginary world of quantities and divisions. When, therefore, Johnson writes of being bored reading Prior, he is employing a literary figuration that restrains metaphysical curiosity in the interests of critical judgment. Time is conceptualized within the science of a three-dimensional world inhabited by 'bodies' subject to inertia and moving through time, in its aspect as space, with measurable, and decreasing, velocity. Johnson represents the inferiority of the poetical experience, its lack of intensity, in relation to the drawn-out experience of time, its extensity. The temporal and the spatial are not confused. Each dimension is necessary to the expression of the other. Johnson repairs experience that philosophy murders to dissect.

Johnson typically relates being to time remedially. There is the unforgiving reality of time's clock and calendar divisions and the anguish that we find in his annals and prayers when the mental calculations are done; but Johnson also has one of the most eloquent accounts in literature of the flux of time, fluid, endless, and indefinable. Johnson tests literary quality against emotions of excitement or boredom, while his advocacy of a 'general nature,' independent of historical time, emphasizes the rich traditions of temporal reflection in his writings. Thus Johnson's philosophical fiction of *Rasselas* (1759), published fifty-nine years after Dryden's rendering of Ovid quoted above, takes the alternate deprivations and healing powers of time as the theme of a philosophical consolation. The situation is the gloomy atmosphere of the travelers' grieving for Pekuah, a young woman presumed dead after a kidnap; the words are spoken by Imlac the poet:

> 'Our minds, like our bodies, are in continual flux; something is hourly lost, and something acquired. To lose much at once is inconvenient to either, but while we glide along the stream of time, whatever we leave behind us is always lessening, and that which we approach increasing in magnitude. Do not suffer life to stagnate; it will grow muddy for want of motion: commit yourself again to the current of the world.' (*Yale* XVI.127)

'Lost' stands against 'acquired' in this passage; 'lessening' is set against 'increasing.' The pendulum swing in this advocacy of self-renewal registers the opposite of mental vagrancy or neurotic vacillation. According to Sherman, Johnson found that 'the imagination, operating upon time, discovers vacuity rather than fullness.'[23] But Sherman may overstate the tragic manifestation of time in Johnson's writings at the expense of its power to recuperate being, a role appreciable in the accelerated 'mingled drama' of Shakespeare where 'the loss of one is the gain of another.' Time is a mode of existence 'obsequious to the imagination,' writes Johnson in his 'Preface' to Shakespeare (*Yale* VII.66), and the imagination itself exists in the condition of time. But in the passage from *Rasselas* 'minds' and 'bodies,' the mental and the corporeal, the temporal and spatial, run together as the Shakespearean 'course [or current] of the world.' And in this collaboration between inward and outward reality, the 'whole system of life is continued in motion' (*Yale* VII.62).

## NOTES

1. But see James McLaverty's Chapter 13, which draws attention to the different recorded versions of poems often thought to have been composed extempore.
2. Johnson refers to his 'vacillation and vagrancy of mind' and determines to 'spend [his] time with more method' (*Yale* I.292).
3. Samuel Johnson, *Prefaces and Dedications*, ed. Allen T. Hazen (New Haven and London: Yale University Press, 1937), 183.
4. See Stuart Sherman, *Telling Time: Clocks, Diaries, and English Diurnal Form, 1660–1785* (Chicago and London: University of Chicago Press, 1996), 191.
5. Fred Parker, ' "We are perpetually moralists": Johnson and Moral Philosophy,' *Johnson After 300 Years*, eds. Greg Clingham and Philip Smallwood (Cambridge: Cambridge University Press, 2009), 15–32.
6. See Greg Clingham, 'Life and Literature in Johnson's *Lives of the Poets*,' *The Cambridge Companion to Samuel Johnson*, ed. Greg Clingham (Cambridge: Cambridge University Press, 1997), 161–91.
7. See also Johnson's letter to Hill Boothby, 30 December 1755 (*Letters* I.117).
8. Henri Bergson, 'Concerning the Nature of Time,' Chapter 3 of *Duration and Simultaneity* (1922); see *Henri Bergson: Key Writings*, eds. Keith Ansell Pearson and John Mullarkey (London: Continuum, 2002), 216.
9. The close relation between comedy and durability appears elsewhere in Johnson's criticism. See e.g. 'Life of Cowley' (*Lives* I.216).
10. *The Plays of William Shakespeare*, ed. Samuel Johnson, 8 vols. (London: Jacob and Richard Tonson et al, 1765), IV.305–6.
11. John Dryden, 'Of the Pythagorean Philosophy,' in *The Works of John Dryden*, eds. H. T. Swedenberg, Jr., et al., 20 vols. (Berkeley, Los Angeles, and

London: University of California Press, 1956–2002), VII.492. See also David Hopkins, *Conversing with Antiquity: English Poets and the Classics, from Shakespeare to Pope* (Oxford: Oxford University Press, 2010), 238–49.

12. 'To his Coy Mistress,' l.22, *The Oxford Authors: Andrew Marvell*, eds. Frank Kermode and Keith Walker (Oxford: Oxford University Press, 1990), 24.

13. Martin Heidegger, *Being and Time*, trans. John Macquarrie and Edward Robinson (Oxford: Wiley-Blackwell, 1962), 456.

14. Immanuel Kant, *Critique of Pure Reason*, trans. Norman Kemp Smith (Houndmills: Macmillan, 1993), 74–9.

15. Johnson's *Dictionary* definitions of *imagination* include its sense as a mental faculty: 'I. Fancy; the power of forming ideal pictures; the power of representing things absent to one's self or others.'

16. *Coleridge's Shakespearean Criticism*, ed. Thomas Middleton Raysor, 2 vols. (London: Dent, 1960), I.176.

17. See Kant, *Critique*, 77. On the tendency to regard time and space as distinct individuals see Anthony Quinton, 'Spaces and Times,' *Philosophy* 37 (1962), 130–47.

18. Henri Bergson, *Time and Free Will: An Essay on the Immediate Data of Consciousness*, trans. Frank Lubecki Pogson (London: George Allen, 1913), 111.

19. 'Sailing to Byzantium,' l.32, *W. B. Yeats: The Poems*, ed. Richard J. Finneran (London: Macmillan, 1983), 194.

20. Lucretius, *De Rerum Natura*, in Dryden's translation, 'Against the Fear of Death' (1685), ll.155–6, in *The Works of John Dryden*, III.52.

21. Rudyard Kipling, 'If—,' l.29, *The Oxford Authors: Rudyard Kipling*, ed. Daniel Karlin (Oxford: Oxford University Press, 1999), 497.

22. Sherman, *Telling Time*, 205–6.

23. Ibid., 205.

# 3

# Johnson and Change

*Robert DeMaria, Jr.*

Herculean constancy and Roman stability are prominent traits in many early descriptions of Johnson's character. For Boswell, Johnson was the 'infant Hercules of Toryism' whose piety was the 'constant... ruling principle of all his conduct' and whose regard for morality was 'steady and inflexible' (*Life* I.38; IV.429, 426). Elsewhere, Johnson's mind is the Roman Colosseum, which endures as a whole, although it houses mighty contests between his gladiatorial judgment and his bestial fears (*Life* II.106). In her short preface to *Anecdotes of the Late Samuel Johnson* (1786), Hester Lynch Piozzi describes Johnson as an oak, Trajan's Column, and the shield of Ajax Telamon (*Johnsonian Miscellanies* I.145 and n.3). In the nineteenth century, as Isobel Grundy explains in Chapter 14 of this volume, Thomas Carlyle took such elevation to its extreme: 'Aloft, conspicuous, on his enduring basis, he stands there, serene, unfaltering.'[1]

In some respects, these characterizations of Johnson are suitable to his thinking on many subjects. Indeed, much of what he asserts on important topics suggests a classical preference for stability that is consistent with the image of Johnson as monumental and unbending, like the muscular statue of him in St. Paul's Cathedral. Johnson hoped, for example, that his *Dictionary* would help stabilize and fix the English language: 'There is,' he said in the 'Preface' to the *Dictionary*, 'in constancy and stability a general and lasting advantage' (*Yale* XVIII.78). As Philip Smallwood has pointed out in Chapter 2, in his literary criticism, too, Johnson described the greatest achievements as the most stable: 'The stream of time, which is continually washing the dissoluble fabricks of other poets, passes without injury by the adamant of Shakespeare' (*Yale* VII.69–70).

Despite such powerful recommendations of stability, however, there is, as always with Johnson, another side to the story. In the 'Preface' to Shakespeare, famous for its praise of the Bard's stability, Johnson also praises his variety:

The interchanges of mingled scenes seldom fail to produce the intended vicissitudes of passion...and though it must be allowed that pleasing melancholy be sometimes interrupted by unwelcome levity, yet let it be considered likewise, that melancholy is often not pleasing, and that the disturbance of one man may be the relief of another; that different auditors have different habitudes; and that, upon the whole, all pleasure consists in variety. (*Yale* VII.67)

Likewise, in the 'Preface' to the *Dictionary*, Johnson's aspirations to control linguistic change bend under the pressure of popular usage and melt into poetic descriptions of variety and mutability. Johnson wants, for example, to make order out of confusion in the carefully arranged series of senses by which the meanings of each word are described. Nevertheless, 'The shades of meaning sometimes pass imperceptibly into each other,' and, as he says a few paragraphs earlier, 'while our language is yet living, and variable by the caprice of every tongue that speaks it, these words are hourly shifting their relations, and can no more be ascertained in a dictionary, than a grove, in the agitation of a storm, can be accurately delineated from its picture in the water' (*Yale* XVIII.91, 89–90).

Looking not at Johnson's imagery but his assertions, we may also find evidence of change or, some would say, changeableness—the pejorative aspect of change, 'inconstancy' and 'fickleness,' as Johnson defines it in his *Dictionary*.[2] The 'Preface' to Shakespeare famously follows passages of Olympian praise with passages of severe condemnation: 'In his comick scenes he is seldom very successful....In tragedy his performance seems constantly to be worse, as his labour is more....In narration he affects a disproportionate pomp of diction and a wearisome train of circumlocution' (*Yale* VII.72–3). On many occasions, as a critic, Johnson adeptly changes his style and his tone to suit the work at hand. In his famous essay on the metaphysical poets in his 'Life of Cowley,' Johnson not only asserts his respect for these poets' powers of mind, he also exhibits an ability to imitate their linguistic licentiousness. Describing the extravagant metaphors of the metaphysicals, he becomes himself extravagant in his imagery: 'they broke every image into fragments: and could no more represent, by their slender conceits and laboured particularities, the prospects of nature, or the scenes of life, than he, who dissects a sun-beam with a prism, can exhibit the wide effulgence of a summer noon' (*Lives* I.201). Johnson was capable of protean mimicry of other kinds. Everyone's favorite example comes from a Presbyterian minister who had dinner with Johnson and Boswell on their celebrated tour of the Hebrides in 1773. Having mentioned the discovery by the naturalist Joseph Banks of a kangaroo, Johnson, with growing animation, 'rose from his chair, and volunteered an imitation of the animal....He stood erect, put out his hands like feelers, and, gathering up the tails of his huge brown coat so as to resemble the pouch of the animal, made two or three vigorous bounds across the room!' (*Life* V.511).

Boswell did not see fit to report this peculiarly un-Herculean episode, and it did not make it into print until 1852, after the death of the long-lived minister. It is just the kind of image of Johnson that Boswell would not admit—not merely because it is undignified; there are undignified images of Boswell's Johnson sweating while eating voraciously, muttering, and clucking like a madman. What really offended Boswell here, I believe, is the quality of mimicry and shape-changing that did not sort with his image of Herculean, Roman, unchanging Johnson. While Boswell did record instances of Johnson contradicting himself or arguing merely for victory, he nevertheless sought a sense of Johnson as massy and immoveable, like the rock from which he rebounds in his refutation of Bishop Berkeley (*Life* I.471). And Johnson projected this sense of massiveness for Boswell as he did for the eulogist Gerard Hamilton, who said Johnson's death 'made a chasm, which…nothing can fill up' (*Life* IV.420).

Unlike Boswell, however, Johnson was on some occasions a defender of change. For example, Johnson excused William Warburton's changed opinion of Alexander Pope, saying, 'surely to think differently, at different times, of poetical merit, may be easily allowed. Such opinions are often admitted, and dismissed, without nice examination. Who is there that has not found reason for changing his mind about questions of greater importance?' (*Lives* IV.41). Johnson changed his own mind about many things, and he saw change as an inevitable aspect of human life. In this Johnson differs from Boswell, Plutarch, and many other biographers who emphasize the fixity of character throughout life.[3] In *Rambler* 151, he gives an account of the changes that are characteristic of man's physical, mental, and emotional life: 'in each part of life some particular faculty [of the mind] is more eminently employed.' At first, he contends, we entertain novelty with 'vivacious and desultory curiosity,' and 'we are delighted with improbable adventures, impracticable virtues, and inimitable characters.' As we mature, however, we 'discard absurdity and impossibility, then exact greater and greater degrees of probability [and] at last become cold and insensible to the charms of falshood.' 'Now,' argues Johnson, 'commences the reign of judgment or reason,' during which knowledge is reduced to 'a certain number of incontestable or unsuspected propositions…[and] compacted into systems.' But this state of mind is not stable either: 'At length weariness succeeds to labour, and the mind lies at ease in the contemplation of her own attainments.… This is the age of recollection and narrative…[when] nothing is…so odious as opposition, so insolent as doubt, or so dangerous as novelty' (*Yale* V.39–40).

Johnson finds a similar pattern in the metamorphosis of the passions in the course of a lifetime. We take pleasure first in our mere experience of the world, then in art, then in systems of power and wealth. At last we sink into fatigue with all this and cling merely to our reputation. In stoical Christian fashion Johnson concludes that we can and should resist these natural patterns as part of the work of salvation: 'to contend with the predominance of successive passions...is the condition upon which we are to pass our time, the time of our preparation for that state which shall put an end to experiment, to disappointment, and to change' (*Yale* V.42). Change is a condition of human life and reacting to it is here made into a test of virtue.

The evolution of mind outlined in *Rambler* 151, like so much of John-son's writing, not only provides a basis for moral injunction; it also re-flects, and in this case predicts, some aspects of his own intellectual life. The reflection is visible in changes in Johnson's prose style between his earliest efforts in the 1730s and 1740s and his last major work, the *Lives of the Poets* (1779–81).

That there are changes in the prose style visible in the *Lives of the Poets* has long been accepted; the reason for these changes has been a subject of debate. Addressing the matter in *The Prose Style of Samuel Johnson*, W. K. Wimsatt, Jr., cited Thomas Babington Macaulay's article on Johnson, which appeared in the eleventh edition of the *Encyclopedia Britannica* (1911). One hundred years later, this still, I think, represents the com-monly received opinion on the subject of Johnson's changed style. Blend-ing literary criticism and biography, Macaulay wrote:

> Since Johnson had been at ease in his circumstances [after receiving his pen-sion in 1762] he had written little and had talked much. When therefore he, after the lapse of years, resumed his pen, the mannerism which he had con-tracted while he was in the constant habit of elaborate composition was less perceptible than formerly, and his diction frequently had a colloquial ease which it had formerly wanted. The improvement may be discerned by a skilful critic in the *Journey to the* [*Western Islands*], and in the *Lives of the Poets* is so obvious that it cannot escape the notice of the most careless reader.[4]

Wimsatt avers that 'in some sense Macaulay is right, that in some way Johnson's writing is "lighter" in the *Lives of the Poets* than in the *Rambler*.' Wimsatt confusingly substitutes 'lighter' for 'easier,' but he still means a style that avoids 'harsh or...daring figures' and 'all unusual...structure of speech,' as Johnson put it when he defined 'easy poetry' in *Idler* 77 (*Yale* II.239). (Johnson was critical of 'the light and the familiar' in style [see e.g. *Lives* I.221], which he saw as bordering on the low and mean. Never-theless, the components of a 'light' or 'easy' style may be identified as:

relatively little syntactical inversion or elaboration, such as parallelism and antithesis, and diction that is plain and generally not Latinate. A 'heavy' style, on the other hand, has more inversion, more hard words, more periphrasis and other figures of speech: at its worst it is ponderous or turgid.)

Having made that concession to Macaulay, Wimsatt cites G. B. Hill's denial that this 'lightness' is due to Johnson having changed his style,[5] and in his chapter entitled 'The Consistency of Johnson's Style,' Wimsatt 'sustains and elaborates' Hill's view. Wimsatt concludes: 'all his life Johnson exhibited different degrees of his own peculiar style both in his talk and in his writing, and...especially in his writing this is to be referred to differences of subject matter.' Further, Wimsatt says, 'a topic on which Johnson was always forced to employ his lightest style was specific literary criticism....This sort of subject matter in a great measure accounts for the lightness of the *Lives*.' His example par excellence of 'this sort of subject matter' is prosody.[6]

There is some truth in Wimsatt's claims, but, even on 'heavier' subjects, such as life and death, or truth and fiction, there are conversational elements of style in the *Lives*. Wimsatt's determination to isolate elements of style from elements of content here leads him away from the obvious fact that Johnson's changes in style cohered with changes in his outlook. Against Wimsatt, I want to argue that Johnson's style in the *Lives* is easier, less encumbered with rhetoric, precisely because at this stage of life he saw life and literature in a way that required a simpler style, not merely because he was obliged to talk about the nuts and bolts of prosody and other critical matters. Rather, Johnson is markedly plainer and simpler—and more conversational—even when he is talking about the same subjects that he had addressed many years earlier. (For evidence that Johnson could modulate his style at will, without change of subject, see *Life* IV.320.)

As the passages I cite below suggest, by the age of sixty-five or so Johnson had come to see life and art in simpler, franker terms, and his style matches that perception. To put it another way, what we might describe as Johnson's style of perception is different in the *Lives* from the style of perception in the work of his middle and early periods, and this is a change that is naturally registered in his writing style. Johnson's late style shows him migrating from 'the reign of judgment or reason' to 'the age of recollection and narrative,' as he called the second and third stages of mental development in *Rambler* 151 (*Yale* V.40).

To show what I mean about the style of the *Lives* I have collected a number of telling passages and distributed them into five groups. In the first group are examples of what Macaulay may have meant by 'colloquial ease' in the prose style of the *Lives*. These little bits are trivial in themselves—like the individual bricks displayed by the estate salesman in the *Jests of Hierocles* (*Yale* VII.62)—but I think they add up in the course of a long work like the *Lives*.

To begin with a very small brick: in the 'Life of Cowley,' after his dissertation on the metaphysical poets, Johnson says, 'It was about the time of Cowley that *Wit*...took the meaning, whatever it be, which it now bears' (*Lives* I.214). It is a bit odd for the great lexicographer to say, 'the meaning, *whatever it be*, which it now bears' (my emphases). Johnson's 'whatever' contains an element of surrender to the difficulty of expressing a very complex idea that seems foreign to his earlier writing, and is more likely to come from conversation. He used 'whatever it be' again in the 'Life of Pope' when talking about the arbitrary ordering of the precepts in the *Essay on Man* (1733–4). This may be stylistic evidence that the age of judgment and reason is yielding to one of greater ease; or, as Johnson put it more plainly in the 'Life of Swift,' 'The love of ease is always gaining upon age' (*Lives* III.206).

Elsewhere in the 'Life of Pope' Johnson concludes a long passage in which he is trying to untangle the complexities of the argument between Pope and Joseph Addison that led to the dissolution of their friendship. He says: 'That the quarrel of those two wits should be minutely deduced, is not to be expected from a writer to whom, as Homer says, *nothing but rumour has reached, and who has no personal knowledge*' (*Lives* IV.25). This is a strikingly colloquial translation of *Iliad* II.486, which contains part of the invocation of the muses just before the catalogue of the ships. Homer invokes the muses because they live on Mount Olympus, and, as goddesses, they are present at all important events and know all, whereas we mortals only hear of such things by rumor and know nothing for certain. In his *Iliad*, Pope made a couplet of the line and put it in parentheses: '(We, wretched Mortals! lost in Doubts below,/But guess by Rumor, and but boast we know)' (*Iliad* II.576–7; *Twickenham* VII.155). Pope takes liberties, but the line is gnomic and has a kind of epic pathos, which he tries to capture. Johnson, on the other hand, is deliberately prosaic and applies the line to his situation as a biographer seeking the kind of truth that can be known only by eyewitnesses. As a result, the phrase 'personal knowledge' stands as a peculiarly modern (and therefore 'light') translation of the omniscience of the gods. Johnson is being playfully self-conscious in constructing divine knowledge in terms of a biographer's knowledge. He has, however, also rendered epic language casually and colloquially in a marked change of style from the days when he took care to render the 'grandeur' of Juvenal in his major poems.[7]

Moving from instances of words or phrases that seem colloquial, there are some passages in which Johnson rephrases in easier terms statements of substantially the same meaning that he made earlier in his career. In the 'Life of Blackmore' (written in 1780), for example, Johnson says, 'While the distributors of literary fame were endeavouring to depreciate and degrade him, he either despised or defied them, wrote on as he had written before, and never turned aside to quiet them by civility, or repress them by confutation' (*Lives* III.85). As John H. Middendorf points out in his note to this passage (*Yale* XXII.774, n.3), Johnson 'spoke of Boerhaave [in 1739] in similar terms' when he wrote:

> he was never soured by calumny and detraction, nor ever thought it necessary to confute them; for 'they are sparks,' said [Boerhaave], 'which, if you do not blow them, will go out of themselves.'[8]

Syntactically, the sentence in the 'Life of Blackmore' is simpler, partly because it uses the active voice throughout, whereas the sentence in the earlier 'Life of Boerhaave' begins with a passive clause, follows with an active, and then goes into indirect discourse. Johnson's diction in the 'Life of Boerhaave' is also more complex: 'calumny' and 'detraction' are close to being personifications, like 'hope' and 'fear,' the figures that 'o'erspread the clouded maze of fate' in *The Vanity of Human Wishes* (ll.5–6; *Yale* VI.92). The sense of animation in these terms is intensified by the quotation from Boerhaave in which he calls them 'sparks,' which can either be blown into life or let die. If there is a hint of personification in the use of 'civility' and 'confutation' in the 'Life of Blackmore,' it is more muted. This later passage is plainer and more colloquial, using alliteration for rhetorical effect, as one might in speech, but eschewing syntactic complication.

To take another example, in the 'Life of Pope' (written in 1781) Johnson defends the importance of *The Rape of the Lock* (1714) against the charge of John Dennis (in *Remarks on Mr Pope's Homer*, 1717)[9] that the poem has no moral: 'The freaks, and humours, and spleen, and vanity of women, as they embroil families in discord, and fill houses with disquiet, do more to obstruct the happiness of life in a year than the ambition of the clergy in many centuries' (*Lives* IV.72). Again, as Middendorf points out, this sentiment appeared much earlier in Johnson's works: in his 1735 translation of Father Lobo's 'observation on the libertine behavior of the Abyssinian princesses,' Johnson wrote: 'Nor has the most insatiable ambition of monarchs either to gain or enlarge an empire been the occasion of more broils and troubles than the intrigues and passions of these women' (*Yale* XXIII.1, 208, n.1, citing *Yale* XV.213). The sentence in the 'Life of Pope' starts out on the subject of unruly women and gradually finds its way to the end by comparing these outrages to the 'ambition of the clergy.' The earlier sentence knows its path from the start because it puts the *comparans*, 'the most insatiable ambition of monarchs,' at the front, while holding the real subject, the *comparatum*, back until the end. The later sentence, despite the elaboration of the subject, is more direct because its true subject is also its principal grammatical subject.

A third group of passages that may show the greater simplicity of Johnson's style in the *Lives* comprises those in which Johnson seems to have written what we might describe as shorthand, 'light' versions of some of his familiar literary themes. It might be objected that in doing so Johnson was merely adjusting his style to suit the audience or the genre. This may be true, but the stylistic adjustment is not superficial. It does not come from mere change of subject, as Wimsatt suggested; it indicates a change in Johnson's intellectual outlook. Given his high regard for biography and literary criticism, Johnson's sense of audience and his relaxation of style in the *Lives* exhibit him at the third intellectual phase he identified in *Rambler* 151—well past the age of discovery, largely beyond the stage of ordering his knowledge, and often recollecting. After desisting from his transcription of Pope's corrections to the proofs of his *Iliad* (the transcriptions were actually made by Hester Thrale and George Steevens), Johnson writes: 'Of these specimens every man who has cultivated poetry, or who delights to trace the mind from the rudeness of its first conceptions to the elegance of its last, will naturally desire a greater number; but most other readers are already tired, and I am not writing only to poets and philosophers' (*Lives* IV.23). Such frank, direct concessions to his reader belong to Johnson's late style.

In the *Lives* Johnson composes his themes in a lighter fashion than he did earlier, because he is writing for general readers and conversationalists, but also because he now sees his common themes in a lighter fashion. For example, discussing Pope's tardy completion of his translation of the *Iliad*, Johnson launches into one of his commonplaces. Readers of Johnson know this theme best in the lamentations about 'sickness and sorrow' and 'frigid tranquility,' which appear in the conclusion of the 'Preface' to the *Dictionary*, but it shows up elsewhere in Johnson's works. The most haunting version is in *Rambler* 207: 'the toil with which performance struggles after idea, is so irksome and disgusting, and so frequent is the necessity of resting below that perfection which we imagined within our reach, that seldom any man obtains more from his endeavours than a painful conviction of his defects' (*Yale* V.311).[10] In the 'Life of Pope' Johnson says, 'Indolence, interruption, business, and pleasure, all take their turns of retardation,' but he concludes more dryly and directly: 'Perhaps no extensive and multifarious performance was ever effected within the term originally fixed in the undertaker's mind' (*Lives* IV.16). Revising for the third edition of the *Lives* (1783), Johnson capped off the already blunt passage with the pithy remark: 'He that runs against Time, has an antagonist not subject to casualties.' There is a kind of proverbial wisdom in this capstone; despite its poetry, it is easier and plainer than that of the *Rambler* or the exhausted lexicographer's expressions of the same theme.

In the *Lives* there are many such examples of simplified expressions of common Johnsonian themes. Here are two from the 'Life of Dryden': 'That book is good in vain, which the reader throws away'; and 'Learning once made popular is no longer learning' (*Lives* II.147, 119). In both cases Johnson follows the proverbial statement with poetic imagery. The first statement leads to the image of the reader as a traveler: of a good book, he says, the 'conclusion is perceived with an eye of sorrow, such as the traveller casts upon departing day.' The second proverb leads to an image almost metaphysical in its flavor: popular learning 'has the appearance of something which we have bestowed upon ourselves, as the dew appears to rise from the field which it refreshes.' These images are poetic, but they are not complex. In fact, the little vignettes in them are remarkably pictorial and, in that sense, explanatory and plain, as befits the age of recollection.

Such vignettes used to illustrate proverbial truths are not uncommon in the *Lives*, and they contribute to the easiness of the writing style. Johnson is hardly recurring to the sixteenth-century Alciati (Andrea Alciato) or seventeenth-century Francis Quarles, the great writers of emblem books for popular audiences, but he is going a little in that direction. In some of his vignettes the image takes the form of a little narrative. In the 'Life of Pope,' for example, Johnson says: 'The man who threatens the world is always ridiculous; for the world can easily go on without him, and in a short time will cease to miss him' (*Lives* IV.35). Then he adds, by way of illustration: 'I have heard of an idiot, who used to revenge his vexations by lying all night upon the bridge' (i.e. London Bridge). In the MS and proof sheet the image was more extreme: the 'idiot' there 'used to enforce his demands by threatening to beat his head against the wall' (*Lives* IV.201). The swiftness with which the world forgets individuals who are out of favor is a recurrent theme in Johnson's works and closely allied to the vanity of human wishes, but he never earlier illustrated it with such a homely little story.

Another group of passages indicative of Johnson's lighter style in the *Lives* comprises those in which Johnson actually tells a story, not so much to illustrate a point as merely to enliven his presentation. Here, Johnson sounds casual, like a raconteur of the sort that ordinarily seems beneath his dignity as a philosophical writer. Often these stories come from intimate correspondents. Johnson's father Michael, for example, provided this anecdote in the 'Life of Sprat':

There prevailed in those days an indecent custom; when the preacher touched any favourite topick in a manner that delighted his audience, their approbation was expressed by a loud *hum*, continued in proportion to their zeal or pleasure. When Burnet preached, part of his congregation *hummed* so loudly and so long, that he sat down to enjoy it, and rubbed his face with his handkerchief. When Sprat preached, he likewise was honoured with the like animating *hum*; but he stretched out his hand to the congregation, and cried, 'Peace, peace, I pray you, peace.'

This I was told in my youth by my father, an old man, who had been no careless observer of the passages of those times.  (*Lives* II.187–8)

The story reflects Sprat's modesty, but it is also just a funny story because of the 'indecent' (i.e. 'unbecoming,' as Johnson defines it) custom captured in the onomatopoetic 'hum,' repeated thrice. The seriousness and 'zeal' of the silly-sounding 'animating hum' makes for burlesque humor. Johnson seems to indulge himself in telling the story both because it is funny and because it was pleasant for him to recall his father, almost as though this were a memoir and not a preface biographical and critical.

Another example of a good story embedded in the text came to Johnson from Gilbert Walmesley, 'one of the first friends that literature procured' him (*Lives* II.178). There are many examples in the *Lives* of Johnson turning a writer's final days into dark humor, and there is a colloquial tone in many of these tales. Speaking of Edmund Smith's removal to a patron's house, where he hoped to work without interruption, Johnson says:

Here he found such opportunities of indulgence as did not much forward his studies, and particularly some strong ale, too delicious to be resisted. He eat and drank till he found himself plethorick: and then, resolving to ease himself by evacuation, he wrote to an apothecary in the neighbourhood a prescription of a purge so forcible, that the apothecary thought it his duty to delay it till he had given notice of its danger. Smith, not pleased with the contradiction of a shopman, and boastful of his own knowledge, treated the notice with rude contempt, and swallowed his own medicine, which, in July 1710, brought him to the grave. He was buried at Hartham. (*Lives* II.177)

The last sentence is the punchline to a dark joke, suitable for the tavern. Smith goes to Hartham as a refuge from the trouble of life, and at Hartham his troubles end: he dies. Just how Walmesley told the story we shall never know, but Johnson is repeating his old friend's tale and taking some pleasure in the recollection as well as the telling.

As a final group of specimens showing the relative plainness and simplicity of Johnson's late style in the *Lives*, I adduce some of his astonishingly blunt statements of biographical fact. These are often preceded by a rejection of the statements of earlier biographers as fictional. The 'Life of

Smith' provides a good example. Having repeated the account of Oldis-worth, Johnson's main source for this life, he says:

> Such is the declamation of Oldisworth, written while his admiration was yet fresh, and his kindness warm; and therefore such as, without any criminal purpose of deceiving, shews a strong desire to make the most of all favour-able truth. I cannot much commend the performance. The praise is often indistinct, and the sentences are loaded with words of more pomp than use. There is little however that can be contradicted, even when a plainer tale comes to be told.
>   EDMUND NEAL, known by the name of Smith, was born at Handley, the seat of the Lechmeres, in Worcestershire. The year of his birth is uncertain. (*Lives* II.173)

The 'plainer tale' is plain both in style and substance. It is blunt about the facts of Smith's life. The same bluntness is present in Johnson's 'tale' telling throughout the *Lives*. The first of the lives, 'Cowley,' provides the para-digm. Rejecting Sprat's biography because 'all is shewn confused and en-larged through the mist of panegyrick,' Johnson declares plainly, 'ABRAHAM COWLEY was born in the year one thousand six hundred and eighteen. His father was a grocer, whose condition Dr Sprat conceals under the general appellation of a citizen' (*Lives* I.191).

Johnson seems to sum up his method in these passages with a plain statement in the 'Life of Addison' ('The rejection and contempt of fiction is rational and manly,' in *Lives* III.24) that embodies the third intellectual phase identified in *Rambler* 151, when we are 'cold and insensible to the charms of falshood' (*Yale* V.40). Johnson had made a similar remark in a different style in his 'Dissertation on the Epitaphs Written by Pope' (1756): 'Let fiction, at least, cease with life, and let us be serious over the grave.'[11] The double use of 'let,' indicating changes in verbal mood (see Johnson's *Dictionary*, senses 2–8), makes the earlier sentence less plain than the later one. In the earlier sentence, moreover, the contempt of fic-tion is restricted to the contemplation of death, whereas in the later there are no restrictions.

The change in Johnson's style visible in the *Lives*, I argue, reflects a change in his attitude towards life. The style of the *Lives* on the whole, al-though Johnson is still capable of rhetorical grandeur when he wishes, is simpler, blunter, and also more conversational in certain ways. It is not so much that Johnson has been at his ease, as Macaulay suggested, but that he has clarified his perception of life and brought it down to plainer outlines and more domestic details. He is recollecting the perceptions distilled in a lifetime of intellectual work, rather than forming those perceptions.

This late Johnson, contemptuous of fiction, is the man who converted his walking stick into a measuring rod on his tour to the Hebrides and regretted the lack of more accurate instruments as he explored a cave and looked on Fingal's Table (*Life* V.318; *Yale*, IX.145–6). This is the Johnson who performed experiments on himself, measuring, for example, his vitality by shaving the hair on his arms and seeing how long it took to return (*Yale* I.297), or calculating his strength by using the pump at Brighton (*Yale* I.342; *Letters* IV.83).

This late Johnson, more concerned with recollection than discovery, is also the man who arranged for an inscribed stone to be laid over the graves of his father, mother, and brother—the members of his immediate family from whom as a young man he rebelled—and who rewrote his relationship with his father in a moving Latin poem about learning to swim: he hears anew his father's soft voice (*blanda voce*) as he struggles with awkward arms ('In Rivum a Mola Stoana Lichfeldiae diffluentem,' l.4, *Yale* VI.342). It is also the Johnson who grew easier and less demanding in society and made new friends in the twilight of life, such as William Bowles, who was fifty-three years his junior, and Frances Burney, only forty-three years younger. Johnson did not like small talk as a young man and even in middle age despised conversation about the weather. He was known for his austere philosophical stance and his condemnation of idle activities such as fishing. In later life, however, he once went so far as to wish he could play cards because 'it generates kindness and consolidates society' (*Life* V.404), and he condescended to talk of the weather (*Life* I.332 and n.2). Johnson may still have been difficult company—silent at times, dominating the conversation mercilessly at others—but there is evidence of a softening and increased sociability, and all this, like his late prose style, is part of the movement into the third phase of his intellectual life.

Johnson did not have a late life conversion or political awakening that radically changed his life and art; he experienced nothing of the sort that makes the late works of Goya, for example, so different from almost everything that came before. However, Johnson did change; he changed in ways that are fundamentally human and healthy, and all these changes are consistent with his change of style in the *Lives of the Poets*. Johnson's late combination of stylistic plainness, frankness, increased interest in the pleasures of friendship, and a desire to be reconciled with one's parents (even posthumously) is not a bad formula for aging profitably and even gracefully. It has its own heroism, which I would oppose to the Boswellian images of Johnson as a classical, Herculean hero. Johnson's late heroism is not the result of changes in his prose style, but it may be that his prose is more than the mere reflection of intellectual changes. By writing more plainly and more directly, when he wished, Johnson helped create and confirm the self of his late years. It may be, as Johnson's exact contemporary the Comte du Buffon said, that 'the style is the man,'[12] but in Johnson's case both sides of the equation were dynamic, interactive, subject to change, and changed by the will of the great spirit who inhabited them.

## NOTES

1. See Chapter 14.
2. Definitions are from the 4th edition of Johnson's *Dictionary* (1773).
3. See also Robert DeMaria, Jr., 'Plutarch, Johnson, and Boswell: The Classical Tradition of Biography at the End of the Eighteenth Century,' in *The Eighteenth-Century Novel*, eds. Albert J. Rivero and George Justice, 6–7 [double issue] (2009), 79–102.
4. See W. K. Wimsatt, Jr., *The Prose Style of Samuel Johnson* [1941] (2nd edn, New Haven: Yale University Press, 1963), 74.
5. Wimsatt cites George Birkbeck Hill, 'Dr Johnson's Style,' *Macmillan's Magazine* LVII (1888), 190–4; Wimsatt, *Prose Style*, 74, n.3.
6. Wimsatt, *Prose Style*, 74, 78, 83.
7. Other examples of colloquial style could include a dash in the middle of a grammatically broken sentence in the 'Life of Pope' and the use of 'possibly' as a colloquial qualifier in the 'Life of Halifax' (*Lives* IV.68; II.190). For Johnson on Juvenal's style, see *Lives* II.143.
8. Johnson, 'Life of Dr Herman Boerhaave,' *The Gentleman's Magazine* 9 (1739), 174.
9. *The Critical Works of John Dennis*, ed. Edward Niles Hooker, 2 vols. (Baltimore: Johns Hopkins University Press, 1939–43), II.330–1.
10. For other versions of the thought, see *The Plan of a Dictionary* (1747) (*Yale* XVIII.28) and *Rambler* 17 (*Yale* III.96).
11. *The Universal Visiter, and Monthly Memorialist* V (1756), 212.
12. 'Le style est l'homme même,' George-Louis Leclerc, Comte de Buffon, *Discours sur le style* (1753), *Oeuvres Complètes de Buffon*, ed. F. D. Pillot, 28 vols. (Paris: Salmon, 1829), I.12.

# 4

# Johnson's Assertions and Concessions: Moral Irresolution and Rhetorical Performance

*John Richetti*

Recording a conversation from 5 April 1776, Boswell observes that Johnson 'loved to display his ingenuity in argument; and therefore would sometimes in conversation maintain opinions which he was sensible were wrong, but in supporting which, his reasoning and wit would be most conspicuous.' Boswell inserts into his account a moment when Johnson was asked about card-playing: ' "Why, Sir, as to the good or evil of card playing"—"Now, (said Garrick,) he is thinking which side he shall take" ' (*Life* III.23–4). Boswell suggests what is clear to any reader of the *Life*, that 'He appeared to have a pleasure in contradiction, especially when any opinion whatever was delivered with an air of confidence; so that there was hardly any topick, if not one of the great truths of Religion and Morality, that he might not have been incited to argue either for or against it' (*Life* III.24). Boswell observes that Johnson 'owned that he often "talked for victory" ' (*Life* II.238). Once, discussing the work of the Scottish historian, William Robertson, he urged objections against it more 'in the ardour of contest, than expressed his real and decided opinion' (*Life* II.238).

The particular occasion for the first of these observations about Johnson's 'pleasure in contradiction' is his response to Boswell's mentioning a new gaming-club 'where the members played to a desperate extent' (*Life* III.23). Irritated, one supposes, by the superficiality of such worries about rich, irresponsible gamesters, Johnson makes the case to Boswell and Henry Thrale that many more people are ruined 'by adventurous trade, and yet we do not hear such an outcry against it' (*Life* III.23). In the aftermath of the latest convulsions of the capitalist order, this is bracingly pertinent, a matter of Johnson's superior insight. And yet it is also evidence of Johnson's love of debate. As Boswell reports of a morning-after conversation from May 1769, Johnson declares himself 'highly satisfied with his colloquial prowess the preceding evening' and says that 'we had good talk.' To which Boswell in a rare moment of candor replies, 'Yes, Sir; you tossed and gored several persons' (*Life* II.66).

These are the satisfactions of self-dramatizing rhetorical performance that, much earlier in the *Life,* Johnson claims that he learned as a younger man to temper or indeed to repress. Speaking of David Hume and 'other skeptical innovators,' Johnson calls them 'vain men [who] will gratify themselves at any expence' (*Life* I.444). It takes one to know one, we might say, and Johnson admits as much in the following startling assertion, made on Thursday, 21 July 1763: 'If I could have allowed myself to gratify my vanity at the expence of truth, what fame might I have acquired. Every thing which Hume has advanced against Christianity had passed through my mind long before he wrote' (*Life* I.444). Johnson imagines himself as a kind of youthful anti-Johnson, the notorious infidel who would have out-Humed Hume in his intellectual bravado.

In Boswell's *Life,* Johnson is something like a decorous Hume who has achieved fame in his own way, in love with the performance of paradox and contradiction, and regularly gratifying his vanity in triumphing over others in conversation. Ready to pounce on merely conventional opinions, he enacts the role that Boswell is eager for him to play for our amusement and, perhaps, our moral and intellectual improvement. As Bertrand Bronson put it in 'Johnson Agonistes,' Johnson often 'could not resist the sheer fun of seeing what could be said in favour of an untenable position.'[1] But there is more to Johnson's contentious nature than fun. Like a traditional rhetorician, he clearly liked to test his powers by arguing to win, by defending paradoxical opinions against ill-considered positions. As the irascible Sir John Hawkins said of Johnson, 'In all Johnson's disquisitions, whether argumentative or critical, there is a certain even-handed justice that leaves the mind in a strange perplexity' (*Hawkins,* 290).[2] My contention is that the performance Johnson favors in conversations is necessarily quite different in a good deal of his moral writing. Often enough, he considers positions he can imagine himself entertaining, not simply triumphing by attacking conventional wisdom but rather dramatizing how slippery or complicated truth is. Even outrageous positions as Johnson examines them may contain some truth or utility (thus perplexing some of his friends like Hawkins, and continuing to puzzle us). Such admissions or concessions may require major modifications of Johnson's opening position, and this recurring rhetorical stance often lends his moral writing both force and remarkable honesty.

Paul Fussell argued persuasively that, in his periodical writing and in the *Rambler* especially, Johnson was simply irresolute. As he bent reluctantly to his twice-a-week task of composing, says Fussell, his thinking was essentially improvisational: 'caught short at deadline-time' and 'working things out ad hoc from page to page.'[3] Through all those qualifying adversatives he is so fond of—those 'yets' and 'buts'—he is 'very close to naked indecision.'[4] For Fussell, Johnson articulates much of the time an 'instinctive skepticism' by which he differs 'from himself, one of Johnson's activities that has not always been sufficiently appreciated.'[5] Fussell is quoting *Adventurer* 107: 'We have less reason to be surprised or offended when we find others differ from us in opinion, because we very often differ from ourselves' (*Yale* II.442). Johnson, Fussell contends, cannot simply be taken 'as an odd wise man who is most interesting because he "says" witty and outrageous dogmatic things upon all occasions.'[6] Boswell and many later commentators have turned him into a sage who emits sententiae, neglecting the dynamic or even destabilizing force of genre and rhetorical occasion on Johnson's various dicta. Fussell instead portrays him as a rhetorician for whom, as he puts it, 'genre, occasion, and human rhetorical purpose are the main determinants of truth.'[7]

This may go just a bit too far, since there are moments such as the review of Soame Jenyns' *A Free Inquiry into the Nature and Origin of Evil* (1757) and the polemical pamphlet against the American rebels, *Taxation no Tyranny* (1775), when Johnson is demolishing positions that he treats with contempt and ridicule (*Yale* X.401–55; XVII.407–15). In this chapter I hope to refine Fussell's readings by focusing on a few key moments from Johnson's periodical essays and from *Rasselas* (1759) that dramatize just how those assertions—and their balancing concessions—add up to a rhetorical performance. Johnson creates situations in which those performative factors—genre, occasion, and rhetorical purpose—are in tension with a strenuous attempt to articulate moral truthfulness in the distinctive concessive situation created by his writing.

For an example of the crucial differences between his recreational conversations and his efforts as a serious moral writer, consider *Adventurer* 85, where Johnson launches a defense of reading against those he calls his 'ingenious contemporaries,' who deny the necessity 'of consulting other understandings than their own.' He notes with incredulity that:

> An opinion has of late been, I know not how, propagated among us, that libraries are filled only with useless lumber; that men of parts stand in need of no assistance; and that to spend life poring upon books, is only to imbibe prejudices, to obstruct and embarrass the powers of nature, to cultivate memory at the expence of judgement, and to bury reason under a chaos of undigested learning   (*Yale* II.412).

In paraphrasing a position he is about to demolish, Johnson expresses it with persuasive force and satirical vigor. The moral essay as he practices it always mandates a concession that articulates a balancing position to whatever is being criticized. But the witty and logical turns that follow have two characteristic Johnsonian strategies for refutation: first, he extracts a contradiction built into the position he's attacking by pointing out that he who rails against his literary predecessors is 'raising prejudices against his own performance...with what particular force does he suppose himself invigorated, that difficulties hitherto invincible should give way before him?' (*Yale* II.413). Second, he notes that originality is rare; the appeal here and often in Johnson's writing is to the reformulation and stylistic renovation of proverbial wisdom that would seem to require no defense: the number of those able 'to make any addition to human knowledge' is extremely small, so that most of mankind necessarily owe their knowledge to the 'information of others.' So he who can store his mind 'with acquired knowledge, and can detail it occasionally to others who have less leisure or weaker abilities,' Johnson avers, 'is by no means to be accounted useless or idle' (*Yale* II.413).

But how can knowledge be most effectively shared with those who possess 'less leisure or weaker abilities'? Johnson doesn't have faith in reclusive instructors, those who lack 'conversation' and are unprepared for opposition. When such a man comes into the world and encounters others 'who, arguing upon dissimilar principles, have been led to different conclusions,' he is like a man 'who having fenced always with the same master, is perplexed and amazed by a new posture of his antagonist' (*Yale* II.415). The analogy is striking, worldly in its suggestive evoking of intellectual life as an athletic contest (although the thought of Johnson as fencer prompts a smile). The art of promoting knowledge in the world, then, requires mixing with mankind and being part of what the eighteenth century called the conversable world, where intellectuals and lay persons meet for mutual intellectual profit. This is a reasonable concession to the conventional position with which Johnson began—that an exclusive involvement with books may get in the way of effective knowledge or hinder the efficient communication of it. But the essay ends with a warning for those who learn to master the art of conversation, since in practicing 'every art of recommending our sentiments' we may fall into a trap, the description of which sounds very much like the combative Johnson who flares up in Boswell's *Life*:

> we are frequently betrayed to the use of such as are not in themselves strictly defensible: a man heated in talk, and eager of victory, takes advantage of the mistakes or ignorance of his adversary, lays hold of concessions to which he knows he has no right, and urges proofs likely to prevail on his opponent,

though he knows himself that they have no force: thus the severity of reason is relaxed; many topics are accumulated, but without just arrangement or distinction; we learn to satisfy ourselves with such ratiocination as silences others; and seldom recall to a close examination, that discourse which has gratified our vanity with victory and applause.    (*Yale* II.416)

Johnson concludes by urging the necessity for moralists 'to fix the thoughts by writing, and subject them to frequent examination and reviews,' which are, he says, the best way to enable 'the mind to detect its own sophisms.' This balance involves reading, writing, and conversing 'in due proportions,' which, taken together, constitute 'the business of a man of letters' (*Yale* II.416). Johnson turns out not to be immune in his writing to the temptations of performative excess. His greatness lies in his ability to balance those moments of triumphantly assertive rhetorical bravura with concessions to alternative positions. As here, this can produce an auto-critique that subjects his own moralizing to rigorous examination, as well as articulating a powerful skepticism about the very possibility of final or stable moral knowledge.

Such skepticism is itself a form of moral insight. Every reader will remember Johnson's contempt for the confident abstractions of those he calls 'speculatists' as well as for what he refers to scornfully as 'declamation' (a word always placed implicitly in scare quotes, while at the same time Johnson implicitly recommends a form of declamation by his exemplary and uniquely eloquent style). For one example, consider the opening of *Rambler* 71 as Johnson ridicules that most banal of moral topics, that ' "life is short," which may be heard among mankind by an attentive auditor, many times a day, but which never yet within my reach of observation left any impression upon the mind.' Indeed, he continues with dark humor, readers will, if they think about their old friends, 'find it difficult to call a single man to remembrance, who appeared to know that life was short till he was about to lose it' (*Yale* IV.8). So the knowledge conveyed by considering the effects of the repeated articulation of the truism that life is brief is nothing less than its irrelevance, since the shortness of life is, in practice, generally forgotten: 'So deeply is this fallacy rooted in the heart, and so strongly guarded by hope and fear against the approach of reason, that neither science nor experience can shake it, and we act as if life were without end, though we see and confess its uncertainty and shortness' (*Yale* IV.11).

The Johnsonian moral essay is dialogical, based on the testing or refining of conventional opinions that requires their fair and balanced articulation, as well as their insertion in actual experience and accurate observation. Over and over again, Johnson tends to the paradoxical, the questioning not just of opinions held by implicit adversaries but even at times of what would seem to be his own thoughtful countering of such opinions. As W. K. Wimsatt, Jr., stated in his analysis of Johnson's prose style, strenuous antithesis was his signature move as a writer, part of what makes his manner unique even among his contemporaries: 'each element is emphatic; it seems special and striven for. He is saying: Mark this difference and mark this.'[8] Wimsatt goes on to note that when the purpose of a writer is 'persuasive' rather than merely 'expository,' 'antithesis may tend to retraction, nullification, or cancellation.'[9] I contend that Johnsonian moral writing can be a sometimes 'perilous balance' (to echo the title of W. B. C. Watkins's book)[10] between the brutal and simple assertiveness that conversation can encourage, and the thoughtful but often confusing concessions and revisions (or in Wimsatt's triad of negations—retractions, nullifications, cancellations) that are promoted by Johnson's mode of writing. Johnson seems aware of the dangers of his antithetical style, and his periodical essays visibly wrestle with these compromises with stable truth. Indeed, Freya Johnston, who traces 'the fluctuations of Johnson's uncertainty across his career,' quotes to good effect a passage from *Adventurer* 107 that would seem to express Johnson's inescapable uncertainty: 'Such is the uncertainty, in which we are always likely to remain with regard to questions, wherein we have most interest, and which every day affords us fresh opportunity to examine: we may examine, indeed, but we can never decide, because our faculties are unequal to the subject: we see a little, and form an opinion; we see more, and change it' (*Yale* II.444).[11] The *Rambler* and *Adventurer* essays that I quote from were written by a man in his vigorous forties for whom such paradoxes might well be a form of intellectual and rhetorical playfulness (and who was not yet the terrified septuagenarian facing death that Watkins chiefly discussed). Even in those essays Johnson nevertheless stages a balance between opinions that tends to be deeply skeptical in its qualifications and its contradictions.

The opening number of *The Rambler*, however, makes a joke of such balancing, as Johnson wonders how to begin, suggesting that perhaps he should claim 'indisputable merit' and 'an exemption from general restraints, and to elevations not allowed in common life.' This strategy may be better than modesty, he observes, since 'there is something captivating in spirit and intrepidity, to which we often yield, as to a resistless power; nor can he reasonably expect the confidence of others who too apparently distrusts himself' (*Yale* III.5). Eventually, he arrives at the position that 'ostentatious display of themselves' by 'diurnal writers' such as he aspires to be is imprudent, but is counterbalanced by their sincerity and thus forgiven by readers thanks to the brevity of such productions. So Johnson presents a tongue-in-cheek mini-drama written in almost self-parodic Johnsonese in which he banishes his uncertainty with a stalemate between 'arrogance and submission,' which he finds 'so nearly equiponderant, that my impatience to try the event of my first performance will not suffer me to attend any longer the trepidations of the balance' (*Yale* III.6, 7).

As a comic prelude to what is a serious moral enterprise, the first *Rambler* is remarkable for the tensions it sets out. Indeed, in *Rambler* 2, Johnson still harps on his uncertainty as he enters this new literary enterprise. That anxiety is closely related to his topic, which is, as he notes, the most banal of moral and psychological themes: the danger of 'the mind of man...losing itself in schemes of future felicity,' which has been 'a commodious subject of raillery to the gay, and of declamation to the serious.' 'Declamation' gives the game away once again, since in the next paragraph Johnson pours scorn on a writer who succumbs to the temptation of 'wantoning in common topics' that enable him 'to shine without labour, and to conquer without a contest' (*Yale* III.9).

A recurring theme of Johnson's moral writing is the avoidance of banality, as he fashions his absolutely distinctive, densely aphoristic idiom that challenges and refines 'common topics.' Here the paradoxical turn in Johnson's argument is to defend our tendency to look to the future, by stressing the defining human necessity of keeping one's eyes on what may come to pass. Hope is a sustaining, essential emotion, even if it is largely illusory. This affirmation of what moralists usually deride is quickly followed by another characteristic turn: the modifying 'yet,' by which Johnson reminds us that 'few maxims are widely received or long retained but for some conformity with truth and nature.' What Johnson chiefly objects to in this case (and in many others) is not so much substance as style—an imperfect or derivative manner, a facile moral rhetoric that expresses an unearned or unexamined confidence. The warning against hope 'may have been recited with too much levity, or enforced with too little distinction' (*Yale* III.11).

How striking, though, that moral generality gives way in the last third or so of the essay to the particular plight of authors who more than any other 'class of the human species' need to be cautioned 'against this anticipation of happiness' (*Yale* III.12). To write and to publish, as Johnson is doing, is to ignore the very warnings he is sounding against hope that the future will be better than the present. Simply to contemplate 'every catalogue of a library' (*Yale* III.13) will show how nearly hopeless it is to aspire to literary fame. Johnson's reflexive and ironic meditation as he sets out on his literary career is a powerful summary of the unforgiving print marketplace of the mid-eighteenth century that dramatizes his anxiety about the whole enterprise upon which he has embarked:

> though it should happen that an author is capable of excelling, yet his merit may pass without notice, huddled in the variety of things, and thrown into

the general miscellany of life. He that endeavours after fame by writing, solicits the regard of a multitude fluctuating in pleasures, or immersed in business, without time for intellectual amusements; he appeals to judges prepossessed by passion, or corrupted by prejudices, which preclude their approbation of any new performance... he that finds his way to reputation, through all these obstructions, must acknowledge that he is indebted to other causes besides his industry, his learning, or his wit.   (*Yale* III.14)

These initiating *Ramblers* mark the direction Johnson's periodical writing will take: the densely aphoristic control of moral possibilities that demolishes conventional moral exposition but often turns back on itself to find some truth even in such flawed reasoning, thereby renovating in specifically Johnsonian terms tired moral commonplaces. But even these renovations often run up against the paralyzing distance between moral formulation and lived experience to which, as Johnson repeatedly insists, he wishes above all to be true. The *locus classicus* for this comically inevitable fate of moral discourse occurs in *Rasselas*. The prince reports to Imlac that he has found the perfect moral teacher: 'a man who can teach all that is necessary to be known, who, from the unshaken throne of rational fortitude, looks down on the scenes of life changing beneath him. He reasons, and conviction closes his periods. This man shall be my future guide: I will learn his doctrines, and imitate his life' (*Yale* XVI.74).

For Johnson the moralist such rhetoric is deeply flawed, since it lacks balance, together with an awareness of qualification, the concession that always accompanies assertion, at least in his writings if not in his conversation. When Rasselas returns to see this master, he finds him grieving for his daughter who has just died. Ingenuously, Rasselas repeats the Stoic doctrines he has been so thrilled by: 'Has wisdom no strength to arm the heart against calamity? Consider that external things are naturally variable, but truth and reason are always the same.' To which the grieving philosopher responds: 'What comfort... can truth and reason afford me? of what effect are they now, but to tell me, that my daughter will not be restored?' (*Yale* XVI.75–6). Such an ending bears out Imlac's earlier warning after Rasselas has told him of his enthusiasm for this teacher: 'Be not too hasty... to trust or to admire the teachers of morality: they discourse like angels, but they live like men' (*Yale* XVI.74). To be sure, Imlac is offering, as he must, yet another generalization, albeit one grounded in his worldly experience, to counter Stoic claims; but perhaps the inevitability of (doomed) moral generalization is Johnson's ultimate irony.

Although Johnson's specific target in this sequence is the absolutism of Stoic pride and its deliberate falsification of normal human emotions (and as such a satiric commonplace as old as philosophy itself), the implications are broader. The moral essay runs up against the built-in irrelevance of abstract moralizing, of any attempt to generalize, and thereby evade the facts of experience. The whole project of the moral essay is, as a result, almost purely negative—to dramatize the comic failure of moral-philosophic searching after final or stable truth. The mordant title of the last chapter—'The conclusion, in which nothing is concluded'—underlines the comedy that attends such searching. If we look back at the *Rambler* essays of the 1750s, *Rasselas* is a darkly explicit repudiation of their moral project—but no more than those essays themselves at times strongly imply. Nevertheless, all Johnson's moral writings, including *Rasselas*, also insist on the inevitability of moral searching as well as, given the massive generality of his style, the extreme difficulty of descending to the particular and the concrete. As Freya Johnston puts it, 'Johnson's suspicion of the general truths to which he is also attracted does not lead simply or directly to espousing the concrete, everyday particular.'[12]

And yet, as Fred Parker argues, the effect of Johnson's style is a positive and energizing skepticism, 'a peculiar combination of definiteness and openness' that expresses 'a skeptical intelligence.' Parker characterizes Johnson's writing as a ratification of the concrete world whereby 'any assertion of a general truth or position is felt as a moment in an ongoing process to which the assertion is not wholly adequate.' For Parker, 'the Johnsonian style insists upon the gap between the activity of thinking and the object of thought.'[13]

Many of Johnson's moral essays have, like *Rasselas*, this reflexive feature; they tend toward a questioning of the efficacy of moral discourse itself, which is derided as a static set of abstractions. In *Rambler* 129, Johnson begins by lumping moralists with other writers who neglect experience: 'instead of casting their eyes abroad in the living world, and endeavouring to form maxims of practice and new hints of theory, [they] content their curiosity with that secondary knowledge which books afford' (*Yale* IV.321). One example he offers from among 'the favourite topicks of moral declamation' is the critique of temerity, of 'imprudent boldness' to attempt things 'beyond our power' (*Yale* IV.321). Who, he asks, can deny the justice of such warnings? Yet in the next paragraph Johnson offers a concretely metaphorical balancing opposite, with its images of frozen immobility: 'but there is likewise some danger lest timorous prudence should be inculcated till courage and enterprise are wholly repressed, and the mind congealed in perpetual inactivity by the fatal influence of frigorific wisdom' (*Yale* IV.322).

Several paragraphs follow of further concessions to the original caution of conventional moralists: 'there is a ridiculous perseverance in impracticable schemes which is justly punished with ignominy and reproach' (*Yale* IV.322). Yet despite this wavering, Johnson returns with great (and daring) insistence to the defense of daring, which he says has been so easily and often censured because it is 'one of the vices with which few can be charged,' and many are therefore ready to condemn this 'vice of noble and generous minds, the exuberance of magnanimity, and the ebullition of genius' (*Yale* IV.323). The balance of the essay tips decidedly in favor of boldness, or at least the necessity of experience that will sweep away the fear of difficulty and reveal 'how much constancy may endure, or perseverance perform' (*Yale* IV.324). At the same time Johnson acknowledges, as is his wont, the futility and indeed the bad faith of moral reasoning, since 'men are generally willing to hear precepts by which ease is favoured' (*Yale* IV.323).

In the final two paragraphs, in the light of the common reluctance to heed calls to bold and risky exertion, Johnson manages his final balancing act by shifting his terms. Since few will take his advice to embrace boldness, everyone should by 'reason and reflection' seek to exercise what he calls 'the latent force that nature may have reposited in him' before the time comes when 'compulsion shall torture him to diligence' (*Yale* IV.324). Johnson in effect lowers the bar in defining temerity; he asks that we should see any avoidance of 'necessity' and embracing of 'choice' (no matter how futile, apparently) as a form of boldness that all should strive for before circumstances force action. And in his final paragraph he in fact further attenuates boldness into a sort of entrepreneurial ambition by noting that modern life, with all that makes possible its 'convenience or elegance,' was at one time unknown and 'believed impossible; and therefore would never have been attempted had not some, more daring than the rest, adventured to bid defiance to prejudice and censure' (*Yale* IV.325). The balance Johnson is always seeking can be said to break down. He seems defeated by what he defines as an almost universal timidity in which 'difficulty is, for the most part, the daughter of idleness' (*Yale* IV.324).

Among the most radical of his balancing acts—and another instance of Johnson's attempt to renovate moral discourse—can be found in my last example from *Rambler* 58, which begins with an account of how 'the love of money' has, since antiquity, been denounced by philosophers, 'how all the powers of reason and eloquence have been exhausted in endeavours to eradicate a desire, which seems to have intrenched itself too strongly in the mind to be driven out.' Despite 'all the wit and reason which this favourite cause has called forth,' he wonders if 'a single convert was ever made; that even one man has refused to be rich, when to be rich was in his power, from the conviction of the greater happiness of a narrow fortune' (*Yale* III.310). Does this universally ignored universal moral bromide prove the irrelevance of moralizing? No, as it happens, for then begins the sly restoration of what looks very much like what I suspect Johnson in conversation would have called 'cant.' We know from the first 'yet' that an attempt to realign and refine the topic is on its way. Johnson warns us that even though the rich have ignored these 'admonitions,' it is rash to say 'they are altogether without use.' Since most of us will not be rich ('far the greatest part of mankind must be confined to conditions comparatively mean'), the denigration of riches helps to restrain our envy of those who attain wealth. Johnson puts this at first in only mildly concessive terms that defend such moralizing by negation: 'those writers cannot be thought ill employed that have administered remedies to discontent almost universal' (*Yale* III.311). But concession provokes more aggressive counter-assertions as he evokes the dramatically benign social and moral consequences of the admonitions against riches that he began by disparaging. It is not just envy of the rich that has been diminished by this moral tradition of despising riches. His claim is that the 'doctrine of the contempt of wealth' has hindered 'that fraud, violence, rapine, and circumvention, which must have been produced by an unbounded eagerness of wealth' (*Yale* III.312). Finally, 'whoever finds himself incited by some violent impulse of passion, to pursue riches as the chief end of being' will hesitate if he considers the advice of all those sages, and such 'examination will seldom fail to repress his ardor, and retard his violence' (*Yale* III.312–13).

Johnson's final paragraphs rehearse a *contemptus mundi* theme. He constructs vignettes that dramatize how wealth's uses are limited, that it 'can neither open new avenues to pleasure, nor block up the passages of anguish,' nor improve the mind, but 'may, by hiring flattery, or laying diligence asleep, confirm error and harden stupidity' (*Yale* III.313). Johnson's recuperation of the moral value of the attack on riches is richly concrete in its evocations of the uses of wealth, but not very convincing. The disastrous cupidity he claims is prevented by the moral campaign against wealth is wildly over-dramatized. However, this *Rambler* can be valued as pure performance, as an instance of arguing to win rather than to convince, and I think that this is how Johnson conceived of it. The essay is rather like a traditional school exercise in rhetoric: prove that an ugly woman is better than a beautiful one, that poverty is better than riches, old age than youth. What matters here and elsewhere in Johnson's periodical writing is often enough the rhetorical cleverness that provokes thought and to that extent at least promotes truth or rather the difficulties of seeing the truth, which may be nearly the same thing. But this is not to say with Fussell that Johnson's moral writing is almost pure performance. Rather, the performative elements in that writing point to—without ever quite stabilizing—the possibility of truth in some final or abstract sense.

Uncertainty stands as a guard against dogmatism and even as a provocation for further investigation. Or, more specifically, we can say with Parker that those performative exertions so visible in Johnson's strenuous prose serve to illustrate that truthfulness (as distinct from truth, *tout court*) lies in the mind's active rumination on the ultimately elusive nature of truth, an impossibly abstract notion in Johnson's moral project that is always difficult to locate and even to affirm.

## NOTES

1. Bertrand H. Bronson, 'Johnson Agonistes,' in *Johnson Agonistes and Other Essays* (Cambridge: Cambridge University Press, 1946), 1–52 (9).
2. W. K. Wimsatt, Jr., cites this passage in *The Prose Style of Samuel Johnson*, 2nd edn (New Haven and London: Yale University Press, 1963), 47.
3. Paul Fussell, *Samuel Johnson and the Life of Writing* (New York: Harcourt Brace Jovanovich, 1971), 161.
4. Ibid., 168.
5. Ibid., 173.
6. Ibid., 156.
7. Ibid., 171.
8. Wimsatt, *Prose Style*, 44.
9. Ibid., 47.
10. W. B. C. Watkins, *Perilous Balance: The Tragic Genius of Swift, Johnson, and Sterne* (Princeton: Princeton University Press, 1939).
11. Freya Johnston, *Samuel Johnson and the Art of Sinking 1709–1791* (Oxford and New York: Oxford University Press, 2005), 2.
12. Ibid., 64.
13. Fred Parker, *Scepticism and Literature: An Essay on Pope, Hume, Sterne, and Johnson* (Oxford: Oxford University Press, 2003), 253, 279, 270.

# 5

# Johnson: Sanity and Syntax

*Philip Davis*

There is a bold challenge offered in Adam Phillips's *Going Sane* when he says that 'No one is famous for his sanity.'[1] Madness seems more exciting: 'sanity,' argues Phillips, 'has no drama. Like the "good" characters in literature, the sane don't have any memorable lines.... In so far as we can imagine them at all, they are featureless, bland, unremarkable.'[2] A number of undramatic qualities get taken for granted in the world: they hardly seem worth writing about, or they seem even inherently non-literary. Sanity may be one such common, unexciting norm—if anything, it is only a basis for achieving something more than merely being sane. Mere 'soundness of mind' is how it is defined in Johnson's *Dictionary*, and even there the illustrative quotation from *Hamlet* has more to do with the protagonist's supposed madness. Too often, sanity is recognized as an achievement only when recovered in the face of chaos and breakdown, not as an everyday form of wise living.

But this chapter claims that Samuel Johnson *is* famous for his sanity—despite later biographical efforts to make him more famous, more 'singular' (as it might have been put in the eighteenth century) for his fear of insanity and fantasy, and his horror of depression, loneliness, and death.[3] The test of the fundamental and unshakeable sanity of Johnson's writing lies, I suggest, in this proposition: that if one had to put into the hands of someone on the knife-edge of serious mental trouble the unselected writings of any one author, then it is the work of Johnson one might risk.

In evidence, here is *Rambler* 29 on the sanity of not anticipating trouble—and the following single sentence, which I want to keep in mind throughout this essay:

> Evil is uncertain in the same degree as good, and for the reason that we ought not to hope too securely, we ought not to fear with too much dejection. (*Yale* III.160–1)

It would not be sane to suffer continual anxiety. Equally, it does not help to try to will a constant hopefulness instead. But to put it thus as two separate thoughts in two distinct sentences will not do here, when the intellect feels, however helplessly, that they must somehow be brought into a relation consonant with the nature of the world. As Saul Bellow's Herzog writes to his favorite dead philosopher, Spinoza, for the sake of sanity itself: 'Thoughts not causally connected were said by you to cause pain. I find that is indeed the case.'[4]

Johnson knew equivalent pain in sensing mental gaps and vacuities, in experiencing contradiction or suffering passivity. Boswell famously wrote of the amphitheater in which Johnson did battle with his demons, even using one to fight another (*Life* II.106).[5] So, between those correlating negatives of *Rambler* 29 ('not to hope too...' and 'not to fear too...'), the very arena of life is shaped by a syntax that, refusing separations even amidst difficult negatives and contrasts, offers no simple middle course. As such, Johnson's way is a lay version of what that great Johnsonian, Samuel Beckett, famously admired in the theology of Augustine—commenting thus on the two thieves crucified beside Christ, one on the right hand, the other on the left:

> I am interested in the shape of ideas, even if I do not believe in them. There is a wonderful sentence in Augustine: I wish I could remember the Latin. It is even finer in Latin than in English. 'Do not despair; one of the thieves was saved. Do not presume; one of the thieves was damned.' That sentence has a wonderful shape.[6]

It was not only between presumption and despair but between their lower fallen versions, hope and fear—described by Johnson's beloved Robert Burton as 'those two battering Cannons and principall Engins, with their objects, reward and punishment, *Purgatory*'[7]—that Johnson lived in disturbance, as between heaven and hell. Emotional life for Johnson was characterized by a basic susceptibility to opposite pairs of feelings, positive and negative, related to the ancient animal sense of basic attraction and repulsion, pleasure and pain, good and evil, across the whole arena of existence. So in his *Dictionary* entry for *balance* (sense 7) as 'Equipoise,' Johnson quotes from Pope's *Essay on Man* (1733–4) as a primal template:

> Love, hope, and joy, fair pleasure's smiling train,
> Hate, fear, and grief, the family of pain;
> These mix'd with art, and to due bounds confin'd,
> Make and maintain the *balance* of the mind.

But to Johnson nothing—including 'the balance of the mind'—was ever so simple as Pope's verse always seemed to him to claim.[8] Upon the primitive basis of opposite forces there formed a whole series of secondary and tertiary combinations, in the complex interrelation of body and mind that the chemistry of human emotions involves. 'As the chemists tell us, that all bodies are resolvable into the same elements, and the boundless variety of things arises from the different proportions of very few ingredients; so a few pains, and few pleasures are all the materials of human life' (*Rambler* 68, *Yale* III.359–60). But those simple few in theory make for a complex many in experience. Although somewhere in Johnson there always remains the classic memory of the Aristotelian mean between emotional extremes, it is overlaid with the painful experience of in-between states of predicament, fallen uncertainty, and ambivalence. In *Rambler* 43, for example:

> Such, indeed, is the uncertainty of all human affairs, that security and despair are equal follies, and as it is presumption and arrogance to anticipate triumphs, it is weakness and cowardice to prognosticate miscarriages.   (*Yale* III.236)

As in some ironic and fallen world, the balanced and symmetrical structure of the writing still does not make the act of balancing easy. The space between the opposites is, ats Johnson well knows, easier to identify on the page than to inhabit in the life. But it is those spaces, 'the shape of ideas,' that most compel Johnson's writing.

Thus it is not only the words 'hope' and 'fear' that matter in that characteristic sentence from *Rambler* 29. Nor is it even the opposition between them. 'Evil is uncertain in the same degree as good, and for the reason that we ought not to hope too securely, we ought not to fear with too much dejection.' Every bit as crucial is the fact that, in this middle earth, evil is uncertain 'in the same degree' as good, and so 'for the reason' that we should not hope too securely, we should not fear too dejectedly either. Both hope and fear here, like security and despair in *Rambler* 43, are fallible for the same reason and to the same degree—occurring as part of the same sentence and of the selfsame structure of life. It is the subtler connective between the contrast of hope and fear that is vital. For what Johnson is about is syntax, and not just discrete feeling—syntax being to Johnson the act of joining, with 'syntactical' defined in the *Dictionary* as 'conjoined, fitted to each other.' 'Hope is necessary,' says Johnson in one paragraph of *Rambler* 67; 'Hope is, indeed, very fallacious,' he adds in the next (*Yale* III.354). But the great work of human art is to put the separate phrases together, as in the *Dictionary* citation from Richard Crashaw which Johnson includes under sense 1 of *hope*:

> Sweet *hope*! kind cheat! fair fallacy! by thee
> We are not where or what we be;
> But what and where we would be: thus art thou
> Our absent presence, and our future now.

But Johnson distrusted too ready a wit for paradox. He wanted to work out intricately the way of shaped understanding, connective by connective. As the psychologist William James was to argue in his *Principles of Psychology*, there aren't merely the basic named feelings of anger, of love, of joy; in the evolution of complex combinations of emotion, there is also an otherwise undefinable feeling of *and*, of *if*, of *but*.[9] And what such complex connective syntax is about is the envisioned structure of the world and the place of human expectations, aspirations, and emotions within it.

'Metaphysical rights entering into common life,' said that great disciple of the school of Johnson, Edmund Burke, are like 'rays of light piercing a dense medium'; by the laws of nature, they are 'refracted from their straight line':

> The primitive rights of men undergo such a variety of refractions, that it becomes absurd to talk of them as if they continued in the simplicity of the original direction.[10]

The rights of men, Burke concludes, 'are in a sort of middle, incapable of definition, but not impossible to be discerned.'[11] Similarly, Johnson's sentences are themselves not straightforward, nor straight lines, but have to work their way to understanding through refractions, in a sort of middle of life. It is not as Plato would have it according to his ideal of pure reason described in Aristotle's *Nicomachean Ethics*: that sentences proceed either from or towards first principles along a racecourse with a beginning, a turn, and an end.[12] Johnson's is rather second-order, fallen, resiliently struggling work. So in *Rambler* 29 that middling enabler-phrase 'for the reason that,' embedded in the midst of the syntax, creates a corresponding disposition towards mental acceptance at the level of the whole sentence. We don't know 'the reason,' only that there is a reason that makes it like this.

What Johnson brings to culmination in his work is the applied use of the humanist periodic sentence. That is to say: a sentence combining a number of distinct thoughts in a number of balanced phrases and clauses, signaling its course through the use of particles and conjunctions acting as markers or signposts, and not mentally complete until it discloses its end. It is vitally different from the basic nuclear sentence, where noun meets verb. It is also distinct from the loose and open style of narrative where one sentence follows another horizontally in time—sometimes all too predictably; sometimes, alternatively, without any prior sense that it was coming, or of where it is going.

Instead of either abstract reason or contingent narrative, Johnson offers a syntax such as the following—against the Stoic theory of preserving an invulnerable state of emotional indifference:

> If by excluding joy we could shut out grief, the scheme would deserve very serious attention; but since, however we may debar ourselves from happiness, misery will finds its way at many inlets, and the assaults of pain will force our regard, though we may withhold it from the invitations of pleasure, we may surely endeavour to raise life above the middle

point of apathy at one time, since it will necessarily sink below it at another. (*Rambler* 47, *Yale* III.256–7)

It is not just the oppositions of joy and grief, happiness and misery, pain and pleasure, of 'raise above' and 'sink below,' that matter here. Just as important structurally are 'If by … but since'; then the complex 'however we may … misery will … pain will … though we may'; and, above all, the final 'may surely … since it will necessarily.' That 'since' is courageously vital: the hard work of sanity lies in a syntax that cannot 'exclude' what is inconvenient or 'shut out' what is painful, but can include what still 'may' be in the face of what undoubtedly 'will.'

We may not 'surely' raise life, but only 'surely endeavour' to do so. In Johnson such syntax is a way of being, a form of experience one learns after one has been several times through the repeated experience of those simple individual emotions, such as pleasure or pain, love or hate, hope or fear, back and forth. It forms a shape beyond the registering of separate momentary emotions. Sanity in Johnson is not one separate thing but that which comes out of a set of hard-won mental connections.

This sense of a complex overall experience in the sentences is far less easily definable than are the separate elements that compose its character. I say 'character' because the writer of such sentences is emphatically not the inexperienced youth of *Rambler* 196, 'who never imagines that there may be greatness without safety, affluence without content, jollity without friendship, and solitude without peace' (*Yale* V.259). In his feeling for the intricate, dense structure of things, 'without' is a preposition so heavy that Johnson almost turns it into a conjunction. He will not leave out what must be thought on, whatever the effect on elegance of style or peace of mind. *Rambler* 134 warns against idleness, in the face of mortality:

> The certainty that life cannot be long, and the probability that it will be much shorter than nature allows, ought to awaken every man to the active prosecution of whatever he is desirous to perform. It is true that no diligence can ascertain success; death may intercept the swiftest career; but he who is cut off in the execution of an honest undertaking, has at least the honour of falling in his rank, and has fought the battle, though he missed the victory. (*Yale* IV.349)

Dictionary Johnson creates his careful linguistic pathway over the verbal stepping stones of 'certainty' and 'probability.' But the way he works would not be so effective if he had tried harder for *more* than 'at least'—if he had, for instance, written more cheerily 'and though he missed the victory, has fought the battle.' Although Johnson will not let down his reader with the order in which he does things, his cannot simply be an effort in mechanical cheering up. To the author who wrote in *Idler* 103 of the 'horrour of the last' (*Yale* II.315), the period must end where life may end, in the very possible threat of missing a final victory and suffering a final defeat. Caught as he is in the middle of life between the lost simplicity of pre-lapsarian origin and the unknowable outcome of a nonetheless certain end, it is the meantime that has to be Johnson's concern. So he writes: 'has fought the battle, though he missed the victory'—where 'though' means both sadly '*notwithstanding* it is true that' and defiantly '*even if* it is true that.' 'Though' is on that Johnsonian knife's edge where resistance and acceptance are found to be unexpectedly close. There are two opposite feelings, but one condition that insists on combining them.

And yet it is precisely Johnson's syntax that Romantics and post-Romantics have disparaged as cumbersome, pompous, and mannered.[13] In 'The Periodical Essayists' (1819), William Hazlitt offered one of the first great challenges to Johnson's style, assailing it as a great, obsessive controlling mechanism for the nerves:

> The structure of [Johnson's] sentences, which was his own invention, and which has been generally imitated since his time, is a species of rhyming in prose, where one clause answers to another in measure and quantity, like the tagging of syllables at the end of a verse; the close of the period follows as mechanically as the oscillation of a pendulum, the sense is balanced with the sound; each sentence, revolving round its centre of gravity, is contained with itself like a couplet, and each paragraph forms itself into a stanza. Dr. Johnson is also a complete balance-master in the topics of morality. He never encourages hope, but he counteracts it by fear; he never elicits a truth, but he suggests some objection in answer to it.   (*Hazlitt*, VI.102)

In seeing so much even whilst liking it so little, this is a brilliantly unsympathetic account. For what Hazlitt manages to expose here is the underlying mechanical temptation in Johnson to believe that the achievement of balance—of almost any kind and by almost any means—is automatically a guarantee of one's being in good shape and order.

As author of the great Romantic *Essay on the Principles of Human Action* (1805), Hazlitt saw all emotions as imaginative anticipations of actions; as deep, pre-conscious adventures in opening and creating a new future.[14] No wonder he would hate a seemingly pre-emptive balance-master whose every hope seemed only to raise a fear, whose every primary truth is challenged by some secondary doubt and complication that swing back upon him like an afterthought from the past. 'He [Johnson] dares not trust himself,' Hazlitt complains: he lives not in 'the immediate impressions of things' but in the timidity of 'morbid apprehension' (*Hazlitt* VI.102).

It is not difficult to imagine Hazlitt reading the following letter from Johnson as though through the italics here inserted as marks of what Hazlitt would call Johnson's unnecessary foreclosure:

Hope is itself a species of happiness, and *perhaps*, the chief happiness which this world affords, *but* like *all* other pleasures *immoderately* enjoyed, the excesses of *hope must be expiated by pain*, and expectations *improperly* indulged *must end in disappointment*. If it be asked, what is the improper expectation which is it dangerous to indulge, *experience* will quickly answer, that it is such *expectation*, dictated not by *reason* but by *desire*; expectation raised *not* by the *common* occurrences of life *but* by the *wants* of the Expectant; an Expectation that requires the *common* course of things to be *changed* and the *general rules* of Action to be *broken*.     (*Letters* I.203–4)

'Immoderately' cannot be left unchecked; Johnson's law requires it to be balanced by later expiation and final disappointment. 'Wants' mean as much 'lacks' as 'desires' to Johnson: into the felt vacancy left by the sense of something missing comes that restless imagination which creates the specific need to try to fill it. 'Expectation,' informed by experience and taught by reason, can alone salvage what in desire or in hope may survive life's testing.

But Hazlitt may be right to suspect that such tutored expectation was impossible to sustain. Johnson did fear the human pendulum and with it the danger of automatic psychological swings from hope to fear, from the rising to the depressing of spirits. For the emotions could work almost unilaterally between themselves, psychologically separated from external objects or creating them delusively or even madly, in their own image, without our even recognizing it. That is why in l.343 of the final verse paragraph of *The Vanity of Human Wishes* (1749) he wrote, 'Where then shall Hope and Fear their objects find?' (*Yale* VI.107)—meaning their proper, external objects. Johnson was in that sense a committed realist, wanting a psychology that was not at its own mercy but sanely anchored in the reality of this fallen world, without either eschewing or anticipating the reality of a world hereafter. Unrealistic Romantic desire would be to Johnson every bit as psychologically mechanical as the mechanisms Hazlitt attributes to Johnsonian distrustful reasoning.

But Hazlitt might retort: Where in this restrictive sanity, which is so often working against the natural human grain, was Johnson's confidence in himself and his fellow creatures? To use Iain McGilchrist's terms, it was as though Hazlitt was a champion of the creative right hemisphere of the brain, challenging in Johnson the Enlightenment's left-hemisphere dominance in symmetrical and pre-emptive reason.[15]

Yet to come back to that key sentence from *Rambler* 29 one last time, it is important that Johnson doesn't choose to write, as he could have: 'and for the reason that we ought not to fear with too much dejection, we ought not to hope too securely.' To read Hazlitt's criticism might be to expect that ordering. But Johnson writes 'and for the reason that we ought not to hope too securely, we ought not to fear with too much dejection.' The pendulum could indeed go in either direction: he has fought the battle, though he missed the victory; he has missed the victory, but he has fought the battle. But for Johnson it must not swing automatically, when within the tight laws of structure there was still, however small, some chance for discretionary choice, some room for vital maneuver. 'The balance is put into our own hands, and we have power to transfer the weight to either side' (*Rambler* 7, *Yale* III.39). As Johnson says in *Rambler* 25: 'A man once persuaded, that any impediment is insuperable, has *given* it, with respect to himself, that strength and weight which it had *not* before' (*Yale* III.138, my emphases). The task is to refuse to be the human screech-owl of *Rambler* 59—emphatically not Johnson, though Hazlitt would almost have it so; a creature that might 'weaken for a time that love of life, which is necessary to the vigorous prosecution of any undertaking' (*Yale* III.315).

Given the choice between definitely making existence worse and trying to make it better, there is no more 'reason' to give up on hope than to give in to fear. What human beings should do is take the bad news that they have learnt from hope and use it for good in relation to fear, moving from one medium to another. 'The cure for the greatest part of human miseries is not radical, but palliative,' as Johnson states in *Rambler* 32 (*Yale* III.75). Within his balanced sentences, there is a palliative effect when the balance is tipped in favor of will rather than theory—cheating as it were for the sake of life, in putting one priority robustly ahead of another when abstract reason could go either way.

To try to play middlingly safe; to pretend to be always neutral or already well-balanced; not to take pleasure now in anything we might later lose: 'is it not like advice, not to walk lest we stumble, or not to see lest our eyes should light upon deformity?' (*Rambler* 32, *Yale* III.179). Sanity in Johnson is not elegantly or effortlessly poised. But amidst its stumblings it is, I repeat, something indeed similar to what we call character:[16] not a primary cure-all for life's ills, but the little second-order difference a person can make, or a person can become, when the balance between good and bad is otherwise wholly poised. It is like the work of the brain's right hemisphere contained and constrained within the realm of the left. So in *Rambler* 47, Johnson writes of sorrow, and especially mourning, that it has no remedy provided by nature:

> it requires what it cannot hope, that the laws of the universe should be repealed; that the dead should return, or the past should be recalled. (*Yale* III.254)

This is characteristic Johnsonian syntax—that of a man whose human powers exist precisely but paradoxically in the realization of their own limitation. There are the 'laws,' and there is also what 'cannot' be, nonetheless still retained and emotionally included within those laws like the human clause within the overall life-sentence, 'requir[ing] what it cannot hope.' Whoever, so to speak, invented the words *what* or *though* or *since* or *yet* or *without* gave Johnson what he needed. For with those little verbal markers, the irresistible but unavailing emotions in the sentences are not made less by their placed limitation, but poignantly felt more, as a result of being involuntarily a part of a world that seems both to summon and to deny them. Sanity does not consist in trying to eradicate the passions but in finding their place for better *and* worse within the overall sentence, offering palliative scope for life. In Johnson's words, 'It is our duty, while we continue in this complicated state, to regulate one part of our composition by some regard to the other' (*Rambler* 17, *Yale* III.97). This rebalancing adjustment is a courageous and encouraging willed extra, the will-to-live that a human being individually brings to existence, like that appeal which Johnson always left open to nature forcing its way in against any closed system.

This brings me, finally, to a second but subsidiary function of Johnson's syntax in the service of sanity. If the first duty of Johnsonian syntax is to locate, and adapt itself to, the structure of existence, a second purpose is lodged in a different dimension—as it were behind the text, as a result of the language's creative repression and silenced frustration. For this second function has to do with the counteracting relations in Johnson between the confining limitation of grammatical space and the potentially expansive concentration of the vocabulary that competes within it. Here Hazlitt is again perceptive, seeing within Johnson's prose an equivalent to the productive tension between the competing demands of rhyme and sense in the verse couplets of Johnson's age.

In his remarks on poor writers in *Idler* 36, Johnson makes clear his distaste both for the writer who '*diffuses* every thought through so many diversities of expression, that it is lost like water in the mist' and for the 'ponderous dictator of sentences, whose notions are delivered in the *lump*, and are, like uncoined bullion, of more weight than use' (*Yale* II.113, my emphases). In between these extremes of the diffusive and the lumpen, Johnson's verbal physics seeks linguistic density. As he suggests in *Rambler* 8, modern philosophers say that the universe is made up of dispersed matter which, if concentrated, could be contained in the shape of a cube of a few feet (*Yale* III.41). What Johnson does in his massy language is compress those energies that, as a singular individual, he felt he had dispersed in time and vacuity. And it is this potentially explosive vocabulary that forms a counter-resistance to the subordinate space left to it within the overall syntactical structure.

For Johnson is the writer who shows within writing what also goes on behind writing. Here is an example from within the density of *Rambler* 14. Against the simple charge of literary hypocrisy, Johnson offers a defense of a man often writing much better than he lives. The *idea* of perfection may be necessary, he says, even if—or especially because—we cannot attain it:

> and he that is most deficient in the duties of life, makes some atonement for his faults, if he warns others against his own failings, and hinders, by the salubrity of his admonitions, the contagion of his example.
>
> Nothing is more unjust, however common, than to charge with hypocrisy him that expresses zeal for those virtues, which he neglects to practise; since he may be sincerely convinced of the advantages of conquering his passions, without having yet obtained the victory, as a man may be confident of the advantages of a voyage, or a journey, without having courage or industry to undertake it, and may honestly recommend to others, those attempts which he neglects himself.   (*Yale* III.76)

Again Johnson struggles for mental equilibrium, fighting for the room in which to allow human mitigation and complexity. The knife-edge insertion, for example, of the word 'some' amidst the balancing acts: 'makes some atonement for his faults, if he warns others against his own failings.' Not complete atonement, not no atonement, but middling, palliative, and not radical, 'some atonement.' It is like the word 'yet' in 'without having yet obtained the victory.' Or, it is like the room found for the insertion of the adverb 'sincerely'—'may be sincerely convinced of the advantages without having yet obtained the victory.' However ethical from a vertical dimension, 'sincerely' has, like 'honestly' later in the sentence, to be incorporated into horizontally going onward, in the midst of a complex life delivering at best only limited efficacy. By the end it is the repeated word 'without' that has to act as the painful fulcrum for the writing. The characteristically Johnsonian inclusion of such little words trigger the feelings that they also partly restrain.

And in particular there are two electrical instants that are, momentarily, almost poetically autonomous within the almost physical drive of the prose syntax. I mean, first, that point at which Johnson says that the writer makes some atonement if he 'hinders, by the salubrity of his admonitions, the contagion of his example.' And then, second, he speaks sympathetically of the man who 'expresses zeal for those virtues, which he neglects to practise.' It is the pendulum's pivotal 'which,' the morally connecting relative, that is so mortifying in the latter of those two instances: zeal which he neglects—what a piece of work is a man! And it is equally painful when a connective such as 'which' is taken away and we are confronted instead by the sudden morally violent juxtaposition of 'salubrity of admonitions' immediately up against 'contagion of examples.' As so often in Johnson it can swing either way, from the salubrity of the one to the contagion of the other. So it is, finally, that a man 'may honestly recommend to others, those attempts which he neglects himself': this is at once a balance of painful contradiction and partial corrective.

By such means the second effect of Johnsonian syntax is achieved: the passing pressure of these general formulations triggers in the reader the sort of singular and particular memories, the private instances, that the writer himself felt beneath the very writing of them. And that is where these private, biographical, and even discreditable matters belong, Johnson believes: in the creative background to general social life, in the silence that is nonetheless here audible as resonant personal subtext. '[Z]eal for those virtues, which he neglects to practise'; 'recommend to others . . . which he neglects himself'; 'the salubrity of his admonitions'; 'the contagion of his example.' There are levels hidden within these lines: discontinuities, fallings off, lost or broken links, unhappy connectives. Even as the sentence goes through and past them, the pressurized nouns and verbs in such painful juxtaposition momentarily open up another dimension within the reader. The reader of *Rambler* 14 thinks silently and privately: I know that I have written or spoken better than I have lived; I know I have not wanted to recall specifically when or how. But that *is* how by repression such specific things, unacknowledged, become generally residual and latent, the minutiae that shake down into the lump called guilt, primed for activation.

'Men more frequently require to be reminded than informed,' as Johnson states in *Rambler* 2 (*Yale* III.14). In this way Johnson's general language finds its resonant power in simultaneously recalling *and* repressing those personal memories. For Johnson emphatically won't do what he describes writers as too often doing—proposing their paper-based schemes in abstract and in theory, in an omission of all surrounding and underlying life, exempt from 'the enticements of hope, the solicitations of affection, the importunities of appetite, or the depressions of fear' (*Rambler* 14, *Yale* III.75). Incorporated mind in Johnson makes the reader almost physically register these besetting difficulties of feeling. For what were verbs—hope *entices*, affection *solicits*, appetite *importunes*, fear *depresses*—are pulled back from being specific events into the solid permanence of nouns, themselves in turn reactivating the force of the other nouns in their immediate environment. It feels like a language so deeply shared as almost to be composing a biological blueprint of the human race.

But without that species-language of a massy diction in a holding syntax, Johnson would be confronted with the chaos he found, for example, in both the person and the poetry of his distressed friend Christopher Smart. Smart's is a case in extreme contrast, which unbalances normative syntax, undoes relative considerations, and subsumes social norms in religious absolutes. For Smart represented an extreme confessional privacy that remained neither silent nor private, but was singular, naked, and idio-syncratically explicit, even to the point of questionable sanity:

> My poor friend Smart shewed the disturbance of his mind, by falling upon his knees, and saying his prayers in the street, or in any other unusual place. Now although, rationally speaking, it is greater madness not to pray at all, than to pray as Smart did, I am afraid there are so many who do not pray, that their understanding is not called into question.   (*Life* I.397)

Yet while Smart stepped outside the normal ongoing system of things in peril of the madhouse, Johnson himself would not risk his all for salvation—and knew too he might be damned even for that. Even in that way Johnson's position remained painfully and self-checkingly honorable—sane in both its achievement and its limitation—precisely for his being unable to escape into the transcendent for reasons inextricably good and bad. 'God be gracious to Samuel Johnson,' prayed Smart, in turn.[17]

Johnson's syntax is wisdom best characterized as mental survival in the very middle of life. But even near the end of it, there is a letter to the Reverend Doctor Taylor (5 May 1784) in which Johnson writes, 'O! my friend, the approach of death is very dreadful.' Then there is this great sentence which may stand, I believe, as almost a final statement: 'I am afraid to think on that which I know I cannot avoid' (*Life* IV.270).[18]

That sentence is profoundly characteristic in the work it does between parts and whole, the human condition and the feelings within it. I am afraid. I am *afraid* to think. I am afraid to *think* on that which I *know*. I am afraid to think on that which I know I *cannot avoid*. The syntax created by 'That which' is what made this paradoxical utterance achievable at the extreme writerly limits of honesty, of sanity, and of mortality alike.

Almost impossibly occupying so many positions at once, it is in every sense one of the greatest life-sentences in English letters, supremely balanced and wholly vulnerable. Despite what Adam Phillips says, the sane do have memorable lines when the sane is Johnson.

## NOTES

1. Adam Phillips, *Going Sane* (London: Penguin, 2006), 35.
2. Ibid., 19.
3. See, for example, Bertrand H. Bronson, 'Johnson Agonistes,' in *Johnson Agonistes and other Essays* (Cambridge: Cambridge University Press, 1946), 1–52.
4. Saul Bellow, *Herzog*, first published 1964 (Harmondsworth: Penguin, 1965), 189.
5. See Arieh Sacks, 'Samuel Johnson on "The Art of Forgetfulness,"' *Studies in Philology* 63 (1966), 582–3: 'The relation between hope and fear is not

merely schematic since hope itself is a kind of fear.' What Sacks has in mind is 'the great anxiety or "uneasiness" which characterizes all "expectation," all projections into the future. . . . Hope and fear are interchangeable in the sense that they sum up the tragic restlessness inherent in man's temporal being, his mind's constant over-reaching of his body.'

6. Quoted in Frank Doherty, *Samuel Beckett* (London: Hutchinson, 1971), 88. Thus Beckett: 'It's Johnson, always Johnson, who is with me. And if I follow any tradition it is his' (120).

7. Robert Burton, *The Anatomy of Melancholy*, eds. Thomas C. Faulkner, Nicolas K. Kiesling et al., 6 vols., rev. edn (Oxford: Oxford University Press, 1992–2000), III.355.

8. See *Lives* IV.76 on Pope's 'wonder-working sounds' dazzling the reader into thinking the obvious to be new and deep.

9. William James, *The Principles of Psychology* [1890] (New York: Dover, 1950), 2 vols., I.245.

10. Edmund Burke, *Reflections on the Revolution in France* [1790], ed. C. C. O'Brien (Harmondsworth: Penguin, 1968), 152–3. See Philip Davis, 'Johnson's Cosmology: Vacuity and Ramification,' in *English Literature, Theology and the Curriculum*, ed. Liam Gearon (London: Cassell, 1999), 173–89.

11. Burke, *Reflections on the Revolution in France*, 152–3.

12. See Aristotle, *Nicomachean Ethics*, trans. Terence Irwin (Indianapolis, IN: Hackett, 1985), 1,095a22–b16.

13. See, for example, Macaulay on Johnson, as discussed in Iain McGilchrist, *Against Criticism* (London: Faber, 1982), 77–81.

14. See Philip Davis, 'The Future in the Instant: Hazlitt's *Essay* and Shakespeare,' in *Metaphysical Hazlitt: Bicentenary Essays*, eds. Upendra Natarajan, Tom Paulin, and Duncan Wu (London: Routledge, 2005), 43–55.

15. Iain McGilchrist, *The Master and his Emissary: The Divided Brain and the Making of the Western World* (New Haven and London: Yale University Press, 2009), esp. Chapter 11.

16. See also Chapter 10.

17. *Jubilate Agno*, Fragment D, l.74, in *The Poetical Works of Christopher Smart*, I: *Jubilate Agno*, ed. Karina Williamson (Oxford: Clarendon Press, 1980), 114.

18. *Letters* IV.312 inserts a comma after 'know.'

# 6

# Johnson's Freud

*Adam Phillips*

METHODIST. *n. s.* [from *method*]
1. A physician who practises by theory.
2. One of a new kind of puritans lately arisen, so called from their profession to live by rules and in constant method.

Johnson, A Dictionary of the English Language (1755)

In Chapter VI of *Rasselas* (1759), 'A dissertation on the art of flying,' the prince talks to the man referred to as 'the artist' about the 'sailing chariot' the latter is building. '[R]esolved to enquire further before he suffered hope to afflict him by disappointment' (*Yale* XVI.24), Rasselas pursues his skeptical enquiry in his search for realistic hope, the implication being that disappointment is created by false expectation, and that, while life isn't inherently disappointing, we can still be disappointed. ' "I am afraid," said he to the artist, "that your imagination prevails over your skill, and that you now tell me rather what you wish than what you know." ' In an anticipation of William Empson,[1] the artist, defending his belief, replies: 'He that can swim needs not despair to fly,' and that 'We are only to proportion our power of resistance to the different density of the matter through which we are to pass' (*Yale* XVI.24–5). For sense 1 of *resistance* Johnson has, in his *Dictionary*, 'The act of resisting; opposition' and, in sense 2, 'The quality of not yielding to force or external impression.' He cites the Bible, Bacon, Waller, and Locke; the affinity with *Rasselas* is evident in his illustrative quotation from Newton's *Opticks* (1704); 'But that part of the *resistance*...is proportional to the density of the matter, and cannot be diminished by dividing the matter into smaller parts, nor by any other means, than by decreasing the density of the medium.' Resistance depends upon, is proportional to, the density of the matter that has to be resisted. It would be unrealistic to be disappointed by the density of the matter.

Clearly it was not part of Sigmund Freud's originality to show us that perception is distorted by wish or, as Rasselas puts it, to the artist, 'you now tell me rather what you wish than what you know.' And resistance was the heart of the matter for Freud, the ways in which the patient, and not only the patient, resists what he knows with what he wishes. Freud, like Johnson, has to be mindful of the density of the matter, of what the analyst and the patient are up against. 'The unconscious—that is to say "the repressed,"' he writes in *Beyond the Pleasure Principle* (1922), 'offers no resistance whatever to the efforts of the treatment. Indeed, it itself has no other endeavour than to break through the pressure weighing down on it and force its way either to consciousness or to a discharge through some real action. Resistance during treatment arises from the same higher strata and systems of the mind which originally carried out the repression.'[2]

The ego—Freud's figure for a part-function of consciousness—has to have what Johnson called, in defining sense 2 of *resistance* in his *Dictionary*, 'the quality of not yielding to force,' from the repressed instincts, or to 'external impression,' from the interpreting analyst. Resistance is the name of the game, and such is the density of the matter—the determined and horrified repudiation of forbidden or unacceptable desire, and of forbidden or unacceptable external reality by the individual, his life organized to refuse its acknowledgment—that a great deal of work has to be done understanding the density of the resisting medium, the person's defensive system. (Johnson writes in *Rambler* 4 of youth needing to be 'initiate[d]' into what he calls 'the art of necessary defence,' *Yale* III.23.) Indeed, it is the analyst's job to nudge the patient, to give him a good description of how he goes about not seeing things. 'There is no doubt,' Freud writes, 'that it is easier for the patient's intelligence to recognise the resistance and to find the translation corresponding to what is repressed if we have previously given him the appropriate anticipatory ideas. If I say to you: "Look up at the sky, there's a balloon there" you will discover it much more easily than if I simply tell you to look up and see if you can see anything' (Freud, *Standard Edition*, XVI.437). When Johnson and Freud write about resistance they write about flying, about the strange matter of air. It was, we should remember, the artist who claimed to understand 'resistance' in *Rasselas*; the man who, eventually, 'waved his pinions awhile to gather air, then leaped from his stand, and in an instant dropped into the lake' (*Yale* XVI.28).

I have made this detour into Freud's writing just to make an obvious and simple point, and it is worth wondering what is gained—and perhaps more importantly what is lost—in the making of such links. We might wonder, for example, what is being resisted in the courting and claiming of echoes and shared preoccupations. Especially when Johnson is, or was, or can be so easily cast as a secret sharer of Freud's, despite the obvious disparities of time and place, of genealogy and profession. So, for example, in Donald Davie's Introduction to *The Late Augustans: Longer Poems of the Later Eighteenth Century* (1958), he has this to say about Johnson that easily finds favor with Freud's picture of the (modern) human predicament. 'This man,' Davie writes:

> who, as critic, insisted on the necessity for common sense to control the flights of the imagination, was the same whose imagination so peopled his solitude that he implored his friend's company in the middle of the night. The man whose vivid emotional life is recorded in his private prayers, whose tender sensibilities led him to maintain for years a household of waifs and strays and unfortunate eccentrics, is the same whose verses observe disciplines equalled in strictness only by Pope's. And this is not paradoxical. For it is the mind which knows the power of its own potentially disruptive propensities that needs and demands to be disciplined.[3]

It is a touching portrait in the service of a poetics; and it could be said that, after Freud, psychoanalysts—and not only psychoanalysts—also divided into those who were on the side of the potentially disruptive propensities of the mind, and those who were rather more interested in the discipline side of things; and what it might mean to be on those sides, so twinned and interanimating as they are. Both Freud and Johnson, it should be said, were among those so struck by the potentially disruptive propensities of the mind that their money was, fairly and squarely, on the disciplines required. 'For it is the mind which knows the power of its own potentially disruptive propensities,' as Davie says, 'that needs and demands to be disciplined.' Clearly, how Johnson and Freud described the mind and those disruptive propensities, and indeed what constituted realistic (or truthful) discipline is, as we say, culturally and historically specific. It is intriguing to read Johnson's 'Prayers' and Freud's *Future of an Illusion* (1927), or his *Civilization and its Discontents* (1930), together, but it reveals almost a different cosmology—a different description of where the stress is, and where the stress should fall. Where, for example, Freud makes the most sweeping generalizations about religion, in his insistent attempt to demystify it, Johnson is most particular about its necessary truths and essential consolations. Freud generalizes to discredit, Johnson generalizes to credit. Johnson warns himself away from 'loose thoughts' (*Yale* I.92); Freud encourages them.

Johnson advises us famously in his 'Life of Cowley' that 'Great thoughts are always general, and consist in positions not limited by exceptions, and in descriptions not descending to minuteness' (*Lives* I.201). (Freud, it should be noted, thought biography impossible, whereas for Johnson it was both instructive and exemplary.) 'The business of a poet,' Imlac argues in *Rasselas*, 'is to examine, not the individual, but the species; to remark general properties and large appearances: he does not number the streaks of the tulip, or describe the different shades in the verdure of the forest' (*Yale* XVI.43). If we can avoid, in our descriptions, descending to minuteness, and look for the species not the individual, then, in Johnson's eighteenth-century aesthetic, we can make our links and connections wherever they are truthfully pertinent; pertinent, that is, to a putatively universal human nature, bearing in mind Philip Davis's description of Johnson as 'so particular a generaliser.'[4]

Johnson's aesthetic frees us, in a way that Freud's does not. For the psychoanalyst it is not great thoughts that are general but defensive ones. Great thoughts may or may not be general for Freud—Freud was interested, as a scientist, in particulars in the service of generalities—but they are, clinically, the least revealing; it is the exceptions, the descending to minutenesss, the examining of the individual that Freud is after. Johnson, that is to say, encourages us to read Freud in a way that Freud cannot encourage us to read Johnson. Johnson might recommend that we read Freud for abiding truths about human nature, or at least to find out whether Freud has such truths to tell. Freud believes that the patient is at his least truthful in the speaking of general truths. Freud, one might say, is interested in what generalization is about, what psychic needs it might serve. He gives us a language in which we can redescribe what people might be up to when they generalize. Freud, indeed, has a method for finding out how people use general truths to hide themselves in. He was not of William Blake's party—'To Generalize is to be an Idiot'[5]—but a distinctive difference is discernible in these shifting criteria.

So when T. S. Eliot in his well-known lecture 'Johnson as Critic and Poet' tries to give an account of how we are to read Johnson, it is the historical question that vexes him; he is insistent that we reduce Johnson if we try and make him modern, and render Johnson our contemporary. 'If we censure an eighteenth-century critic,' Eliot writes:

> for not having a modern, historical and comprehensive appreciation, we must ourselves adopt towards him, the attitude the lack of which we reprehend; we must not be narrow in accusing him of narrowness, or prejudiced in accusing him of prejudice. Johnson had a positive point of view which is not ours; a point of view which needs a vigorous effort of imagination to understand.[6]

Part of this vigorous effort of imagination, Eliot believes, requires that we not be bewitched by our contemporary vocabularies in our redescriptions of the past, something that seems rather easier in the breach. He wants us to have a sense of historical context, but not a historicism that can be used to diminish the emotional impact of the writing. 'A contemporary critic,' he writes, 'would produce another, and more complicated account, which would probably be influenced by the study of sciences of more recent growth. The modern account would fit in better with our mental furniture, but would not necessarily be more true for this reason.'[7] It is the burden of the present to distract us from the past. He urges us, particularly in writing about Johnson (and Dryden), to accept that critics 'concerned with literature as literature, and not with psychology or sociology,' are more likely to have what he calls 'enduring usefulness.'[8]

'In our own day,' Eliot goes on—and he does go on—'the influence of psychology and sociology upon literary criticism have been very noticeable'; and even though this has, he says with faint disdain, 'enlarged the field of the critic,' 'this enrichment has also been an impoverishment.' For Eliot, this is not a contradiction in terms because it has been a particular kind of impoverishment: 'an impoverishment for the purely literary values, the appreciation of good writing for its own sake, have become submerged when literature is judged in the light of other considerations.'[9] Johnson, Eliot felt, was particularly prone to this kind of impoverishing view of his work because he wrote in what Eliot calls, rather amazingly, 'a settled society' in which there was 'a definite and limited public, in the midst of which there would be a smaller number of persons of taste and discrimination, with the same background of education and manners'; whereas Eliot, who delivered these lectures in 1944, was living 'amongst the varieties of chaos in which we find ourselves immersed to-day.'[10] In this light, we should value Johnson because he is not our contemporary; and we make him our contemporary and thus radically misrecognize him, by foisting on his writing other considerations, such as the modern vocabularies of sociology and psychology (the 'literary,' in this view, presumably becomes everything that is not sociology or psychology). Like Davie, Eliot implicitly acknowledges that Johnson in particular—like Coleridge, but not like Dryden or Arnold—is a poet-critic who tempts us to be, as it were, psychological about him. Johnson seems to be a writer for whom what we now think of as psychological descriptions seem particularly illuminating, or perhaps just well suited. By being so vividly a character but not a character-type—by being so observed and biographied and sustained, as Chapter 14 argues, as a culture-hero—Johnson's writing all too easily calls up in us psychological thoughts; and Freudian thoughts in those of us for whom, if there is such a thing as psychology, it is psychoanalysis.

For literature students of my generation, Walter Jackson Bate was the authority on Johnson, and Bate could not resist, four years before Norman O. Brown's *Life Against Death* (1959), seeing Johnson and Freud as essentially related. 'Few classical moralists,' he wrote in *The Achievement of Samuel Johnson*, 'are closer to Freud than Samuel Johnson, or have so uncanny a sense of what repression can mean.'[11] So it may be worth, briefly, testing this claim, and what, if anything, it impoverishes. What is at stake, for both Johnson and Freud, is whether sanity—or rather, what kind of sanity—depends upon the acknowledgment of reality.[12] They both give an account in their writing of what it might be not to go mad. To be interested in repression is to be interested in the necessities it serves. It is to picture what an unrepressed life might be like.

The 'Uncanny,' in the sense Freud gave it in his paper on the subject, is an experience of something apparently new that is a disguised version of something from the past (*Standard Edition*, XVII.217–52). If, in Bate's view, Johnson had an incomparably uncanny sense of what repression can mean, then he must have been, though clearly not an influence on Freud's thought, a precursor. Freud's picture of repression is something old disguised as something new, not simply a redescription of something that has been around one way and another, and in one place and another, for some time. 'That it is vain to shrink from what cannot be avoided, and to hide that from ourselves which must some time be found, is a truth which we all know, but which all neglect,' Johnson writes in *Idler* 41 (*Yale* II.129). This is not startling because it reminds us of Freud, but because of its accuracy, its realism, its precision of diction and syntax; it is vain to shrink from what cannot be avoided because it is at once futile and self-flattering, futile because self-flattering (rather than, say, self-evoking).

Freud's concept of repression was not new, according to Bate; the truth is that Johnson knew about what Freud later called repression; that is, indeed, what Bate asserts. Johnson, he claims in *The Achievement of Samuel Johnson*, 'really anticipates the psychoanalysis of the twentieth century,' though not, he is keen to clarify, in terms of the kind of psychological *aperçus* that psychoanalysts have found in Johnson's writing. 'Johnson's own sense of the working of the human imagination,' he argues, 'probably provides us with the closest anticipation of Freud to be found in psychology or moral writing before the twentieth century.'[13] Anticipation is a looking forward, a foreseeing, but not necessarily an accurate conceiving. This uncanny anticipation of Freud, he writes:

> is not to be found in simple thrusts that cut through a sentimental and complacent idealism about human nature. It is to be found in Johnson's studied and sympathetic sense of the way in which the human imagination, which is blocked in its search for satisfaction, doubles back into repression, creating a 'secret discontent', or skips out diagonally into some sort of projection. The result, of course, is not a series of formal analyses.[14]

Freud does, of course, write about the imagination, though it is not one of his technical terms (the word appears 174 times in James Strachey's translation of his works). And it matters that Freud does, under the aegis of science, perform a series of formal analyses—that is, writes in a quite different genre or register—and that, for Johnson, repression and projection are not key words. In Bate's account, Johnson has nothing to add to Freud; there are no revisions to Freud's account, however implicit, in Johnson. In this tacit progress myth, it is one-way traffic. Bate doesn't propose a rereading of Freud in the light of Johnson, he just encourages us to see the ways in which, to put it as crudely as possible, Johnson was years ahead of his time; Johnson's work, whatever else it is, is more good proof and illustration of the veracity of Freud's account. It is clearly part of the achievement of Samuel Johnson to anticipate Freud.

We are more likely to think now that it is the formal and historical— the cultural—differences between Johnson and Freud that are significant, even if it is the aphoristic *aperçus*, what Bate calls the 'simple thrusts that cut through a sentimental and complacent idealism about human nature,' that are striking.[15] When, for example, Johnson writes in *Rambler* 134, 'To act is far easier than to suffer,' or, in *Rambler* 32, 'The cure for the greater part of human miseries is not radical but palliative,' the psychoanalyst will prick up her ears (*Yale* IV.347; *Yale* III.175). Indeed, a case could be made—a tradition could be constructed—in which Johnson and Freud would figure, of writers working on a realistic account of human suffering; a genre of the 'real,' so to speak, as indicated by Henry James's definition of what is real as that which it is impossible not to know.[16] A tradition we might read for its occasional insights, and eccentric know-how (neither Johnson nor Freud, as writers and as critics of other people's writing, was interested in what Eliot calls, in an obscure phrase, 'literature as literature').[17] So, when Bate says of Johnson, 'Few classical moralists are closer to Freud than Johnson, or have so uncanny a sense of what repression can mean,'[18] we might take him to be saying, these writers are preoccupied by how people go about not knowing the things they know; and by how they render themselves unrealistic and, in that sense, unreal, by disavowing truths about themselves, and about the way the world is. (Both Johnson and Freud believe in a Reality Principle, even though only Freud calls it that.) People become unrealistic in the service of self-protection, and this is the most unrealistic thing about them.

Anyone interested in repression is interested in what requires repression and why. The real, in this sense, is whatever wishing and willing cannot change, whatever cannot be transformed by redescription. 'Be not too hasty,' says Imlac, 'to trust, or to admire, the teachers of morality:

they discourse like angels, but they live like men' (*Yale* XVI.74). The realism inheres in the semantic progression from one word to the next. Trust is a form of admiration, and in our eagerness to trust we are prone to admire. We know how men live but not how angels discourse. Our potential—in this case for the good—has to be bound up with what we can actually know about ourselves. The speculative can't afford to float free of experience. Both Johnson and Freud write, in quite different languages, about how the possible can only be a version of the real. As Bate wrote, in a sentence that no one could write now: 'The perennial value of Johnson's example is that the *real* issues are still not dead.'[19] When Bate reprises *The Achievement of Samuel Johnson* in his famous biography of Johnson, the stress falls rather differently. Certain things are made rather more explicit. 'But the part of Johnson that really anticipates psychoanalysis,' he writes (omitting this time round 'and it should be stressed that it is only a part'):

> is not to be found in simple thrusts that cut through a complacent sentimentalism about human nature. It is to be found in Johnson's studied and sympathetic sense of both inner 'resistance' and what in psychoanalysis are called defence-mechanisms, or, in Johnson's phrase, 'the stratagems of self-defence'. In particular he anticipates the concept of 'repression' as he turns on the way in which the human imagination when it is frustrated in its search for satisfaction, doubles back into repression, creating a secret discontent, or begins to move ominously into various forms of imaginative projection. The result, of course, is not a series of formal analyses.[20]

The 'simple thrusts that cut through a sentimental and complacent idealism about human nature' have become 'simple thrusts that cut through a complacent sentimentalism about human nature'; sentimentality, Bate intimates, is the more pernicious form of idealism. But what Bate has most notably added, or rather changed, is that Johnson's studied and sympathetic sense is no longer of the way in which the human imagination deals with frustration. It has become, more starkly, a sense of 'resistance' and 'defence-mechanisms,' with Bate running the Freudian term alongside Johnson's 'the stratagems of self-defence.' This is where, for Bate, Johnson and Freud echo each other: resistance, stratagems of self-defense, repression. As in the earlier text, Bate concludes—and it is not an insignificant qualification—'the result, of course, is not a series of formal analyses.' Of course, Freud pioneered a therapeutic method that might make us more realistic, and a model of the mind that we could use to picture our conflicts; Johnson had neither a method nor a system, but he did have religion and a way of writing and of reading. And both Johnson and Freud were obsessed by conflict, by the impossibility (and the danger) of imagining life without intractable conflict.

Freud, Bate believes, helps us with Johnson, gives us a language to redescribe Johnson's preoccupations; and Bate helps us see Johnson as a kind of phantom precursor of Freud. 'What we most value in the eighteenth century,' Bate writes in his *The Burden of the Past and the English Poet*, '[is] its recognition of fact without the surrender of the ideal'.[21] Freud we can value for his recognition of fact and his analysis of the function of ideals. As so-called moralists, both Johnson and Freud want us to have realistic hopes, whatever that phrase might mean. But what is the problem that is being solved in reading them together? I can only see them as in some tradition of moral realism, as writers wanting to give an account of our evasiveness; and of them both being able to do this because they believe in something they both call human nature. And this, in a sense, frees us to read them each in the light of the other. So it is equally pressing to wonder what Johnson might be able to tell us about Freud; and if that question is verging on the unintelligible, why that might be so. A Freudian reading of Johnson is clearly plausible, but what would a Johnsonian reading of Freud be like? The language of certain descriptive writers—and Freud is one—can be turned into schools and movements and methods and approaches; they lend themselves to this. It is part of their intent. But there are other descriptive writers—and Johnson is one—with whom this cannot be done; writers that are useful for all the ways in which they cannot be used. 'Human experience,' Boswell quotes Johnson as saying, 'which is constantly contradicting theory, is the great test of truth' (*Life* I.454); and a theory constantly contradicted is not much of a theory, though it may be something better, or at least something else. You can train to be a Freudian, but not a Johnsonian. Everyone sounds, or can be made to sound, Freudian, but only one person, it seems, sounds Johnsonian. And that, too, is real.

## NOTES

1. William Empson, 'Aubade,' in *Collected Poems*, ed. John Haffenden (London: Allen Lane, 2000), 70. 'The heart of standing is you cannot fly.'

2. *The Standard Edition of the Complete Psychological Works of Sigmund Freud*, ed. and trans. James Strachey, 24 vols. (London: Vintage, 2001), XVIII.19. Further references are to this edition and are given in the text.

3. Donald Davie, *The Late Augustans: Longer Poems of the Later Eighteenth Century* (London: Heineman, 1958), xxii–xxiii.

4. Philip Davis, *In Mind of Johnson* (London: Athlone Press, 1989), 292.

5. William Blake, 'Annotations to Sir Joshua Reynolds' Discourses' (*c.*1808), in *The Complete Writings of William Blake: With Variant Readings*, ed. Geoffrey Keynes (London, New York, and Toronto: Oxford University Press, 1966), 451.

6. T. S. Eliot, *On Poetry and Poets* (New York: Farrar, Straus, and Giroux, 1969), 164.

7. Ibid., 189.

8. Ibid., 190.

9. Ibid., 191.

10. Ibid., 191–2.

11. Walter Jackson Bate, *The Achievement of Samuel Johnson* (New York: Oxford University Press, 1955), 67.

12. See Philip Davis, Chapter 5.

13. Bate, *Achievement*, 94.

14. Ibid.

15. Ibid.

16. Henry James, *The Art of the Novel: Critical Prefaces*, ed. Richard P. Blackmur (New York: Charles Scribner's Sons, 1962), 31–2: 'The real represents to my perception the things we cannot possibly not know, sooner or later, in one way or another; it being but one of the accidents of our hampered state, and one of the incidents of their quantity and number, that particular instances have not yet come our way.'

17. Eliot, *On Poetry*, 190.

18. Bate, *Achievement*, 67.

19. Walter Jackson Bate, *Samuel Johnson* (London: Chatto & Windus, 1978), 405.

20. Ibid., 306.

21. Walter Jackson Bate, *The Burden of the Past and the English Poet* (London: Chatto & Windus, 1971), 129.

# 7

# Fault Finding in Johnson's
## *Lives of the Poets*

*John Mullan*

Great critics are often remembered by their antipathies, and Johnson's *Lives of the Poets* is famous for its author's evident dislike of some of his celebrated poets: Milton and Swift, notoriously, but also the sycophantic Dryden and the self-admiring Pope. The *Lives* is remembered for its dismissive treatment of some works now universally admired: Milton's 'Lycidas,' Donne's poems, or Pope's *The Dunciad*. Good explanations have been offered for all these antagonisms without much notice being taken of a kind of groundswell of complaint that characterizes all the *Lives*. We perhaps tend to read one or a few *Lives* at a time and do not necessarily recognize that those passages in which Johnson catalogues the faults of any given writer are typical of the work as a whole. Each one of his *Lives* was intended as the introduction to the poet's works, and each time Johnson undertook the task of introduction he looked for what his poet had done amiss. Finding the faults of poets was one of his most consistent concerns.

It is worth noticing first of all just how disproportionate Johnson's fault finding can be. His 'Life of Dryden,' for example, culminates in 'a general survey of Dryden's labours' whose conclusion could sound like a ringing celebration: 'To him we owe the improvement, perhaps the completion of our metre, the refinement of our language, and much of the correctness of our sentiments' (*Lives* II.155). Yet the preceding 'survey' has consisted almost entirely of an enumeration of Dryden's faults. 'He...sometimes connects religion and fable too closely without distinction. He descends to display his knowledge with pedantick ostentation;...He is sometimes unexpectedly mean....It was indeed never in his power to resist the temptation of a jest....He had a vanity, unworthy of his abilities, to shew, as may be suspected, the rank of the company with whom he lived, by the use of French words' (*Lives* II.151–2). Johnson then takes breath to declare that these are 'his faults of affectation,' and that they are but the half of it: 'His faults of negligence are beyond recital. Such is the unevenness of his compositions, that ten lines are seldom found together without something of which the reader is ashamed' (*Lives* II.152).

When this section of the life ends with Johnson comparing Dryden's transformation of English poetry to Augustus's adornment of Rome—'he found it brick, and he left it marble'—the reader might be surprised to rediscover Johnson's high opinion of the poet's achievements. There is often, in the *Lives*, this imbalance between the general significance claimed for a poet's achievement, and the closely observed stylistic detail of his infelicities. Denham, for instance, is to be admired for his 'improvement of our numbers,' but the paragraphs that follow enumerate only his faults of versification: the use of imperfect rhymes, the laying of 'the weight of rhyme' on 'a word too feeble to sustain it,' the repeated use of the same rhyme word (*Lives* I.240–1). These 'petty faults' do not detract from 'the strength of his composition,' his compression of 'much meaning in few words' (*Lives* I.239), yet they need to be pointed out.

Faults always mattered to Johnson and some of the most famous passages of his criticism consist of fault finding. 'Shakespeare with his excellencies has likewise faults, and faults sufficient to obscure and overwhelm any other merit' (*Yale* VII.71). This sentence in his 'Preface' to Shakespeare brings to an end perhaps the most eloquent celebration of Shakespeare's 'excellencies' ever written. It is remarkable not because we have long since learned not to find fault with the greatest English writer, but because Johnson unnecessarily suggests that Shakespeare's faults might be enough to cancel out all that is admirable in his work. It is as if he were anxious to show that he has not merely succumbed to the dramatist's genius. He needs to provide a lengthy anatomy of Shakespeare's faults as evidence that he has maintained his critical judgment. Indeed the most famous passage of vindication in the 'Preface'—Johnson's debunking of the unities—comes as a digressive episode in what has been a litany of 'deviations from the art of writing' (*Yale* VII.75). Critics are right to find fault, to want to find fault, with Shakespeare, but 'his neglect of the unities' is not one of them.

Johnson's fault finding produced memorably provocative judgments. In the *Lives*, we might think of those 'Critical Remarks' in the 'Life of Cowley' that display and deprecate the habits of metaphysical poetry. These have become famous because the category of metaphysical poetry has long been so significant, and therefore Johnson's judgments, against Donne in particular, have needed refutation. What is rarely remarked is that his proceedings against Donne and Cowley are typical of what goes on in many other *Lives*. Take the treatment of *Absalom and Achitophel* (1681) in his 'Life of Dryden.' Johnson begins by acknowledging it as a poem widely admired—'so well known, that particular criticism is super-fluous' (*Lives* II.135). He will not need the passages of quotation and exemplification that have been his critical method elsewhere. He will simply endorse posterity's seeming verdict: 'If it be considered as a poem political and controversial, it will be found to comprise all the excellences of which the subject is susceptible' (*Lives* II.135). These 'excellences' are 'raised to such a height as can scarcely be found in any other English composition.' Thus his brief paragraph of praise ends, definitively it would seem. Yet it cannot rest, but turns to something else. 'It is not, however, without faults' (*Lives* II.135). The critic must awake from his daze of admiration. There follow four paragraphs detailing the faults of *Absalom and Achitophel*, some of which—inelegance, irreligion, defective allegory, tedious sententiousness—sound damning (*Lives* II.135–6). The ratio of praise to fault finding is characteristic of the *Lives*. When Johnson describes the achievements of poets he often writes as if he is summarizing what we already know; when he is explicating their faults, he seems to be perform-ing fresh, sharp critical analysis.

To the modern reader, the movement from commendation to disap-probation can read like a negation of the first of these. Treatments such as that accorded to Gay's *Trivia* (1716) seem to damn with borrowed praise, which is bestowed in order to be undermined: 'To *Trivia* may be allowed all that it claims; it is spritely, various, and pleasant…yet some of his decorations may be justly wished away' (*Lives* III.101). Johnson then lam-basts the mythological digressions in the poem, the mock-classical fables narrating the invention of pattens or the shoeblack's parentage: 'On great occasions, and on small, the mind is repelled by useless and apparent falsehood' (*Lives* III.101). We might think that Johnson simply fails to catch the tone of Gay's ingeniously trivial fancies, but his distaste goes beyond this. Typically, he brings an emphasis to his fault finding ('re-pelled,' 'useless,' 'falsehood') that contrasts sharply with his praise.

Many faults that Johnson finds are, as here, offences against propriety. These include the errors of diction that he identifies in the works of several writers. Where he detects the inappropriate use of 'harsh' vocabulary or 'terms of art' in Dryden's poetry, he hardly feels the need to argue his case (*Lives* II.124, 133). Mere exemplification will do. Quoting three stanzas of *Annus Mirabilis* (1667), he italicizes the nautical vocabulary (*okum, mallet, shrouds*, etcetera) and simply adds the observation: 'I suppose here is not one term which every reader does not wish away' (*Lives* II.134). There are also deeper improprieties, such as Dryden's habit of connecting religious with mythological allusions—'the improper use of mythology' (*Lives* II.128). Johnson quotes passages from *Astraea Redux* (1660) in which Dryden first of all invokes pagan sea gods, and then Christian revelation.

But then Dryden is a morally careless writer, caught up in his own inventiveness. Thus Johnson deprecates *All for Love* (1678), which may have 'the fewest improprieties of style or character' but does have 'one fault equal to many, though rather moral than critical, that by admitting the romantick omnipotence of love, he has recommended as laudable, and worthy of imitation, that conduct which, through all ages, the good have censured as vitious, and the bad despised as foolish' (*Lives* II.96).

Johnson often wishes to provide a counterbalance to praise that has too easily been given to a poet. But examine a piece like his 'Life of Waller' and the urge to find fault seems something deeper rooted than an aversion to habitual admiration. After conceding that 'among Waller's little poems are some, which their excellency ought to secure from oblivion,' he sets out to show how others are less 'successful': 'sometimes his thoughts are deficient, and sometimes his expression' (*Lives* II.47–8). His critical examination of Waller's verse is a catalogue of such deficiencies—a parade of passages exemplifying 'unmusical' numbers, 'hyperbolical' notions, 'unnatural' or 'remote and unconsequential' images, feeble conclusions, or 'weak' and 'attenuated' thoughts. And these are just in the section devoted to his lyrical poetry. Johnson's following treatment of Waller's 'panegyrical' verse exhibits predictable scorn for a poet so 'lavish' of praise, but even here he has time to remark 'feeble' conclusions or 'mean' or 'extravagant' figurative language (*Lives* II.50–1). Only after pages of faults, in which every quotation is used to exhibit something to be deplored, does the critic arrive at a consideration of 'the softness and smoothness of his Numbers,' for which he is most often admired (*Lives* II.54). Even here Johnson finds it easiest to notice the 'abatements' in 'his excellence of versification,' duly catalogued. After all this fault finding, the opening of the final paragraph is inadvertently platitudinous: 'But for the praise of Waller, though much be taken away, much will remain' (*Lives* II.55).

Even some of the shorter lives, where there has been no particular examination of the author's poetry, end with what feels like a mandatory summary of poetic faults. He cannot resist ending his 'Life of Watts,' whom he admires for his piety, with a paragraph that quickly collects his poetic faults: 'He writes too often without regular measures, and too often in blank verse; the rhymes are not always sufficiently correspondent. He is particularly unhappy in coining names expressive of characters. His lines are commonly smooth and easy, and his thoughts always religiously pure; but who is there that, to so much piety and innocence, does not wish for a greater measure of sprightliness and vigour?' (*Lives* IV.110). His brief 'Life of Collins,' whom he had known, consists mostly of a description of his character that had first appeared in the *Poetical Calendar* in 1763, but it too has to conclude with a résumé of faults:

To what I have formerly said of his writings may be added, that his diction was often harsh, unskilfully laboured, and injudiciously selected. He affected the obsolete when it was not worthy of revival: and he puts his words out of the common order, seeming to think, with some later candidates for fame, that not to write prose is certainly to write poetry. His lines commonly are of slow motion, clogged and impeded with clusters of consonants. (*Lives* IV.122)

Some faults, Johnson thinks, need merely stating to be recognized. Others, however, are discovered only by a kind of close reading that later critics were to imitate, and that many readers still find abruptly revealing. In his fault finding, Johnson hunts down logical inconsistency, especially in the use of allegory, simile, or metaphor. An example of the first of these is Milton's 'undoubtedly faulty' (*Lives* I.291) representation of Sin and Death in *Paradise Lost* (1667): 'That sin and death should have shown the way to hell, might have been allowed; but they cannot facilitate the passage by building a bridge, because the difficulty of Satan's passage is described as real and sensible, and the bridge ought to be only figurative.' Figurative language itself is often found irrational or absurd. He convicts Addison of illogical and mixed metaphors in a couplet from his *Letter from Italy* (1704), and dedicates a lengthy paragraph to the demonstration that a much-admired simile in *The Campaign* (1705) is merely tautological repetition (*Lives* III.24–5). Most memorably, he finds fault with the incongruous or hyperbolical analogies to be found in the poems of Cowley and Donne over page after page of condemnation by quotation.

Yet the tone of his comments on extracts from Donne suggests something paradoxical about Johnson's critical scrutiny in the *Lives*: the discovery of faults can be a kind of compliment. This is not just a question of reading between the lines of Johnson's judgments; he himself concedes that where faults are not to be found, it is because achievements and ambitions are limited. He describes the Earl of Roscommon as 'perhaps the only correct writer in verse before Addison,' expanding the judgment to declare that 'if there are not so many or so great beauties in his compositions as in those of some contemporaries, there are, at least, fewer faults' (*Lives* II.20–1). Faultlessness can be a kind of failure: 'He is elegant, but not great; he never labours after exquisite beauties, and he seldom falls into gross faults' (*Lives* II.23). Johnson was aware that writers before him had noticed a kinship between ambition and faultiness. In his 'Life of Browne' (1756), he cited Browne's own observation from *Religio Medici* (1643)—'To have great excellencies, and great faults, "magnae virtutes, nec minora vitia, is the poesy," says our author, "of the best natures." This poesy may be properly applied to the style of BROWNE.'[1] As Johnson continues: 'He has many "verba ardentia," forcible expressions, which he would never have found, but by venturing to the utmost verge of propriety; and flights which would never have been reached, but by one who had very little fear of the shame of falling.'[2]

In contrast, the faultlessness of Addison's verse is exactly its limitation: 'His poetry is polished and pure; the product of a mind too judicious to commit faults, but not sufficiently vigorous to attain excellence. He has sometimes a striking line, or a shining paragraph; but in the whole he is warm rather than fervid, and shews more dexterity than strength. He was, however, one of our earliest examples of correctness' (*Lives* III.136). Equally, if poems are too slight or unremarkable, their faults are not worth discovering. When he looks at Waller's lyrics, Johnson writes: 'Of these petty compositions, neither the beauties nor the faults deserve much attention' (*Lives* II.50).

It is telling that one of the three passages quoted in his *Dictionary* to illustrate the word *faultless* is a couplet from Pope's *Essay on Criticism* (1711) expressing the necessity of faults: 'Whoever thinks a *faultless* piece to see,/Thinks what ne'er was, nor is, nor e'er shall be.' When Johnson examines Pope's *The Rape of the Lock* (1714), he listens to John Dennis's complaints of its superfluous machinery and lack of connection between set pieces, appearing almost to agree, before he turns away with an exclamation: 'These perhaps are faults, but what are such faults to so much excellence!' (*Lives* IV.72). Faults are the surprising evidence of the attention that we should pay to a poet. Dryden has some 'faults of a ... generous and splendid kind' (*Lives* II.151), his failings the consequence of his ambition. He was endeavoring 'after the grand and the new' (*Lives* II.150). Johnson's characterization of this inclination will probably sound genuinely equivocal to the unschooled reader: 'He delighted to tread upon the brink of meaning, where light and darkness begin to mingle; to approach the precipice of absurdity, and hover over the abyss of unideal vacancy' (*Lives* II.149–50). The well-versed Johnsonian will know this for mock-heroic disapprobation, but the less knowing reader would be right to hear something grand in at least the first half of that sentence. It takes some wonderful critical phrase-making to do justice to Dryden's poetic adventures. Equally, Dryden's 'negligence' was born of his superiority to his contemporaries Waller, Denham, and Cowley. 'Standing therefore in the highest place, he had no care to rise by contending with himself' (*Lives* I.152). His hasty preference for what first occurred to him was the symptom of a justified confidence in his own abilities.

When Johnson tracked down faults, he wrote as if he were performing the accepted duties of a critic. *Critick* was, after all, defined in his *Dictionary* as 'A man skilled in the art of judging of literature; a man able to distinguish the faults and beauties of writing.' The ideal is repeated in the

*Lives* when he praises Watts—'his judgement was exact, and he noted beauties and faults with very nice discernment'—or Edmund Smith: 'He had great readiness and exactness of criticism, and, by a cursory glance over a new composition, would exactly tell all its faults and beauties' (*Lives* IV.109–10; II.177). We might remember, in the opening of the 'Preface' to Shakespeare, the phrasing of a critical commonplace: 'The great contention of criticism is to find the faults of the moderns, and the beauties of the ancients. While an authour is yet living we estimate his powers by his worst performance, and when he is dead we rate them by his best' (*Yale* VII.59). Or his summary near the end of the 'Preface' of the purposes of the notes to his edition: 'The notes which I have borrowed or written are either illustrative, by which difficulties are explained; or judicial, by which faults and beauties are remarked; or emendatory, by which depravations are corrected' (*Yale* VII.102).

Faults and beauties: these are what a critic is expected to notice. Thus the comment on the poems in Cowley's *The Mistress* (1647): 'it is not necessary to select any particular pieces for praise or censure. They have all the same beauties and faults, and nearly in the same proportion' (*Lives* I.217). Or his comment on Pope's *Dunciad* (1728–43): 'The beauties of this poem are well known; its chief fault is the grossness of its images' (*Lives* IV.75). The coupling was conventional in the eighteenth century. Here is Joseph Warton in *The Adventurer* in 1753: 'I am inclined to think that a few observations on the writings of SHAKESPEARE will not be deemed useless or unentertaining, because he exhibits more numerous examples of excellencies and faults of every kind than are, perhaps, to be discovered in any other author.'[3] The essay that follows mentions the absence of 'unity' in his 'fables' and his sometimes 'blameable' diction, 'which is obscure and turgid'—but then embarks on an unimpeded celebration of his powers. Acknowledging faults as one aspect of praise is a common critical reflex, as in Oliver Goldsmith's comment on Shakespeare: 'I admire the beauties of this great father of our stage as much as they deserve, but could wish, for the honour of our country, and for his honour too, that many of his scenes were forgotten.'[4]

The convention of pairing faults with 'beauties' is what Johnson has in mind near the end of his consideration of *Paradise Lost* in his 'Life of Milton,' where he denies that he will follow it: 'Such are the faults of that wonderful performance *Paradise Lost*; which he who can put in balance with its beauties must be considered not as nice but as dull, as less to be censured for want of candour, than pitied for want of sensibility' (*Lives* I.292). But putting faults in the balance with beauties is exactly what Johnson has just done. Indeed, their proportions have been nicely measured against each other, and Johnson has done the poem the compliment of devoting equal space to both.

What is unusual about Johnson is his resistance to what we might call the culture of beauties. By the time that he was writing the *Lives*, there were many volumes of 'beauties' available to the polite reader. The *OED* gives as the earliest example a 1737 title, *The Beauties of the English Stage, consisting of all the celebrated passages, soliloquies, similies, descriptions and other poetical beauties in the English plays*. Anthologies of 'beauties' might have begun in the late 1730s, but the use of the word in literary analysis is older, as in the title of Joseph Spence's *An Essay on Pope's Odyssey: in which some particular beauties and blemishes of that work are considered* (1726). It appears in the title of an anthology of extracts from 1724, *Thesaurus dramaticus. Containing all the celebrated passages, soliloquies, similies, descriptions, and other poetical beauties in the body of English plays, antient and modern, etc.* From the mid-eighteenth century, however, there was a proliferation of such anthologies, as the appreciation of beauties became an essential aspect of genteel reading—and, connectedly, of the discovery of English Literature. Most collections of beauties presented the highlights from the writings of a particular author, but others, like Goldsmith's *The Beauties of English Poesy* (1767), collected for the discerning consumer a selection displaying the highlights of 'modern' literature.

This is the context for Johnson's apparent determination to remember the faults of poets. Sometimes the coexistence of 'beauties' and 'faults' in the *Lives*—the swift turning from one to the other—is more like doublethink than broad-mindedness. Two consecutive paragraphs from the 'Life of Pope' about his *Essay on Man* (1733–4) provide an extreme example of this (*Lives* IV.77). In the first, Johnson concedes that the content of the poem is common wisdom, but wonders at its 'blaze of embellishment' and 'sweetness of melody': 'The vigorous contraction of some thoughts, the luxuriant amplification of others, the incidental illustrations, and sometimes the dignity, sometimes the softness of the verses, enchain philosophy, suspend criticism, and oppress judgement by overpowering pleasure.' Yet he is not overpowered, for the next sentence begins a paragraph informing us that the *Essay on Man* contains 'more lines unsuccessfully laboured, more harshness of diction, more thoughts imperfectly expressed, more levity without elegance, and more heaviness without strength, than will easily be found in all his other works.' The critical self-correction is so complete as to be unintentionally comical.

Why does Johnson feel compelled to turn so quickly away from appreciation into fault finding? Partly it seems to be a distaste for praise that is peculiar to the *Lives*. It is Johnson's response to the tales of flattery and self-flattery that he finds himself telling. Here the biography surely inflects the criticism. Johnson's disenchantment is his recoil from all the praise and self-praise with which he meets. In the very first paragraph of his first 'Life,' he is telling us that Thomas Sprat has shrouded Cowley's life in 'the mist of panegyrick' (*Lives* I.191). Panegyric will certainly not be his inclination. Johnson feels that many of the authors he discusses have been involved in the giving and receiving of congratulation. Poets have praised patrons and patrons have superciliously praised the efforts of poets. Praise has been the medium in which poets have basked. Reporting that the youthful compositions of the late seventeenth-century poet George Stepney were once thought wonderful, he shakes his head: 'One cannot always easily find the reason for which the world has sometimes conspired to squander praise' (*Lives* II.65). Johnson is determined not to admire so readily. It is his contrary spirit to refuse to repeat easy critical judgments, and sometimes this means bestowing unexpected praise—as on Richard Blackmore, mocked into absurdity by Pope, but included in the collection at Johnson's request and admired for his ability to 'reason in verse' (*Lives* III.85). For the most part, however, this refusal is a refusal to admire.

Johnson gave his own explanation of the importance of fault finding in *Rambler* 93, when he said that the faults of a good writer were 'dangerous' because of 'the influence of his example'; they needed to be 'discovered and stigmatized, before they have the sanction of antiquity conferred upon them' (*Yale* IV.134). This is Johnson the umpire of correctness, the critical criterion belonging to his age that we now find most difficult to value, or even recognize. There were conventions governing diction, allusion, poetic form, and generic consistency that a poet should try to observe. The critic's job was to detect him in any failures to do so. Yet there is some evidence that contemporaries thought Johnson went too far in this endeavor. John Duncombe, reviewing the *Lives* anonymously in the *Gentleman's Magazine*, found himself having to 'lament...that, in some instances, his criticisms are too minute and too severe to be approved by "readers uncorrupted by literary prejudices."'[5] Duncombe retorted to Johnson with his own phrase from his 'Life of Gray.' 'Through the whole of his performance the desire of praise, excepting in the case of some very favourite author, is almost always overpowered by his disposition to censure,' wrote Edmund Cartwright in the *Monthly Review*, 'the slightest blemish is examined with microscopical sagacity' (*Lives* IV.531). But Johnson had a more individual, more personal reason for wanting to find faults. This was his desire that poetry should not fool us. Poetry should pass the tests of reason and experience. He would not be blinded by technique or fooled by a blur of fine-sounding words. If Dryden, led on by his own inventiveness, should knowingly write 'nonsense,' then Johnson would call it such (*Lives* II.150). Poets are themselves seduced into faulti-ness by the temptation to produce something to admire. The 'unskilful allegory' of Sin and Death in *Paradise Lost* is, says Johnson, 'one of the greatest faults of the poem; and to this there was no temptation, but the author's opinion of its beauty' (*Lives* I.191).

Thus his account of Thomas Gray's poetical extravagance, which aroused considerable controversy amongst the first readers and critics of the *Lives*: 'In 1757 he published *The Progress of Poetry* and *The Bard*, two compositions at which the readers of poetry were at first content to gaze in mute amazement' (*Lives* IV.178). It was thanks to a few critics who championed these poems that their status was assured, and 'many were content to be shewn beauties which they could not see.' Johnson's subse-quent close reading of 'the two Sister Odes' acknowledges the 'cumbrous splendour' of Gray's poems, but catalogues the examples of incoherence, illogicality, and even meaninglessness that he finds as he reads through them. Sometimes the skeptical spirit in evidence in this reading of Gray amounts to a suspicion that poetry is out to trick the reader. When John-son 'examines' Pope's *Essay on Man*, he wonders at the evidence of the poet's 'genius' (*Lives* IV.76). Here he finds 'the dazzling splendour of imagery, and the seductive powers of eloquence,' but they are deployed exactly in order to 'dazzle' and to 'seduce.' The poem consists of common-places made to seem wonderful by the poet's 'ornaments': 'Never were penury of knowledge and vulgarity of sentiment so happily disguised.' With his 'blaze of embellishment' and 'sweetness of melody,' Pope, in effect, has set about deceiving the reader. Seeing through Gray or Pope is more important than calling the bluff of minor writers—but this needs doing too. The third and last section of the 'Life of Prior' begins: 'Prior has written with great variety, and his variety has made him popular' (*Lives* III.58). It then sets about cataloguing the faults and failure of his verse, in a sequence of Prior's mythological poems, as if undoing the spell he has managed to cast:

> Venus, after the example of the Greek epigram, asks when she was seen *naked and bathing*. Then Cupid is *mistaken*; then Cupid is *disarmed*; then he loses his darts to Ganymede; then Jupiter sends him a summons by Mercury. Then *Chloe* goes a-hunting with an *ivory quiver graceful at her side*; Diana mistakes her for one of her nymphs, and Cupid laughs at the blunder. All this is surely despicable; and even when he tries to act the lover without the help of gods or goddesses, his thoughts are unaffecting or remote. (*Lives* III.59)

Poets, by getting poetical, bemuse themselves.

The belief that good criticism involves undeceiving the reader is behind Johnson's treatment of metaphysical poetry in his 'Life of Cowley.' When he examines individual conceits he tussles with the rationality of individual poems. We see this again in his discussion of Pope's epitaphs, a piece written long before the *Lives* were projected and appended to his 'Life of Pope.' He subjects the epitaphs to a discipline of stringent close reading, detecting the instances of flabby phrase-making, tautology, or simple illogic that the solemn form might conceal. He offers what is, in effect, his analysis of faults to 'young students in poetry' (*Lives* IV.81). This kind of exercise makes him sometimes seem a critic whom we still imitate, an advocate of the kind of close reading that became standard in the twentieth century. Fault finding often appears to us the most foreign inclination of Johnson's criticism, yet it has helped form some of our own most persistent habits of reading. Divested of its concern with propriety and 'elegance,' Johnson's fault finding becomes what we now call practical criticism, where we find that the reader most attentive to a poem's subtleties is the reader who is not tricked by them.

## NOTES

1. David Fleeman, ed., *Early Biographical Writings of Dr Johnson* (Farnborough: Gregg International, 1973), 465.
2. Ibid., 467.
3. Joseph Warton, *Adventurer* 93 (1753), reprinted in *Shakespeare: The Critical Heritage*, ed. Brian Vickers, 6 vols. (London: Routledge & Kegan Paul, 1974–81), IV.64.
4. Oliver Goldsmith, *An Enquiry into the Present State of Polite Learning in Europe* (1759), in *Collected Works of Oliver Goldsmith*, ed. Arthur Friedman, 5 vols. (Oxford: Clarendon Press, 1966), I.326.
5. [John Duncombe], 'Impartial and Critical Review of New Publications,' *Gentleman's Magazine* 51 (1781), 276.

# 8

## Johnson and Genius

*Lawrence Lipking*

In the preface to his monumental life of Isaac Newton, *Never at Rest*, Richard S. Westfall deliberately parts company with Samuel Johnson. *Rambler* 60, he notes, had argued for the 'irresistible interest' of any good biography because all of us recognize ourselves in other people's lives: 'We are all prompted by the same motives, all deceived by the same fallacies, all animated by hope, obstructed by danger, entangled by desire, and seduced by pleasure' (*Yale* III.320). A common humanity unites the reader and the writer with the subject of the life, according to Johnson. Yet after more than twenty years of study, Westfall can find no way to measure himself against Newton: 'He has become for me wholly other, one of the tiny handful of supreme geniuses who have shaped the category of the human intellect, a man not finally reducible to the criteria by which we comprehend our fellow beings, those parallel circumstances of Dr Johnson.'[1] Newton seems more, or other, than human, a genius who at once defines and goes beyond the bounds of intellect. He is not like us, he belongs to another species.

Westfall's sense of Newton's otherness reflects a shift in notions of genius that had already become acute when Johnson wrote. The *Dictionary* documents those changes. Its definition of *genius* begins with 'The protecting or ruling power of men, places, or things'—the tutelary spirit who presides over birth (from Latin *genere*, 'to beget'). Poetry still harbored such spirits in Johnson's time. Though Christ had put them to flight forever according to Milton's ode 'On the morning of CHRIST's Nativity' (1629), Milton himself appointed Lycidas 'the Genius of the shore,' and poets such as Thomas Gray perpetually called on Father Thames or 'Genii of the stream.'[2] In one respect, that older sense of *genius* seems quite egalitarian; Socrates enjoyed his own daimon or genius, yet so might a city, a grove, or a slave. But as those genii vanished from the earth, *genius* came to refer instead, as in Johnson's fourth sense, to a 'Disposition of nature by which any one is qualified for some peculiar employment'—an inborn faculty or aptitude.

There is nothing superhuman about such talents; according to this definition, anyone might own some natural portion of genius. Thus even the humble physician Robert Levet employed a 'single talent,'[3] which might be described as a kind of genius for ministering to the afflicted. Johnson quotes lines 60–1 of Pope's *Essay on Criticism* (1711) to illustrate the point: 'One *Science* only will one *Genius* fit;/So *vast* is Art, so *narrow* Human Wit' (*Pope* I.245–6).[4] The plurality of sciences or forms of knowledge ensures that different sorts of genius will be distributed among many different sorts of people, since any particular human intelligence must be narrowly focused. If Newton had a genius for mathematics, another person might have a genius for trade.[5] This was the standard sense of the word well into the eighteenth century.

Yet that definition began to strike many critics as too confining. Already in the seventeenth century, contemporaries declared that Newton not only *had* but *was* a genius; in the terms of the *Dictionary*, 'A man endowed with superior faculties' or mental power. Potentially, those superior powers might lift him far above his fellow beings. As soon as the *Principia* appeared in 1687, Edmond Halley's adoring Latin ode worshiped its genius as one of a kind: 'Arise, ye mortals, put aside earthly cares;/And from this recognize the force of a heaven-born mind,/From the life of the herd far and away removed.../Nor can any mortal come closer to touching the gods.'[6] Halley concedes that Newton is (just barely) a mortal. But the imagery draws freely on Lucretius's famous assertion that Epicurus, his idol, must be considered a god whose genius 'surpassed the human race'; and the same Latin phrase later appeared beneath Roubiliac's heroic statue of Newton in the chapel of Trinity College, Cambridge.[7] Nor did other poets hesitate to call the great man 'godlike.' In an age when an 'insuperable line'/The nice barrier 'twixt human and divine' barred mortals from rising higher in the Great Chain of Being, Newton alone ascended.[8] After his death no eulogist failed to note that he had long ago been made one with the immortals whom now he joined. And many years later, Johnson remarked 'that if Newton had flourished in ancient Greece, he would have been worshipped as a Divinity.'[9]

By that time, the association of genius with something godlike, beyond the ordinary scope of human beings, had begun to prevail. The vogue of Longinus, in the late seventeenth century, exalted the sublime above 'correctness.' Dryden preferred 'the sublime Genius that sometimes erres, to the midling or indifferent one which makes few faults, but seldome or never rises to any Excellence,' and Addison found 'more Beauty in the Works of a great Genius who is ignorant of the Rules of Art, than in those of a little Genius who knows and observes them.'[10] But the next generation went further, reserving *genius* for the sublime and great; for many critics, the middling or little genius would be a contradiction in terms. The title of Joseph Warton's *Essay on the Genius and Writings of Pope* (1756, 1782) exploits a cunning ambiguity: it might refer to Pope's special talents, but in context it might also cast doubt on whether he deserved to be called a true poet or genius. Significantly, Warton dedicated his essay to Edward Young, whose *Conjectures on Original Composition* (1759) would slight the skillful artist and revere the inspired creator: 'Hence Genius has ever been supposed to partake of something divine.'[11] A mystery surrounded the visions of such demigods. In the mid-eighteenth century, a flurry of aestheticians attempted to capture the elusive, ineffable spirit of genius.

A proper grasp of genius preoccupied Johnson as well; he kept returning to the theme in writing and conversation. Yet he objected to both of the popular definitions, the special talent and the sublime afflatus. Each of these placed a drastic, binding curb on what most people—those without the right sort of genius—could hope to do. Like Pope's pet doctrine of the ruling passion, they tended 'to produce the belief of a kind of moral predestination, or over-ruling principle which cannot be resisted' (*Lives* IV.44). Johnson fiercely defends free agency. Definitions that restrict genius to privileged individuals are 'bugbears,' intended to scare young people, according to *Rambler* 25: 'It is natural for those who have raised a reputation by any science, to exalt themselves as endowed by heaven with peculiar powers, or marked out by an extraordinary designation for their profession; and to fright competitors away.' But 'since a genius, whatever it be, is like fire in the flint, only to be produced by collision with a proper subject, it is the business of every man to try whether his faculties may not happily co-operate with his desires' (*Yale* I.139). Genius can be known only by what it achieves, not by some hidden potential or secret spirit.

The attack on 'peculiar powers' runs through Johnson's career. The beginning of the *Lives of the Poets* dismisses 'that peculiar designation of mind, or propensity for some certain science or employment, which is commonly called Genius. The true Genius is a mind of large general powers, accidentally determined to some particular direction' (*Lives* I.191). Most discussions of genius, like those of Dryden, Addison, John Dennis, Edward Young, William Sharpe, William Duff, and Alexander Gerard, had looked for one essential quality: most often a capacity for invention, or what would later be called the creative imagination.[12] Johnson too makes use of that consensus. 'Genius is shewn only by invention,' he wrote in *Idler* 40 (*Yale* II.125), and the final paragraph of the 'Life of Milton' begins with a summary judgment: 'The highest praise of genius is original invention' (*Lives* I.294). But elsewhere he raises other standards, accommodating them to the powers of the poet under discussion, and *genius* takes on other meanings. In Dryden it consists of 'that energy which collects, combines, amplifies, and animates' (*Lives* IV.65)—a position close to Gerard's; in Pope it weds invention and imagination to judgment and 'colours of language' (*Lives* IV.78). This seems to resonate with Hazlitt's pendulum; *genius* swings round with a pliancy that might be construed as oscillation or, more positively, as flexibility and balance. Yet, for Johnson, the unmoving center remains that mind of large general powers. Even invention earns its praise because it bears the stamp of such a mind.

Johnson's conception of genius puts him at odds with many influential critics; it touches his deepest sense of how works of art are made. 'There is nothing so little comprehended among mankind as what is genius,' he told Frances Burney:

> They give to it all, when it can be but a part. Genius is nothing more than knowing the use of tools; but there must be tools for it to use: a man who has spent all his life in this room will give a very poor account of what is contained in the next.
>
> [Miss Burney:] Certainly, sir; yet there is such a thing as invention? Shakespeare could never have seen a Caliban.
>
> [Johnson:] No; but he had seen a man, and knew, therefore, how to vary him to a monster.[13]

This argument addresses a phantom third party. Edward Young had offered another opinion in maintaining that genius partook of something divine: 'A *Genius* differs from a *good Understanding*, as a Magician from a good Architect; *That* raises his structure by means invisible; *This* by the skilful use of common tools.'[14] Johnson responds by speaking up for the tools. Great poems, he insists, are not magic, conjured out of the air like one of the flashy, collapsible castles in old romances. Instead, they depend on solid construction, built from materials made to last. A genius, however inspired, could accomplish nothing without experience and proper tools, any more than a carpenter without wood or tools could raise a house. Nor is good understanding in any way the opposite of genius.

Thus Johnson decisively cuts the ground from under received positions on genius. A long quarrel had shaped the debate, the rival claims of art (or French rules) and of nature (or English inspiration). For Dryden, Dennis, Addison, and other patriotic critics, the national honor seemed at stake in this dispute. Above all, the greatness of Shakespeare needed defending. Foreigners who mocked his want of art were insulting the genius of England, and their shallow enslavement by rules showed only how little they knew about the graces that art could not reach. In this respect, the magic celebrated by Young could function as a critical trump card; genius proved itself precisely by its contempt for or indifference to rules. Yet Johnson refuses to accept the facile contrast of art with nature. To a thoughtful critic, a mind of large general powers like Shakespeare's incorporates whatever serves its purpose. That such a genius freely breaks some artificial rules does not imply any want of judgment, for Johnson. Rather, it demonstrates that the best artist cares most of all for an art that will follow nature, an art that uses every means to mirror all of life. This 'is an art/ That nature makes,' in Shakespeare's words; 'the art itself is nature.'[15] From this perspective the opposition of understanding to genius, or learning to inspiration, seems groundless sophistry. 'Shakespeare, however favoured by nature, could impart only what he had learned,' a knowledge gathered from observation more than from books, according to Johnson's 'Preface' to Shakespeare (*Yale* VII.87). A true genius makes use of the tools he has and turns them to his advantage. In this respect, art and nature seem indispensable allies.

Nevertheless, the topic of genius often exposes tensions in Johnson. It rouses his well-honed sense of competition, not only by provoking him to contradict rival theories but also by tempting him to compare his powers with those of other people. Both tendencies are on display in a conversation reported in *The Journal of a Tour to the Hebrides* (15 August 1773). In Edinburgh, Boswell is showing off his famous friend to his old professor William Robertson, and the talk naturally turns to strong-minded men. Johnson begins by praising Edmund Burke's gift of speech: if you were alone with him for five minutes, 'he'd talk to you in such a manner, that, when you parted you would say, this is an extraordinary man. Now, you may be long enough with me, without finding anything extraordinary' (*Life* V.34). The self-consciousness of this last remark (was Robertson expected to deny it?) extends to other hints of competition. When Robertson suggests that Burke has wit, and when Boswell says that Burke can listen, Johnson flatly contradicts them (after Burke read those dismissive comments in print, his friendship with Johnson chilled). But another issue is raised by Burke's abortive youthful attempt to follow the law. Johnson said:

> he could not understand how a man could apply to one thing, and not to another. ROBERTSON said, one man had more judgment, another more imagination. JOHNSON. 'No, Sir; it is only, one man has more mind than another. He may direct it differently; he may, by accident, see the success of one kind of study, and take a desire to excel in it. I am persuaded that, had Sir Isaac Newton applied to poetry, he would have made a very fine epick poem.' (*Life* V.34–5)

On this favorite theme Johnson's fervor carries him away. If Newton had the slightest talent for poetry, he certainly managed to conceal it. Yet the example of genius is quite revealing. First, it seems oddly personal, like the tacit rivalry with Burke. As soon as Johnson brings up Newton in conversation, he thinks of another powerful mind, a candidate closer to home. '"I could as easily apply to law as to tragick poetry." BOSWELL. "Yet, Sir, you did apply to tragick poetry, not to law." JOHNSON. "Because, Sir, I had not money to study law. Sir, the man who has vigour, may walk to the east, just as well as to the west, if he happens to turn his head that way"' (*Life* V.35). The thought of what he might have achieved in another field often makes Johnson touchy. The author of *Irene* (1749) cannot have taken much satisfaction from applying to 'tragick poetry,' nor did he confess to any sense of calling as a writer. His career had indeed been 'accidentally determined,' when he applied himself to the business of the *Gentleman's Magazine* or when the booksellers commissioned him to put the *Dictionary* together. Yet no one could deny that Johnson had 'a mind of large general powers.' Did Newton remind him of his own genius? The question was potentially embarrassing because it suggested that he might have misused or frittered away his talents. When Newton was asked how he had made his discoveries, he is supposed to have replied 'by always thinking unto them.'[16] But Johnson had not applied himself to any one pursuit; sometimes he had walked to the east, sometimes to the west.

Moreover, he knew that some people walk faster and farther than others. Johnson 'was fully conscious of his own superior powers,' according to Boswell, and praised Robertson for being too prudent to argue with him (*Life* V.371). Yet without such testing of one mind against another, most human intercourse would languish. A contest for superiority animates every good conversation, Johnson told Boswell; an adversary such as Burke would call forth and exhaust all his powers.[17] From this perspective, genius itself consists in winning or leading the unending race to outstrip everyone else. Apparently, Newton had gained the palm in that race. Johnson honors his standing among men of mind; to think of genius was to think of him, because he had no peer. At one time, such honor had tended to be reserved for men of letters or other creative artists. When Johnson awarded *Paradise Lost* the first or second place 'among the productions of the human mind,' he also elevated poets: 'By the general consent of criticks, the first praise of genius is due to the writer of an epick poem, as it requires an assemblage of all the powers which are singly sufficient for other compositions' (*Lives* I.282). But Newton's powers were greater yet. He could have made a very fine epic poem in the unlikely event that he had applied himself, Johnson claims, but he chose instead to comprehend the system of the world. Evidently the human mind could produce some work that surpassed the best of poets. This rearranged the terms of competition. Among the illustrious men of modern times, according to Johnson in *Adventurer* 131, perhaps only

Bacon had 'any pretensions to dispute with [Newton] the palm of genius or science' (*Yale* II.482).

Yet Newton's example also raises other questions, which are even more searching: his work had effectively undermined the time-honored theory, or the world-system, that had sustained most older standards of genius. The Great Chain of Being had once furnished a template for the existing social and intellectual order. It was as if distinctions among human beings were preordained by a series of stations, inscribed in the cosmos itself. But by Johnson's time the Great Chain had begun to tremble. In fact, in the long run Newton's own findings doomed and dissolved it. A cosmos of visible plenitude, held together by uninterrupted, unbroken links without any gap, could not survive the new universe of vast empty spaces, a void with tiny particles that gravity invisibly held in place. Each of the three principles on which A.O. Lovejoy would base his Great Chain—plenitude, continuity, and gradation—turned out to be riddled with holes.[18] Johnson probed them himself in the searing review of Soame Jenyns (1757), which argued that 'infinite vacuities' must lie between any two steps of the scale (*Yale* XVII.404). Vacuity preoccupied Johnson; according to Hester Thrale, 'the vacuity of Life' was 'his favourite hypothesis, & the general Tenor of his reasonings commonly ended in that' (*Thaliana,* I.179). But whether or not his sense of life was influenced by Newton's empty cosmos, his sense of genius reflected a break in the Chain of Being. A hierarchy of wit had once placed human beings on a scale, ascending by degrees from brutes below, one step removed from beasts, to those whose rank and mind, however exalted, could never leap up to the brightness of angels. According to Epistle II of Pope's *Essay on Man* (1733–4), 'Superior beings, when of late they saw/A mortal Man unfold all Nature's law,/Admir'd such wisdom in an earthly shape,/And shew'd a NEWTON as we shew an Ape' (*Pope*, III.i.59–60). But long before West-fall, as we have seen, Newton struck many mortals as wholly other—perhaps as someone able to read the mind of God. Even Pope had succumbed to that sense of awe. His dazzling, oft-quoted epitaph—'Nature, and Nature's Laws lay hid in Night./God said, *Let Newton be!* and all was *Light*'[19]—envisions its hero as an intellectual *fiat lux*, a new creation. God manifests intelligent design by conceiving Newton, a secondary Word, born as it happened on Christmas Day, who comprehends His plan. Such genius exceeds any scale. In this respect, the general powers of Newton's mind resemble gravity, a power that draws together every individual part and absorbs them all into a coherent whole. The sheer mass of his intellect marks him as one of a kind.

Yet Johnson does not accept that glorification. The thought of Pope's epitaph was obvious, he objected; 'the words *night* and *light* [were] too nearly allied'; and, in the Latin caption that introduces Newton, 'the op-position of *Immortalis* and *Mortalis*, is a mere sound, or a mere quibble; he is not *immortal* in any sense contrary to that in which he is *mortal*.'[20] Hyperbole like this seems impious as well as empty. For genius, as John-son defines it, always retains its ties to the twilight where human beings live, a disenchanted world neither all light nor all dark. Significantly, the *Dictionary* refers to a 'protecting or ruling power,' not to a deity or *genius loci*. The god that had haunted older notions of genius, the spirit or daimon that inhabited men and governed their actions, must yield to the one true God. Nor should that God ever be equated with Nature's Laws. Johnson draws a similar lesson, with some satisfaction, from Newton himself. Reviewing *Four Letters from Sir Isaac Newton to Doctor Bentley, Containing Some Arguments in Proof of a Deity* in the *Literary Magazine* in 1756 (a year before he took on Jenyns), he is pleased 'to observe how even the mind of *Newton* gains ground gradually upon darkness.' The material-ism or Deism that some readers had associated with Newton's mathemati-cally regulated cosmos, and that Johnson could not abide, is decisively rejected by the *Letters*, as Johnson affirmed: 'there can be no regular system produced but by a voluntary and meaning agent. This the great Newton always asserted.'[21] And only God could have created the universe and kept it from falling apart; no natural cause could have done it. Newton's hu-mility in acknowledging this, and his confession of how much he does not know, prove him to have been the right sort of genius.

A mind of that sort, a mind that understands its own limitations, will never think of effacing or rivaling God. An unvarying principle runs through Johnson's frequent and varied statements on genius: even su-premely gifted minds are always and only human. Milton and Newton expand our sense of what is possible but do not exhaust it. Thus Johnson demystifies and normalizes the cult of genius. As much as he admires the power of great thinkers and poets, he never calls them godlike. It is telling that his most eloquent praise of poetic genius occurs in the 'Life of Pope,' a writer whom Joseph Warton had accused of wanting the afflatus of a true poet. In refuting this charge, Johnson swings his pendulum once more. Now, the definition of genius follows a mind like Newton's, a mind never at rest. Good sense must lend its support, but 'Pope had likewise genius; a mind active, ambitious, and adventurous, always investigating, always aspiring; in its widest searches still longing to go forward, in its highest flights still wishing to be higher; always imagining something greater than it knows, always endeavouring more than it can do.'[22] The restless movement of this passage, piling on clauses, trying to catch the vaulting, unceasing energy of its subject, mirrors the valiant effort it honors. Johnson clearly admires not only Pope's exertions but also the spur of his discontent, unsatisfied even with brilliant work that other poets might envy. In these terms, genius consists primarily of aspiration, an unremitting desire to be great. Such ardor possesses one critical virtue: it is instructive. Not many of us can dream of rising to Milton's sublimity or to Newton's grasp of the cosmos, but anyone might try to imitate the work ethic of Pope. As a moralist as well as a lover of poetry, Johnson values this inspiring example of a talent well spent. Aspiration encourages others to follow; the man-made wings on which Pope soared might well fit the shoulders of somebody else.

Nonetheless, the pendulum kept swinging. In the long run, Johnson's effort to humanize genius was destined to fail. As everyone knows—and everyone is not necessarily wrong—Romantic writers made a new fetish of genius and inspiration, approving exactly the fallacy against which Johnson had warned Frances Burney: 'they give to it all, when it can be but a part.' 'The power of poetry is from a *genius*,' Coleridge said, '*i.e.*, not included in the faculties of the human mind common to all men';[23] and Blake, in every way, gave all to genius. Curiously, Newton himself was partly responsible for this vision of the isolated and quasi-divine creator, 'Voyaging through strange seas of Thought, alone (in Words-worth's words)'.[24] He liked to insist that his inventions were entirely his own; when asked where he got the lenses for his telescope, he 'said he made them himself & laughing added if I had staid for other people to make my tools & things for me, I had never made anything of it.'[25] Moreover, hardly anyone could understand him. The profundity or even incomprehensibility of the *Principia* confirmed that its genius occupied a separate sphere, outside the reach of groundlings; it was a mystery, like his own favorite book, the Revelation of John.[26] In time a reaction set in against his self-sufficiency, which seemed too calculating. 'If an author owes a product to his genius,' Kant famously argued, 'he himself does not know how he came by the ideas for it'; and Kant then drew a logical conclusion: Newton was far too rational to be considered a genius.[27] Blake and his twentieth-century disciple Czesław Miłosz agreed with that verdict; in their imaginations, Newton reigned as the Prince of the Land of Ulro—anti-Christ, anti-Creator, anti-Genius.[28] That too is a tribute to the power of his mind.

For Johnson, however, mere greatness could never be a sufficient excuse for turning one's back on the world. The sublime independence of some-one like Milton, whose 'appetite of greatness' disdains to acknowledge how much he shares with his fellow beings, troubles the definition of genius. No one ought to be proud of being singular, as if that were a virtue. Thus the distance from common humanity that Westfall would later remark in Newton disturbed Johnson too. On principle, he believed that every life, closely examined, was much like the lives of others. Moreover, he had a personal stake in the issue. One way of describing Johnson's own life would mark a perpetual struggle between two drives or images of the self: on one side, the pride and fear of knowing that he was not like other people, whether because his powers were greater or because, in the lonely fortress of his mind, compulsive fantasies fought for his soul; on the other side, a willful submission to duty and everyday tasks, in which his self-esteem depended on understanding and identifying with the lives and thoughts of ordinary people. A pious humility vies with extreme competitive urges. Thus he *wanted* to feel that others were like him and he was like others. This was not easy. But Johnson contrived an ingenious solution: as a writer and critic, he tried to represent and bow to the common reader (just like another great eccentric, Virginia Woolf). Somehow he would tune himself to that reader's opinions. There is something heroic about this surrender; deliberately and voluntarily the great man stoops, as if in prayer.

Moreover, he thought that he had found an ally in Newton. *Adventurer* 131, 'Singularity censured,' begins with paradoxical praise for a singular man who did not regard himself as anything special. 'It is an eminent instance of Newton's superiority to the rest of mankind, that he was able to separate knowledge from those weaknesses by which knowledge is generally disgraced; that he was able to excell in science and wisdom, without purchasing them by the neglect of little things; and that he stood alone, merely because he had left the rest of mankind behind him, not because he deviated from the beaten tract' (*Yale* II.482). Johnson follows an orthodox biographical line trumped up by Newton himself, who had an interest in keeping his heresies secret. In memory the great man's later life as Master of the Mint and President of the Royal Society came to suggest a faithful public servant; his Arianism, alchemical studies, and petty jealousies were unknown or forgotten. But in any case, Johnson cares far more about the legend of modesty and probity than about particular facts. Men of genius, on whom others fawn, are all too often wrapped up in themselves; and scholarly authors, wrestling in silence with their thoughts, tend to inhabit a world of their own. This was a peril that Johnson knew well. But Newton seemed to have overcome it; his humility showed that even the most superior thinker might have something in common with Robert Levet, a good man doing his duty every day.

In this way, Newton sets an example for singular people like Johnson. The competitive fire that sometimes consumed both men, and the extreme introspection that often locked each of them in solitude as dark as the astronomer's lonely turret in *Rasselas* (1759), might be redirected to doing good and thinking of other people. Such coming out of oneself is not at all incompatible, in Johnson's eyes, with the peculiar powers of genius; Newton's superiority is augmented by it. Nor will Johnson ever give up his effort to humanize genius. Strange bedfellows, the mathematician who shattered the Great Chain of Being and the writer who spoke for the common reader join forces as servants of God and the public. Thus Johnson, unlike Westfall, finds a part of himself in Newton—or at least in the Newton whom he imagines and wants to resemble. The great genius of modern times proves worthy of his powers precisely by not being vain about them; he knows that in the end he is a man like anyone else. And Johnson is comforted by that measure of genius. The life of Newton, he can see, might well have been his own.

## NOTES

1. Richard S. Westfall, *Never at Rest: A Biography of Isaac Newton* (Cambridge: Cambridge University Press, 1980), ix.
2. For 'Father *Thames*' see Thomas Gray, 'Ode on a Distant Prospect of Eton College' (1747), l.21, in *The Poems of Thomas Gray, William Collins, Oliver Goldsmith*, ed. Roger Lansdale (London and Harlow: Longmans, Green, and Co., 1969), 58; for 'genii of the stream' see Gray, 'Ode on the Death of a Favourite Cat' (1747), l.15, in Lonsdale, 82.
3. 'On the Death of Dr Robert Levet,' l.28 (*Yale* VI.315).
4. 'Science' means 'branch of knowledge' or 'trained skill'; 'art' also implies trained skills, as opposed to 'nature'; and 'wit' means 'intelligence.'
5. Johnson quotes Arbuthnot: the Romans 'had no great *genius* for trade.' A classic modern argument for heterogeneous mental powers is Howard Gardner, *Frames of Mind: The Theory of Multiple Intelligences* (New York: Basic Books, 1983).
6. '*Surgite Mortales, terrenas mittite curas;/Atque hinc cælingenæ vires dignoscite Mentis,/A pecundum vita longe lateque remotæ…/Nec fas est propius Mortali attingere Divos*'; Edmond Halley, 'Ode on this Splendid Ornament of our Time and our Nation, the Mathematico-Physical Treatise by the Eminent Isaac Newton,' ll.27–9, 48. Reprinted in Eugene Fairfield MacPike, ed., *Correspondence and Papers of Edmond Halley* (Oxford: Clarendon Press, 1932), 205–6.
7. The inscription (1755) inserts 'Newton' in the line from Lucretius, '*qui genus humanum ingenio superavit*'; *De rerum natura*, 3.1043.
8. The 'nice barrier' (pronounced *bareer*) comes from Francis Fawkes's 1755 translation of Halley's 'Ode,' reprinted in MacPike, *Papers of Edmond Halley*, 207–8.
9. Reported by Sir William Jones; *Life* II.125n.
10. John Dryden, 'The Authors Apology for Heroique Poetry; and Poetique Licence' (1677), in *The Works of John Dryden*, ed. H. T. Swedenberg, Jr., et al., 20 vols. (Berkeley, Los Angeles, and London: University of California Press,

1956–2002), XII: *Plays: Amboyna, The State of Innocence, Aureng-Zebe*, ed. Vinton A. Dearing (1994), 87; Addison, *Spectator* 592 (10 September 1714), in Donald F. Bond, ed., *The Spectator*, 5 vols. (Oxford: Clarendon Press, 1965), V.28.

11. Edward Young, *Conjectures on Original Composition. In a Letter to the Author of Sir Charles Grandison*, 2nd edn (London: A. Millar and R. and J. Dodsley, 1759), 27.

12. James Engell surveys theories of genius in *The Creative Imagination: Enlightenment to Romanticism* (Cambridge, MA: Harvard University Press, 1981).

13. Frances Burney, *Diary & Letters of Madam D'Arblay*, eds. Charlotte Barrett and Austin Dobson (London: Macmillan, 1904–5), II.271 (25 November 1784).

14. Young, *Conjectures on Original Composition*, 26.

15. Polixenes in *The Winter's Tale*, IV.iv.91–2, 97.

16. This familiar quotation, which first appeared in print in 1833, probably derives from a French phrase, 'en y passant sans cesse,' in a note (not published until the 1780s) to Voltaire's book on Newton (1736). But Newton himself often expressed similar sentiments about the merit of 'patient thought.' See Westfall, *Never at Rest*, 105n.

17. *Life* II.444, 450. Cf. *Adventurer* 84 and 85 (*Yale* II.406–17).

18. A. O. Lovejoy, *The Great Chain of Being: A Study of the History of an Idea* (Cambridge, MA: Harvard University Press, 1936).

19. 'Epitaph. Intended for Sir Isaac Newton, in Westminster-Abbey' (1730), in Pope, *Works*, VI: *Minor Poems*, eds. Norman Ault and John Butt (1954), 317.

20. 'Isaacus Newtonius:/Quem Immortalem/Testantur, *Tempus, Natura, Cælum*:/Mortalem/Hoc marmor fatetur'; Lives IV.91.

21. Samuel Johnson, *Literary Magazine* (15 June 1756), I.89–90.

22. *Lives* IV.62. Cf. IV.65 and IV.78.

23. Thomas Middleton Raysor, ed., *Coleridge's Miscellaneous Criticism* (London: Constable & Co., 1936), 172.

24. Wordsworth, *The Prelude* (1850), III.63.The line was inserted in 1838/39.

25. Recorded by John Conduitt, Newton's nephew-in-law, in 1726; *Early Biographies of Isaac Newton, 1660–1885* ed. Rob Iliffe (London: Pickering & Chatto, 2006), I.163.

26. Newton's (posthumously published) *Observations upon the Prophecies of Daniel, and the Apocalypse of St. John*, edited by his nephew Benjamin Smith (London: J. Darby and T. Browne, 1733), reflect his lifelong interest in Revelation.

27. *Critique of Judgment* (1796), trans. Werner S. Pluhar (Indianapolis: Hackett, 1987), 175–8.

28. Czesław Miłosz, *The Land of Ulro*, trans. Louis Iribarne (New York: Farrar, Straus, and Giroux, 1984), 158–82.

# 9

# Johnson Personified

*Freya Johnston*

In a celebrated essay marking Johnson's 250th birthday, Bertrand Bronson observed that an antipathy towards generalization hampers our reading of eighteenth-century literature:

> We have moved from a taste for the abstract...to a preference for the concrete. The fact permeates our judgements and makes it very difficult for us to meet the eighteenth century on its own ground, to experience aesthetic satisfactions comparable to theirs. It may be that one day the pendulum will swing back. Meanwhile, it is a capital duty of criticism...to try by imaginative sympathy and understanding to allow for and correct the ever-present displacement. Nowhere, perhaps, is the necessity more acute than in the field of eighteenth-century personification.[1]

This chapter, following Bronson's lead, seeks to understand how eighteenth-century personification works. In so doing, one of its aims is to appreciate why Johnson might have thought his 'allegory of human life,' *The Vision of Theodore, the Hermit of Teneriffe, found in his cell* (1748), 'the best thing he ever wrote' (*Life* I.192).

Johnson's *Vision* appeared in *The Preceptor*, Robert Dodsley's two-volume textbook pitched at young readers, where it is described as a warning against 'bad habits' (*Yale* XVI.191–2, 179–80). Narrated in the first person by Theodore, *The Vision* is addressed to the 'Son of Perseverance, whoever thou art.' The opening line admonishes us to 'read, and be wise,' anticipating the first line of a later Johnsonian fiction—'attend to the history of Rasselas prince of Abissinia'—another work to include the cautionary narrative of a hermit (*Yale* XVI.7, 80–3). Theodore retires to the foot of Mount Teneriffe; almost half a century later, he resolves to see the top. Tiring of his arduous climb, he finds himself at a mental crossroads, 'forming alternately excuses for delay, and resolutions to go forward.' He is about to fall asleep when a supernatural 'protector' appears before him and instructs him to 'Attend,' 'observe,' and 'survey' the allegorical Mountain of Existence and 'be wise' (*Yale* XVI.197–8)—a reprisal of the opening line of *The Vision*, which also anticipates the first lines of *The Vanity of Human Wishes* (1749) and another 'Survey' of the human condition.[2] Theodore obeys, and sees at the foot of the mountain a crowd of people accompanied by the 'modest virgin' Innocence (*Yale* XVI.199). As the cohort moves upwards, Education replaces Innocence, and Reason, preceded by Religion, succeeds Education as the monitor. A 'troop of pygmies'—or Habits—also attend the travelers, occasionally buttressing their progress but more often enchaining them with the shackles of Appetite and Passion. The 'unhappy followers of Reason' cannot withstand them (*Yale* XVI.210). Some pilgrims, guided by Religion, make their way to the 'temple of Happiness.' Others are devoured by Ambition, Avarice, Intemperance, Indolence, Despair, and Pride. As Theodore contemplates the scene his protector calls out: 'Remember, Theodore, and be wise, and let not Habit prevail against thee' (*Yale* XVI.212).

As personifications, Habits are complex, unpredictable entities, capable of promoting both good and bad conduct. When they are able to combine with Appetite and Passion, their effect is wholly destructive; yet if they can be trained to cooperate with Religion, they will vigorously drive off those same destructive forces (*Yale* XVI.201–9). So although they typically prove inimical to happiness, without their cooperation happiness is rarely achieved. Habits are resistant to service, inherently mobile and aggressive, but:

> if by a timely call upon Religion, the force of Habit was eluded, her attacks grew fainter, and at last her correspondence with the enemy was entirely destroyed. She then began to employ those restless faculties in compliance with the power which she could not overcome; and as she grew again in stature and in strength, cleared away the asperities of the road to Happiness…few were able to proceed without some support from Habit, and…those whose Habits were strong advanced towards the mists with little emotion, and entered them at last with calmness and confidence (*Yale* XVI.209).

One of the most dangerous things about Habits, 'so minute as not easily to be discerned,' is that they seem at first glance ridiculous, unworthy of the 'precepts of vigilance' that they call forth: 'the followers of Education…did not think it possible that human beings should ever be brought into subjection by such feeble enemies' (*Yale* XVI.200–1). In reality, however, these are subtle, violent, predatory shape-shifters whose 'stature' is 'never at a stand'; from such feeble beginnings are forged the usually inescapable 'chains of Habit' (*Yale* XVI.201, 206). The central lesson of *The Vision* is therefore that Habits must be kept under the watchful command of their human possessors, who will otherwise become their victims; only when relentlessly monitored, fought, and subdued will Habits be coerced, at last, into positive behavior. But their auxiliary role is reluctantly admitted in the tale.[3] More often than not, these Habits sound like the 'wild beasts' or 'apprehensions' that Boswell imagined doing combat with Johnson within the 'vast amphitheatre' of his mind: 'After a conflict, he drove them back into their dens; but not killing them, they were still assailing him' (*Life* I.106).[4] The pageant of human existence reveals to Theodore that 'Habits were so far from growing weaker by these repeated contests, that if they were not totally overcome, every struggle enlarged their bulk and increased their strength; and a Habit oppos'd and victorious was more than twice as strong as before the contest' (*Yale* XVI.207).

Although Johnson's *Vision* is aimed at a youthful audience, he tells us that it occurs in the forty-eighth year of Theodore's retreat (*Yale* XVI.195), thereby underlining the lifelong necessity of such 'contests' with the self. Further evidence of Johnson's battles to oppose and conquer 'sinful habits' crops up throughout the *Diaries, Prayers and Annals* (e.g. *Yale* I.131, 137, 143, 149); his tenth Sermon includes the comment that 'The longer habits have been indulged, the more imperious they become...they can be subdued only by continued caution and repeated conflicts' (*Yale* XIV.114). Johnson always delighted in the possibility of escaping or reforming his habits. One of the few positive moments in the 'Life of Swift' comes when he mentions his subject's reaction to the 'disgrace' of obtaining his degree 'by *special favour*':

> He resolved from that time to study eight hours a-day, with what improvement is sufficiently known. This part of his story well deserves to be remembered; it may afford useful admonition and powerful encouragement to men, whose abilities have been made for a time useless by their passions or pleasures, and who, having lost one part of life in idleness, are tempted to throw away the remainder in despair. (*Lives* III.189)

In a poetic context, in order to enforce through admonition and encouragement such a lesson—which 'well deserves to be remembered'—and in order to make plain the necessarily self-divisive combat that it involves, Johnson might have personified both 'Passion' and 'Despair.'[5]

Personification—'The attribution of human form, nature, or characteristics to something; the representation of a thing or abstraction as a person' (*OED Online*, *personification* 1a)—is an eighteenth-century term (the *OED* dates it back to 1728); 'not merely an artificial device of poetic expression,' it was also 'an important element within the range of human experience.'[6] Johnson's contemporaries praised the trope for its boldness and sublimity, and for its ability to conjure up urgent and affecting, yet concise, pictures; above all, they admired its capacity to unite the particular and the general, the imagination and the senses.[7] Personification is also a natural companion to all forms of life-writing, since biography's claim to praise was said to derive from its reducing general historical narratives into the more compelling form of single human beings. As Dryden argued:

> the examples of virtue are of more vigor, when they are thus contracted into individuals. As the Sun beams, united in a burning-glass to a point, have greater force than when they are darted from a plain superficies; so the vertues and actions of one Man, drawn together into a single story, strike upon our minds a stronger and more lively impression, than the scatter'd Relations of many Men, and many actions... the Reader is more concern'd at one Mans fortune, than those of many.[8]

Johnson outlined a similar case for biography in *Rambler* 60:

> Histories of the downfal of kingdoms, and revolutions of empires, are read with great tranquillity.... Those parallel circumstances, and kindred images, to which we readily conform our minds, are, above all other writings, to be found in narratives of the lives of particular persons.   (*Yale* III.319)

The moral efficacy of life-writing is also that of personification. In both cases, what occurs is a form of incarnation, whereby the otherwise merely general or speculative is made human and hence more forcefully engages the reader's imaginative sympathy.

In Johnson's hands, personification achieves the unlikely feat of making solemnity both active and compelling. When *Rambler* 168 celebrates 'the force of poetry' as 'that force which calls new powers into being, which embodies sentiment, and animates matter' (*Yale* V.127), it is describing (among other things) how the personifying impulse manifests itself. In his *Dictionary* definition of *personification*, Johnson stresses the transformative nature of the process; it is a 'change' from the static to the active. That dynamic, life-giving aspect is further brought out by the fact that it is not the word *personification* that he chooses to exemplify. Rather, he gives us an instance of personification in practice, as if he were writing a handbook of rhetoric instead of a dictionary (this movement from defining a literary term to giving an instance of it in practice also occurs in his entry for *quatrain*, cited by Charlotte Brewer in Chapter 11 of this volume). So Johnson flows seamlessly from the theory of personification to animating example:

> PERSONIFICATION. Prosopopœia; the change of things to persons: as,
>    Confusion heard his voice.
> *Milton*. [*Paradise Lost*, III.710]

James Beattie's definition seems, by contrast, inert: 'That figure, by which things are spoken of *as if they were* persons, is called *Prosopopeia*, or Personification.'[9]

Personifications in *The Vision of Theodore* are continuous with the often malevolent energy of abstract agents in *The Vanity of Human Wishes*, and another trace of Johnson's personifying impulse survives in a draft version of the latter work. Here, we catch a glimpse of him transforming human beings, rather than things, into personified abstractions. An early version of l.29 of the poem ran: 'Historians tell where rival Kings command.' Johnson subsequently changed this to 'Let Hist'ry tell where rival Kings command' (*Poems* 416, 116). One necessary consequence of personification is made clear from such a change: when abstractions are given a voice and a role, less prominence and agency can be accorded to people. Yet Johnson, while he is removing the power to speak from actual historians in favor of an abstract, personified 'Hist'ry,' is now energizing his poem through an injunction to the reader. He is asking us rather than telling us something, inviting his audience to grant him permission to continue.

*The Vanity of Human Wishes* begins: 'Let Observation with extensive View,/Survey Mankind, from *China* to *Peru*' (ll.1–2, *Poems* 115). To open a poem or a paragraph thus is to assume a certain resistance on the reader's part; 'Let…' is less straightforward as an imperative than (for instance) 'Say….' It could mean no more than 'Permit…,' but in Johnson's hands the command seems more pressing, more demanding of a response than that, as if to say 'I urge you….' This may be because his 'Let' possesses a religious impetus akin to that of the opening line of George Herbert's 'Antiphon' (1633): 'Let all the world in ev'ry corner sing…'[10] In Christopher Smart's *Jubilate Agno* (1758–63) the verses beginning 'Let…' tend, as Harriet Guest notes, to address public matters, while personal material belongs in the 'For…' verses. 'Let' implies a voice that is general, even universal, in its appeal.[11] And yet, to instruct or request people to 'let' something be the case also implies that they will need to be won over to your point of view. 'Let' therefore has built into it the possibility that such persuasion won't be successful. It is, in fact, an antagonym, harboring antithetical meanings: *To let*, as Johnson's *Dictionary* explains, is both 'To allow; to suffer; to permit' and 'To hinder; to obstruct; to oppose.'[12] The pendulum swings between these two possibilities throughout Johnson's writing. His use of 'Let' in verse resembles his use of 'Sir' in conversation, in order to change argumentative gear, as it is recorded throughout Boswell's *Life* (see e.g. I.439–41). Both words are local proofs of Johnson's lifelong contention, exemplified in *The Vision of Theodore*'s battle against personified Habits, that 'To strive with difficulties, and to conquer them, is the highest human felicity; the next is, to strive, and deserve to conquer' (*Yale* II.455).

Johnson's sense of a potential resistance to his words is strongest in the dramatic prologues he wrote for other people. In such works, too, the links between personification, pageantry, and impersonation are brought to the fore. Dramatic prologues assume the presence of an audience waiting to be entertained, perhaps noisily indifferent to the spectacle before them, and a group of people onstage who are professional impersonators. Here, then, personification is to be understood not only as a poetic trope, but also as a form of acting: 'A dramatic representation...of a person or character' (*OED Online, personification* 3).[13] A scurrilous *roman à clef, The Amours of Carlo Khan* (1789), noted with relish the effect on female actresses of 'the frequent personification of *loose* characters.'[14] Thus personification can become synonymous with personation; *To personate* is, according to Johnson's *Dictionary*, 'To represent by a fictitious or assumed character, so as to pass for the person represented,' as well as 'To represent by action or appearance; to act.' Both definitions apply to his 'Drury-Lane Prologue' (1747). The author is not the person who speaks the lines; the person who does pronounce them, David Garrick, is an actor-manager for whom the personification of characters (loose and upright) is a professional calling:

> When Learning's Triumph o'er her barb'rous Foes
> First rear'd the Stage, immortal SHAKESPEAR rose;
> Each Change of many-colour'd Life he drew,
> Exhausted Worlds, and then imagin'd new:
> Existence saw him spurn her bounded Reign,
> And panting Time toil'd after him in vain:
> His pow'rful Strokes presiding Truth impress'd,
> And unresisted Passion storm'd the Breast.    (ll.1-8, *Poems* 107)

Johnson's first personification, Learning, is opposed to a crowd of anonymous foes; virtuous abstractions in his work tend to be singular. The effect, as in a biography, is to make us more sympathetic to an embattled individual than we would be to the abstract idea alone. The figure of 'Learning' anticipates that of the scholar in *The Vanity of Human Wishes*, who, just to complicate matters, is himself warned about the pursuit of 'fatal Learning' (ll.135–74, *Poems* 121–4). It might be argued that the Yale edition of Johnson's poetry skews the emphases of the 'Drury-Lane Prologue', since it retains from the quarto pamphlet in which the *Prologue* was originally published the capital letters for 'Learning' and 'Time,' but removes those given to 'Triumph,' 'Foes,' 'Stage,' 'Change,' 'Life,' 'Worlds,' 'Reign,' 'Strokes,' 'Truth,' 'Passion,' and 'Breast.' While personification can operate independently of typographical distinction (in other words, a noun doesn't have to be capitalized in order to be a personification), it is tempting to think that the eighteenth-century text bristles with nouns on the edge of personification in part because *every* noun has a capital letter. There is no differentiation between nouns on this score, and hence any one of them might become an agent and participant in the drama (being on the edge of drama is, by definition, what a prologue should be). Part of the urgent excitement of this opening salvo derives from the sense that everything is ripe for animation; after all, this is the quality for which Shakespeare is being praised—exhausting worlds and imagining new ones. So it would make more sense to have no capital letters than two in a modern printing of the passage. To single out 'Learning' and 'Time' via such capitalization is also to do some of the work that Johnson's reader might have been expected to undertake in determining the threshold of personification (Donald Davie has argued that 'Personifications and generalizations are justifiable according as they are "worked for" '),[15] and in weighing up the importance of one abstract agent compared to another. If 'passion' is storming the breast, is it any less active a force than 'panting Time'? Passion is in fact the more successful of the two, since Time fails to catch his victim.

Perhaps Johnson had in mind that figure of 'panting Time' when he devised the following caveat on the use of personifications: 'The employment of allegorical persons always excites conviction of its own absurdity; they may produce effects, but cannot conduct actions; when the phantom is put in motion, it dissolves; thus *Discord* may raise a mutiny, but *Discord* cannot conduct a march, nor besiege a town' (*Lives* IV.71). 'Panting Time' does indeed seem to be invoked solely in order to excite a conviction of his own absurdity. He is personified neither as creator nor destroyer but simply as a hapless, comic threat. Paul Alkon points out Johnson's originality here: 'While this [portrait] echoes conventional images of time menacing the artist, Johnson reverses the usual outcome by showing time as the exhausted loser: a Falstaffian figure of fun, not terror.'[16] In the 'Life of Pope' (1781), Johnson treated the race with time more warily: 'he that runs against Time, has an antagonist not subject to casualties' (*Lives* IV.16). The context determines how each personification is construed.[17] Shakespeare's boundless creative fertility ensures that he lives on and continues to conquer, thereby defeating time (part of this may be a thought about Shakespeare's rejection, 'by design' or 'by happy ignorance,' of the dramatic unities of time and place; Johnson supports 'Such violations of rules merely positive,' *Yale* VII.79). In the 'Life of Pope,' however, Johnson is considering 'the distance . . . between actual performances and speculative possibility,' a favorite theme that necessarily exposes human efforts as vulnerable, often as futile (*Lives* IV.16). That same 'distance,' incidentally, is perhaps what drives Johnson to create personifications: beings who combine the 'speculative possibility' of mere abstraction with the 'actual performances' of human agents.

In the 'Life of Milton,' Johnson had already sounded a cautionary note as to the limits of personification:

> To exalt causes into agents, to invest abstract ideas with form, and animate
> them with activity, has always been the right of poetry. But such airy beings

are, for the most part, suffered only to do their natural office, and retire. Thus Fame tells a tale, and Victory hovers over a general, or perches on a standard; but Fame and Victory can do no more. To give them any real employment, or ascribe to them any material agency, is to make them allegorical no longer, but to shock the mind by ascribing effects to non-entity.    (*Lives* I.291)

His sense of the potentially runaway effects of personifications when they are given '*real* employment' (my emphasis) is incorporated into the plot of *The Vision of Theodore*. Habits need to be controlled, or they will control you: applied to personifications, we might say that there is a risk that fictions will begin to operate as realities.[18] If an abstract 'habit' becomes a fully realized individual agent called 'Habit,' it may beguile us as an independent, sympathetic, comic creation when we should be resisting and subduing it to didactic purposes. However, if it remains no more than abstract, it won't compel our attention or curiosity at all. So when reading allegorical fiction, or any writing populated with abstract entities, we need to stay mindful of fictions and realities, and how to distinguish between them; or perhaps better, how to adjust and maintain equilibrium between the claims made by each side.

The personification of 'want' (in the sense of penury or indigence) in 'The Ant' (1766), Johnson's paraphrase of Proverbs 6:6–11, might be said to unite the idea of time as comically impotent (as in the 'Drury-Lane Prologue') with the traditional idea of time as genuinely predatory:

> How long shall sloth usurp thy useless hours,
> Dissolve thy vigour, and enchain thy powers?
> While artful shades thy downy couch enclose,
> And soft solicitation courts repose,
> Amidst the drousy charms of dull delight,
> Year chases year, with unremitted flight,
> Till want, now following fraudulent and slow,
> Shall spring to seize thee like an ambush'd foe.    (ll.9–16, *Poems* 154)

Here, the initial impression of 'want' as 'slow' itself turns out to be 'fraudulent'; a creeping poverty will eventually become sudden ambush. Want has no need to hurry because, like Time (as time is understood in the 'Life of Pope'), he'll get his man in the end. Glossing this passage, Donald Davie remarks that:

> The process of beggary is gradual, yet indigence comes on a sudden. Johnson's 'spring' is faithful to this painful paradox, as true to his Scripture as to the human experience of the Bankruptcy Court. And the method is...stripping the action of adverbs ('deceitfully', 'slowly') and transferring the sense of them to the personified agent, making them prosaic and logical, with a sobering ring, like the fine 'fraudulent'.[19]

'Want' is treated differently in Johnson's lines 'On the Death of Dr Robert Levet' (1783):

> In misery's darkest caverns known,
>     His useful care was ever nigh,
> Where hopeless anguish pour'd his groan,
>     And lonely want retir'd to die.   (ll.17–20, *Poems* 234)

If 'want' in 'The Ant' is the predatory enemy of man, here it is personified as the human victim of that same rapacity; it is something that menaces human beings, and something that is an essential part of human suffering; both outside and inside us, alien and native. Similar contrarieties are involved in Johnson's treatment of hope; it makes us vulnerable and ridiculous, but to attempt to banish hope is absurd.[20] Johnson's personified 'Habits' in *The Vision of Theodore*, like the figure of 'want' in 'The Ant,' seem laughably insignificant, but they ensnare us for life. How can we oppose them if they form an element of our psyche? Or is it part of their armory of tricks to convince us that we can't be rid of them? Since young people are *The Vision*'s target audience, it seems fitting that some abstract qualities are represented as not quite part of them, at least not yet. These readers aren't fully formed. They aren't yet old enough, perhaps, to have attained reason; their experience of religion will be limited, their education is unfinished, and their characters are unfixed. They haven't yet succumbed to or learned how to rein in their habits, so it makes sense to construe those habits as separate entities. Here and elsewhere Johnson's powerfully realized personifications allow him to ask, urgently but impersonally, how much of human behavior is under human command, and whether we possess the capacity to shape, change, or escape ourselves. The answer to that question is perhaps more optimistic in *The Vision of Theodore* than it is in the poem on Levet, although both works suggest that our grip on our own lives is at best limited and that reason alone will not confer the ability to govern ourselves. That ability has to be developed and exercised through practical, lived experience, not through the intellect alone. Self-control is therefore a property of individual growth and not the result of decision, however informed such decisions might be.

In 'Levet,' the particular human frailty indicated by 'want' (like that of 'anguish') pushes so insistently at the personified abstraction that we might forget it is abstract at all. We seem to be faced with a real, suffering individual. As John Ogilvie put it in 1774: 'The great art' of personifying abstractions 'lies in painting these with strokes that in order to be discriminating must be particular'—only not so particular as to lose the sense of their general applicability to the fate of all human beings.[21] A lack of further specificity is appropriate in this poem; we are, after all, in the darkness of 'caverns' (it is hard to see clearly; Levet is 'Obscure' [l.10] in more ways than one); there is dignity and propriety in refusing to identify any more pointedly than this the suffering and dying poor. Bronson sums up the resources and motives governing such personifications:

> To generalize was, in fact, to be civilized, and in poetry, no matter how intensely one might feel, it was not decent to autobiographize. Hence the crucial importance and intense satisfaction found in personified abstractions. The device enabled one to particularize in socially, intellectually, and aesthetically acceptable forms.... Thus [eighteenth-century writers] first translated personal experience to decorous generalization; and then, without surrendering the general, re-individualized it by means of personification, by this combination of opposites they gained access to a kind of aesthetic tension hardly present where the particular alone finds explicit statement.[22]

In a passage from the 'Life of Pope,' discussed by James McLaverty in Chapter 13 of this volume, Johnson wrote that some authors 'form and polish large masses by continued meditation, and write their productions only when, in their own opinion, they have completed them' (*Lives* IV.63). McLaverty notes that Johnson himself 'exemplified' this method of composition, and cites one instance of his producing a poem 'almost extempore' following 'a state of meditation'; another, in which Johnson told Boswell that, when he wrote verses, 'I have generally had them in my mind, perhaps fifty at a time, walking up and down in my room; and then I have written them down' (*Life* I.148–9).[23] We might paraphrase Davie here: if, in 'The Ant,' 'The process of beggary is gradual, yet indigence comes on a sudden,' so too Johnson's writing seems to unite a process of gradual evolution with a conclusive burst of activity.

That combination of a period of meditating or contemplating, in which nothing is committed to paper, followed by a rapid, seemingly impromptu process of writing verses down, may indeed (as McLaverty argues) be inadequate as a model to account for the multiple, often collaborative versions of Johnsonian texts. But one thing to be said for it is that it chimes with eighteenth-century accounts of how personifications come into being—James Beattie describes the trope as 'bold,' but also relates it to 'long acquaintance' with 'things inanimate' and 'passion, especially of long continuance.'[24] The idea of meditation followed by sudden performance also squares with Johnson's explanations of how he trained himself to speak in company, and hence to write—by arranging his thoughts and expressions long before he uttered them:

> by reading and meditation, and a very close inspection of life, he had accumulated a great fund of miscellaneous knowledge, which, by a peculiar promptitude of mind, was ever ready at his call, and which he had con-

stantly accustomed himself to clothe in the most apt and energetick expression...he had early laid it down as a fixed rule to do his best on every occasion, and in every company; to impart whatever he knew in the most forcible language he could put it in...by constant practice, and never suffering any careless expressions to escape him, or attempting to deliver his thoughts without arranging them in the clearest manner, it became habitual to him. (*Life* I.203–4)

Such 'constant practice' may have begun in social situations akin to that described in the elaborately titled 'To MISS—On her playing upon the Harpsichord in a Room hung with some Flower-Pieces of her own Painting' (1746): a work in which youth, education, experience, and seduction are construed through personifications, and in which you can perhaps detect, behind the arras of Johnson's 'youth,' the raw young poet at a gathering in Lichfield:

> When STELLA strikes the tuneful string
> In scenes of imitated Spring,
> Where Beauty lavishes her pow'rs
> On beds of never-fading flow'rs;
> And pleasure propagates around
> Each charm of modulated sound;
> Ah! think not, in the dang'rous hour,
> The nymph fictitious, as the flow'r;
> But shun, rash youth, the gay alcove,
> Nor tempt the snares of wily love.
>
> When charms thus press on ev'ry sense,
> What thought of flight, or of defence?
> Deceitful Hope, and vain Desire,
> Forever flutter o'er her lyre;
> Delighting, as the youth draws nigh,
> To point the glances of her eye;
> And forming, with unerring art,
> New chains to hold the captive heart.
>
> But on those regions of delight,
> Might Truth intrude with daring flight,
> Could STELLA, sprightly, fair and young,
> One moment hear the moral song,
> Instruction with her flow'rs might spring,
> And Wisdom warble from her string.
>
> Mark, when from thousand mingled dyes
> Thou see'st one pleasing form arise;
> How active light, and thoughtful shade,
> In greater scenes each other aid;
> Mark, when the diff'rent notes agree
> In friendly contrariety;

> How passion's well-accorded strife
> Gives all the harmony of life:
> Thy pictures shall thy conduct frame,
> Consistent still, though not the same;
> Thy musick teach the nobler art
> To tune the regulated heart.    (*Poems* 98–9)

This is a stilted piece, but its awkwardness seems in tune with the occasion it records; a beautiful young woman shows off her accomplishments to a select group, one of whom finds it difficult to contain his passion for her physical charms. Whether or not this 'youth' is Johnson personified, he retained enough memory of the poem to misquote it twice in the *Dictionary*, under *modulate* (as the work of *Anon.*) and *strife* (where it is attributed to Johnson). *Modulate* and *strife* together sum up this poem's 'friendly contrariety'; it is a work that discovers 'similitude in dissimilitude,' a kind of small-scale *concordia discors*,[25] and one that yet performs a sense of being socially ill at ease, unresolved, ambitious, and unplaced.

We cannot establish for certain the relationship between 'MISS—' or 'STELLA' and the person who lies behind these guises (probably Alicia Maria Carpenter, *Poems* 97), but that inability to pin identities down itself reflects the pendulum's swing from truth to fiction and back again throughout poem. How can we reach the individuals through and around Johnson's abstract agents, who act as masks or veils for reality? (In 'The Winter's Walk' [1747], another '*Stella*' is implored to 'screen me from the ills of life' [l.20]; the name 'Stella' is itself such a screen, *Poems* 101.) How can we distinguish real people from the personifications of 'Beauty,' 'pleasure,' 'love,' 'Hope,' and 'Desire'? If Johnson's 'youth' is also the voice of the poem, there is a shift from the second to the third person at l.15, so that the object of address now also becomes the subject and 'Ah! think not…' becomes a self-directed caution not to give in to 'wily love'; that shift is mirrored in the change from describing Stella in the third person (l.21) to shaping her future conduct in the second person (ll.25–36). Johnson is fond of the verb 'point' (l.16), but here it lacks direction although it possesses force, suggesting a writer whose aim remains, at this early stage in his career, unsure. Hope and Desire may be pointing Stella's glances, but we don't find out where those glances end up, nor what they do to those who receive them.

The poem embodies and meditates on forms of containment and release, conformity and contrariety. How is a poet to impose order on a scene of amorous confusion; how can he escape imprisonment, whether by love or habit? One way Johnson begins to do so is through the balance of opposing qualities and forms: sight is juxtaposed with sound (ll.25–8, ll.29–33); painting is juxtaposed with music (ll.33–6). There are repeated rhymes—string/spring (ll.1–2, ll.23–4); art/heart (ll.17–18, 35–6)—and redefinitions through such repetitions: 'art' first describes the merely seductive activity of Stella's eyes as they enchain the 'captive heart,' but it appears a second time in loftier guise as 'the nobler art,' capable of tuning 'the regulated heart' rather than bent on disturbing and enslaving it. It is as if the Habits of Theodore's *Vision* have been trained to serve the cause of Religion, rather than yielding to that of Appetite. The poem's key personifications—Truth, Instruction, Wisdom (ll.20, 23, 24)—are virtuous agents in a scene whose moral implications are otherwise hard to discern. The youth has tried to escape the alcove, snares, and charms of hope and desire; at the end of the poem, however, he directs Stella to place herself within the 'frame' (l.33) of knowledge and virtue. Art will point the way, setting due bounds to human conduct by its own decorous example. The conclusion of 'To MISS –' is therefore synonymous with the lesson urged on young readers by *The Vision of Theodore*: 'let not Habit prevail against thee' (*Yale* XVI.212). With its marriage of earthly and unearthly attributes, its yoking of the abstract to the human, personification is what gives life and force to the moral.

## NOTES

1. Bertrand H. Bronson, 'Personification Reconsidered,' in *New Light on Dr Johnson: Essays on the Occasion of his 250th Birthday*, ed. Frederick Whiley Hilles (New Haven: Yale University Press, 1959), 193–4.
2. *The Vision of Theodore* was published in April 1748; by November, Johnson had completed *The Vanity of Human Wishes*. 'The religious exhortation of the conclusion [of *The Vanity*] enforces the lesson of... *The Vision of Theodore, the Hermit of Teneriffe*.' *The Poems of Samuel Johnson*, ed. David Nichol Smith and Edward Lippincott McAdam, 2nd edn, rev. J. D. Fleeman (Oxford: Clarendon Press, 1974), 110–11. All references are to this edition and are given in the text. This edition is cited in preference to Yale for reasons that are outlined later in the chapter.
3. On habits in *The Vision of Theodore*, see also Chapter 10.
4. See also Chapters 3 and 5 for discussion of this passage in Boswell's *Life*.
5. 'Passion' is twice personified in the 'Drury-Lane Prologue' (ll.8, 32; *Poems* 107).
6. Earl Reeves Wasserman, 'The Inherent Values of Eighteenth-Century Personification,' *PMLA* 65 (1950), 439.
7. See e.g. James Beattie, 'On Poetry and Music,' in *Essays* (Edinburgh: William Creech; London: Edward and Charles Dilly, 1776), 274–9; John Ogilvie, *Philosophical and Critical Observations on the Nature, Characters, and Various Species of Composition*, 2 vols. (London: for George Robinson, 1774), II.182–7.
8. John Dryden, 'The Life of Plutarch' (1683), in *The Works of John Dryden*, eds. H.T. Swedenberg, Jr., et al., 20 vols. (Berkeley, Los Angeles, and

London: University of California Press, 1956–2002), XVII: *Prose, 1668–1691: An Essay of Dramatick Poesie and Shorter Works*, eds. Samuel Holt Monk and A. E. Wallace Maurer (1971), 274.

9. Beattie, 'On Poetry and Music,' 548 (my emphasis).

10. 'Antiphon,' in *The Works of George Herbert*, ed. Francis Ernest Hutchinson (Oxford: Clarendon Press, 1941), 53.

11. *The Poetical Works of Christopher Smart*, I: *Jubilate Agno*, ed. Karina Williamson (Oxford: Clarendon Press, 1980); Harriet Guest, *A Form of Sound Words: The Religious Poetry of Christopher Smart* (Oxford: Clarendon Press, 1989), 141–2.

12. On the 'double use of "let," indicating changes in verbal mood' in Johnson's *Dictionary*, see Chapter 3.

13. On personification as a form of rhetorical training, see Arthur F. Kinney, 'Continental Poetics,' in *A Companion to Rhetoric and Rhetorical Criticism*, eds. Walter Jost and Wendy Olmsted (Oxford: Blackwell, 2004), 80–95.

14. *The Amours of Carlo Khan* (London: John Lever, [1789]), p.124. *OED Online* gives no examples pre-1814 of *personification* in this sense. On the author as a mere 'imposter,' akin to a 'player,' see *Boswell's Column*, ed. Margaret Bailey (London: William Kimber, 1951), 356–7; on Johnson himself, post-Boswell, as a 'personification,' see Walter Scott in *Johnson: The Critical Heritage*, ed. James T. Boulton (London: Routledge & Kegan Paul, 1971), 420.

15. Donald Davie, *Purity of Diction in English Verse and Articulate Energy* (Harmondsworth: Penguin, 1992), 41.

16. Paul Alkon, 'Johnson and Time Criticism,' *Modern Philology* 85 (1988), 545.

17. On time as a destructive agent in Johnson, see Chapter 2.

18. Imlac, analyzing 'Disorders of intellect,' warns that 'fictions' can 'begin to operate as realities, false opinions fasten upon the mind, and life passes in dreams of rapture or of anguish' (*Yale* XVI.150–2).

19. Davie, *Purity of Diction*, 35.

20. On the folly of attempting to eradicate hope, see *Yale* XVI.72–6.

21. Ogilvie, *Philosophical and Critical Observations*, II.184.

22. Bronson, 'Personification Reconsidered,' 224–5.

23. See Chapter 13.

24. Beattie, 'On Poetry and Music,' 274.

25. On 'Johnson's commitment to a fruitful fusion of opposites,' see Jean Hagstrum, 'Johnson and the *Concordia Discors* of Human Relationships,' in *The Unknown Samuel Johnson*, eds. John J. Burke, Jr., and Donald Kay (Madison: University of Wisconsin Press, 1983), 50.

# 10

# The Creation of Character

## Jane Steen

This chapter investigates the creation of character in Johnson's prose, arguing that, for him, as for a range of biblical writers, character is formed in response to the altercations of experience. The image of the pendulum nicely describes the back and forth of lived existence, drawing attention to the place of character development as a literary device as well as a moral requirement in Johnson's writing. For Johnson, sympathy and virtue are enhanced in those who will engage with life's full swing. In his writing, not least in the *Life of Savage* (1744), *The Vision of Theodore* (1748), and in certain *Rambler* essays (1750–2), he offers his readers paradigmatic warning and example to guide them in their own response to experience.

*An Account of the Life of Mr Richard Savage* (1744) is a complex work, which invites us to read it on different levels.[1] Savage was, and remains, enigmatic. The man called Richard Savage, whom Johnson met when he first came to London, through their work on the *Gentleman's Magazine*, claimed to be the illegitimate son of Earl Rivers and Lady Macclesfield. Even today, however, his parentage remains uncertain.[2] In Johnson's account, which is based on Savage's,[3] he was rejected by his mother and put to nurse, school, and an apprenticeship largely through the influence of his maternal grandmother. Learning of his parentage, he ran away from his apprenticeship and spent much of his life thereafter trying to make contact with his supposed mother. Johnson relates that Savage was deprived of a legacy from his presumed father (who was told that the child had died in infancy). What is certain is that Savage killed a man in a brawl in 1727, and that he died imprisoned and impecunious in Bristol in 1743. Johnson describes a life apparently circumscribed by Savage's early experience and the expectations he subsequently cherished. The hallmark of Savage's life is not balance and stability amidst the ebb and flow of events, but rather an imbalance induced by his predictable, repeatedly destructive nature. We might say that Savage's life was determinedly played out in only one section of the arc described by the pendulum's swing.

Johnson describes this lopsided life in ways calculated to require nuanced reading. He records, for example, that it was Savage's 'peculiar Happiness, that he scarcely ever found a Stranger, whom he did not leave a Friend; but it must likewise be added, that he had not often a Friend long, without obliging him to become a Stranger' (*Life of Savage*, 60). The first part of the chiasmus leads its readers to expect its completion in the second; but where the sentence's structure suggests consistency and closure, its content is contradictory and implies betrayal. Readers, duped by the balanced honesty of Johnson's prose into tolerating his subject, may find themselves shocked both at the behavior described and at the readiness with which it was condoned. Only gradually do we see that such experience mirrors Johnson's own understanding of Savage, if not Savage's understanding of himself.

If Boswell is to be believed, Savage's insinuation into Johnson's life was indeed deceptive. Savage, for Boswell, took Johnson from his better self (*Life* I.161–4). Johnson himself suggests the deep malevolence of this duplicity in the *Life of Savage* by enhancing already sinister scenes with echoes of parallel experiences in the psalms of the *Book of Common Prayer*. This paradigmatic use of biblical writing is one to which we shall return. These sinister scenes, however, turn our image of Savage from one of difficult but abandoned child to dangerous and treacherous foe.

Both scenes involve Savage's attempts to see his alleged mother. The first is short and graphic: '*Savage* was at the same Time so touched with the Discovery of his real Mother, that it was his frequent Practice to walk in the dark Evenings for several Hours before her Door, in Hopes of seeing her as she might come by Accident to the Window, or cross her Apartment with a Candle in her Hand' (*Life of Savage*, 12). The second is a longer narrative of Savage's unauthorized entry into Lady Macclesfield's house, an event that, in the biography, Johnson places after the 1727 brawl mentioned above:

> Mr. *Savage*, when he had discovered his Birth, had an incessant Desire to speak to his Mother, who always avoided him in publick, and refused him Admission into her House. One Evening walking, as it was his Custom, in the Street that she inhabited, he saw the Door of her House by Accident open; he entered it, and finding none in the Passage, to hinder him, went up Stairs to salute her. She discovered him before he could enter her Chamber, alarmed the family with the most distressful Outcries, and when she had by her Screams gathered them about her, ordered them to drive out of the House that Villain, who had forced himself in upon her, and endeavoured to murder her. (*Life of Savage*, 36–7)

Both passages are uncomfortable in themselves. In the first, the shadows that hide Savage's mother from him also conceal Savage from Lady Macclesfield. If she is elusive, he is an emotionally starved and desperate figure, haunting her street, or even, in modern parlance, stalking her. In the second, the Savage who enters unbidden and unexpected is, in Johnson's biography, one who has already been proved capable of the murder that Lady Macclesfield fears.

Johnson, far from offering any explicit comment to highlight this dangerous Savage, is ostensibly at pains to exonerate him. Johnson tells the reader that the attempted house-entry occurred earlier in Savage's life than the point at which it appears in his biography, hence pre-dating the murder of 1727. Its biographical place supposedly emphasizes not Savage's wild nature but Lady Macclesfield's implacable dislike. Johnson tells us that she used the incident to jeopardize any possibility of a Royal Pardon, seemingly seeking to ensure that Savage died for his crime (*Life of Savage*, 37). Such convolution, however, is in vain: the reader knows, and cannot un-know, of what Savage is capable. Lady Macclesfield's ignorance evokes rather than curtails sympathy towards her: the danger she supposed is, for the reader, all too conceivable.

Johnson's casting of these events in the biography has, however, literary precedents. The echoes found here of the *Book of Common Prayer* psalms, mentioned above, draw out more clearly not only an implicit malevolence in Savage but also the way in which Johnson himself was deceived by his companion. The psalms are appointed to be read at Morning and Evening Prayer on a repeated cycle, so that all 150 psalms are recited monthly. Johnson was familiar with them from his own private reading and devotion, and from his attendance at public worship. His knowledge is attested by his use of their phrases in his correspondence, sermons, and prayers.[4] Psalms 55 and 59 in particular lament the presence of those who prowl by night, symbolizing and causing disquiet.[5] The psalmist associates them with 'unrighteousness and strife in the city' (Psalm 55:9). 'They grin like a dog, and run about through the city' (Psalm 59:6). Psalm 55 mourns that these night-walkers were not enemies but compatriots and sometime friends: 'It is not an open enemy that hath done me this dishonour: for then I could have born it. Neither was it mine adversary that did magnifie himself against me: for then peradventure I would have hid myself from him. But it was even thou, my companion: my guide, and my own familiar friend' (Psalm 55:12–14). The psalmist was deceived. His companion's words 'were smoother than oyl, and yet be they very swords' (Psalm 55:22). Both psalmist and enemy misinterpreted and responded erroneously to experience: the enemy became an enemy even to a friend; the friend trusted where trust was misplaced. For all Johnson's condemnation of Lady Macclesfield in the *Life of Savage*, and his sympathy for his friend, these echoes of the psalms provide a foil against which Savage becomes a deeply perfidious companion.

Johnson, like the psalmist, is awakened to his situation. Although anyone, he writes:

> however cautious, may be sometimes deceived by an artful Appearance of Virtue, or by false Evidences of Guilt, such Errors will not be frequent; and it will be allowed, that the Name of an Author would never have been made contemptible, had no Man ever said what he did not think, or misled others, but when he was himself deceived.   (*Life of Savage*, 46)

The *Life of Savage* shows Johnson's clear-eyed appreciation of Savage, his realization that he too has been deceived, and his communication of the ease with which that deception occurred as he replicates it in prose. It also demonstrates Savage's failure to learn from experience:

> By imputing none of his Miseries to himself, he continued to act upon the same Principles, and follow the same Path; was never made wiser by his Sufferings, nor preserved by one Misfortune from falling into another. He proceeded throughout his Life to tread the same Steps on the same Circle; always applauding his past Conduct, or at least forgetting it, to amuse himself with Phantoms of Happiness, which were dancing before him; and willingly turned his Eyes from the Light of Reason, when he it would have discovered the Illusion, and shewn him, what he never wished to see, his real State.   (*Life of Savage*, 74)

Experience, for Savage, was something to be ignored or reinterpreted. He therefore failed to engage with its diversity and to attain the kind of character that this chapter discusses. Such character, acquired precisely through engagement with the vagaries of experience, is discussed in the theological writing to which we now turn, beginning with Paul's letter to the Romans. Character in this sense can, moreover, take written form to guide, as well as warn, others.

In Romans 5:3–5, Paul reflects on the effect of the events through which he lives: 'we glory in tribulations also: knowing that tribulation worketh patience; And patience, experience; and experience, hope: And hope maketh not ashamed; because the love of God is shed abroad in our hearts by the Holy Ghost which is given unto us.'[6] The noun here translated as 'experience' is related to a verb that the New Testament uses to indicate testing and proving. Elsewhere in Greek biblical literature, it refers to the proving of God's servants by suffering, as precious metals are tested in fire: it is, for example, the first verb in the Septuagint version of Psalm 66:9 ('thou, O God, hast proved us: thou also hast tried us, like as silver is tried').

Testing both demonstrates and clarifies composition. The contribution of patient endurance is so integral to the refining effect which Paul discusses, that modern biblical versions refer not to 'experience' but to 'character.' Written reflection on opposition and response is not, however, for the benefit of the individual alone. Paul's pedagogic method makes his own testing a template for his hearers (and, subsequently, readers), allowing them to make sense of comparable fluctuations in their experience. The Pauline paradigm becomes the vehicle by which Christians in different circumstances can follow their Lord, imitating Paul just as Paul imitated Christ (cf. also 1 Corinthians 11:1).

Paul's discussion of the testing of experience in Romans 5 draws on his discussion of the untested mind in Romans 1:28. The untested mind is, for Paul, one that is unsuccessfully tested; it is shown by the refining process to be base metal. Such a mind results directly from a deliberate refusal to acknowledge God as God. Throughout Romans, Paul reminds his hearers of the foundational place of ideas of testing and proving in what he writes. Justification and righteousness are inseparable from testing, because testing describes the experiential process of growth in the Christian life that justification initiates and righteousness enables. We might suggest that Savage's inability to learn from suffering and his ready refusal of the light of reason contribute to a picture of his as, in Pauline terms, an untested mind.

Johnson's *Dictionary* bears witness to his familiarity with the use of the verb *to prove* in the sense of 'testing' as well as 'demonstrating': his first definition of *prove* (v.n.) is 'To make…tryal,' and his fourth, 'To be found in the event.' His second definition of *prove* (v.a.) is 'to try; to bring to the test,' and his third, 'to experience.' His diary attests to his knowledge of the Bible, and to his facility with the Greek text (*Yale* 1.102, 137). Familiarity with the methods of biblical literature would have come with this knowledge and, as we have seen in the *Life of Savage*, biblical literature influenced his writing. Johnson was also familiar with the patristic and scholastic authors who developed this Pauline thinking, not least Augustine of Hippo and Thomas Aquinas.[7] As Paul afforded a glimpse of his evangelistic struggles so that his life could provide a pattern for others, so Johnson's prose offers worked examples of the lessons that experience provides.

In a similar way, Augustine wrote his *Confessions* to reflect on the experiential formation of character in Christian believers. He could not rest in his initial conversion or his attainment of ecstasy. He had to discover how constantly to live the life of a Christian, instituting patterns of behaviour that rather liberate to permit choice than limit to force compulsion.[8] These patterns must become established dispositions or habits and, in *On the Good of Marriage*, Augustine discusses how potential dispositions are made actual. He cites Job as someone whose inclination to patience was known to God but only brought out when Job is 'tested by trial.' For Augustine, it is cultivated habit or cast of mind which 'ensures that something is done when required; when it is not done, it is possible to do it, but there is no need.'[9]

Some eight hundred year later, in the *Summa Theologiae*, Thomas Aquinas turned to these words of Augustine in discussing the relation between action and habit. As Johnson explores in *The Vision of Theodore, Hermit of Teneriffe* (1748), habits might be for good or ill; good habits, or virtues, are dispositions of mind and will that shape individual action for good. Aquinas argued that this shaping for good is teleological: virtuous action is at least in part action directed to the right end.[10] Cultivated dispositions are the means by which action is consistently properly directed, and the human being orientated to God. We may fairly say that for Aquinas, Augustine, and Paul, the person of character has been proved and refined by tests coming from the swings of experience. The life of such a person, alert to the good and to the divine, and habitually acting accordingly, may provide in life and in literature an exemplar for imitation or rejection.

Johnson's indebtedness to the Scriptures, the Church Fathers, and the divines of the Church of England, is indisputable. John Hawkins attributed a 'tincture of enthusiasm' in Johnson's religion to 'the perusal of St. Augustine and other of the fathers' (*Hawkins*, 101). Michael Suarez has noted Thomas Aquinas's place in Johnson's library, and has shown that saturation in the liturgies of the Church of England brought with it exposure to 'a Christian tradition going back not only to Thomas Cranmer and his contemporaries, but also to the early centuries of the church.'[11] Johnson attributed his first serious thinking about religion to the influence of William Law (*Life* I.68–9). The *Dictionary* demonstrates his wide reading in the English divines, the Bible, and the liturgy, as does his discussion of sermons in *Life* III.247–8.[12] It is therefore not surprising that his moral prose is shot through by ideas congruent with the 'Christian morality...collected from the moralists and the fathers,' which Hawkins lists among Johnson's catalogue of planned publications (*Hawkins*, 52–4). In the *Vision of Theodore* and in the *Rambler*, Johnson continued to appropriate both the theological understanding of character and the methods for its cultivation discussed above.

Thomist habit and Pauline mind are both apparent in *The Vision of Theodore*. As Chapter 9 has already discussed, Johnson frequently espouses a sense of the primarily negative nature of habit, but in *Theodore*, he also discusses the beneficial effects of good habit. The allegory shows travelers toiling up the Mountain of Existence towards the temples of Happiness, helped or hindered by those whom they encounter, and not least by Habits. The young on the Mountain are under the care of Education, and when Education keeps Appetite separated from Habits, Habits 'would very punctually obey command, and make the narrow roads in which they were confin'd easier and smoother' (*Yale* XVI.201). After their time with Education, however, pilgrims on the Mountain come under the care of Reason. To ignore Reason is all too quickly to become lost in the maze of Indolence. Yet, as we have seen in the *Life of Savage*, Reason's quality must also be tested and proved by the pendulum-swing of experience. Reason alone cannot achieve happiness or cultivate beneficial Habits. Those who follow only Reason risk Intemperance, Avarice, Tyranny, and Despair. For Johnson, Reason, like the successfully tested mind in Paul's writing, must turn to God. Only when Reason enlists in the service of Religion, can she safely direct followers along her way, which is 'so far as it reached, the same with that of Religion' (*Yale* XVI.209). Even then, Thomist Habit plays its part. Theodore observed 'that few were able to proceed without some support from Habit, and that those whose Habits were strong advanced towards the mists [of Happiness] with little emotion, and entered them at last with calmness and confidence; after which they were seen only by the eye of Religion' (*Yale* XVI.209).

The tested and proved Reason of *The Vision of Theodore* reappears in various *Rambler* essays. In *Rambler* 162, reason is 'the great distinction of human nature, the faculty by which we approach to some degree of association with celestial intelligences' (*Yale* V.95). Reason's purpose in regulating conduct is active, not merely speculative: 'as the excellence of every power appears only in its operations, not to have reason, and to have it useless and unemployed, is nearly the same' (*Yale* V.95). Reason discerns, and directs, the good that must be done. Johnson's understanding of reason here is similar to that of Richard Hooker, from whom he took the first illustrative quotation under *reason* in the *Dictionary*: '*Reason* is the director of man's will, discovering in action what is good; for the laws of well-doing are the dictates of right *reason*.'[13] Active engagement with experience develops capacity and self-knowledge.

To discuss this process, Johnson returns to the biblical metaphor of testing metal seen above: 'that fortitude which has encountered no dangers, that prudence which has surmounted no difficulties, that integrity which has been attacked by no temptations, can at best be considered but as gold not yet brought to the test, of which therefore the true value cannot be assigned' (*Yale* V.36). Johnson's imagery here is close to that found in the Book of Job. Job declares that God 'knows the way that I take; when he has tested me, I shall come out like gold' (Job 23:10). Robert DeMaria has noted the similarities between the aphorisms of the

*Rambler* and the sentiments of Job 14:1: 'man *that is* born of a woman *is* of few days, and full of trouble.'[14] Seven of Johnson's surviving sermons take their texts from this Old Testament Wisdom tradition, of which two are expositions of the Book of Job. It is not by 'unactive speculation' that such trials are endured and surmounted (*Yale* XVI.211), and as much for the *Rambler* as for *Theodore*, the price of reason's absence is languishing existence in the habitation of ignorance and indolence.

The development of character requires repeated engagement and trial, with habit as a necessary adjunct, in the *Rambler* as much as in *Theodore*. Habit may be deployed in the development of virtue as well as in the thwarting of temptation. Thus *Rambler* 28 decries those who lack habit, that Thomistic disposition of the mind and will which repeatedly disposes the individual to good: 'One sophism by which men persuade themselves that they have those virtues which they really want, is formed by the substitution of single acts for habits' (*Yale* III.153). In *Rambler* 43, Johnson calls habit to his aid, insisting it is 'of the utmost importance' that those who wish to distinguish themselves 'add to their reason, and their spirit, the power of persisting in their purposes; acquire the art of sapping what they cannot batter, and the habit of vanquishing obstinate resistance by obstinate attacks' (*Yale* III.235).

Johnson, however, does not stop at recommendation or description. He reinforces the instruction to engage with experience, and to be formed by so doing, by methods that assist his readers to do as he recommends. The remainder of this chapter looks at examples of three of these approaches: Johnson's prose style, his fictitious vignettes, and his reminders of human mortality.

Johnson's prose style can possess an internal rhythmic (and pendulum-like) weight, which reinforces his message that persistence is needed to acquire character. In *Rambler* 155, for example, Johnson writes that 'to do nothing is in every man's power; we can never want an opportunity of omitting duties. The lapse to indolence is soft and imperceptible, because it is only a mere cessation of activity; but the return to diligence is difficult because it implies a change from rest to motion, from privation to reality' (*Yale* V.64). The soft, sibilant sounds of 'lapse,' 'indolence,' 'soft,' and 'imperceptible' insinuate themselves, serpent-like, into the mind, their effortless smoothness anticipating the ease of 'cessation.' The hammering 'd's of 'diligence' and 'difficult' must then jolt readers out of their stupor, with the gentle ending of 'diligence' providing a memory of that from which we are awakened. The essay thus allows readers mentally to experience the temptation against which Johnson cautions, inoculating them against its effects by laying an experiential pattern in their minds. The provision of warning and remedy is comparable to that of novels, which

Johnson discusses in *Rambler* 4: they serve 'not only to show mankind, but to provide that they may be seen hereafter with less hazard' (*Yale* III.22).

This experiential methodology finds further expression in Johnson's fictitious vignettes. In a manner comparable to the Pauline recounting of experience and response which we have seen above in Romans 5, these offer examples of conduct that describe, and assist the reader to internalize, patterns of behavior to be imitated or rejected in the formation of character by experience. Johnson's vignettes address various common states, situations, and activities, including ageing, card playing, collecting, commerce, marriage, and seeking service. Some are in the form of short narratives; many take epistolary form, and may take their discussion beyond the scope of a single essay. *Rambler* 130 and 133, for example, are letters from Victoria, a beauty marred by smallpox and offered the opportunity to change in response to her experience. Victoria's very name implies that she will indeed heed her companion's advice to 'consider yourself, my Victoria, as a being born to know, to reason, and to act' (*Yale* IV.345).

Victoria is one of several correspondents in the *Rambler* whose tale proposes appropriate change in response to circumstance. Others include Pertinax (*Rambler* 147), recovering from disputatious skepticism, and Melissa (*Rambler* 75), who must manage anew without fortune or favor. Their need for reasoned resilience asks the readers of their stories to enquire into their own resources with which they might face adversity and to triumph (*Yale*.V.17–22; IV.28–33).

Other *Rambler*s depict extremes of behavior in which experience is used, Savage-like, to warn and admonish. Gelidus, the ice-man of *Rambler* 24, provides one such extreme of behavior, in his incapacity for human sympathy (*Yale* III.132–4). Another is Quisquilius (whom we might call 'Mr Rubbish') in *Rambler* 82. Quisquilius is a destructive and passionate collector of curiosities, led from the path of wisdom by indulging his hobby. He regrets his absence from 'that happy generation who demolished the convents and monasteries, and broke windows by law' (*Yale* IV.65). He once 'accepted as a half year's rent for a field of wheat, an ear containing more grains than had been seen before upon a single stem' (*Yale* IV.67). He gratifies his passion, squanders his ability, and wastes his patrimony. When the creditors come calling, Quisquilius is theatrical: 'I submit to what cannot be opposed' (*Yale* IV.70). Readers, imagining the hand at the brow, are not sympathetic.

Johnson, however, turns our attention inward, writing the next *Rambler* on curiosity-hunting. It is 'never without grief' that he finds one who 'will not easily be brought to undergo again the toil of thinking, or leave

his toys and trinkets for arguments and principles, arguments which require circumspection and vigilance, and principles which cannot be
obtained but by the drudgery of meditation' (*Yale* IV.75). His challenge
to his readers is powerful: what were their responses to Quisquilius? Did
they dismiss as rubbish one over whom Johnson can grieve? What will
they make of their own lives: will they laze with the lotus eaters or hazard
'again to the dangers of the sea' (*Yale* IV.75)?

With Quisquilius and his like, however, this essay returns to its starting
point. These imaginary heroes, like Savage, neither engage with the ebbs
and flows of experience, nor gain from its rhythms the habit and disposition to know and to choose what is good. The fictitious personalities are
circumscribed by their narratives, but Savage was not (or should not have
been) and neither are Johnson's readers. Johnson, despite his sympathy
with such individuals, nevertheless inhabited and continued a literary,
moral, and indeed religious tradition that encouraged such learning from
experience as would refine and form reasonable and godly character. He
expressed his hope in *Rambler* 208 that his 'professedly serious' essays 'will
be found exactly conformable to the precepts of Christianity' (*Yale* V.320)
and it is fitting to conclude with *Rambler* 185, where the implications of
those precepts are once again reinforced by Johnson's description of 'character.' He writes 'The utmost excellence at which humanity can arrive, is
a constant and determinate pursuit of virtue, without regard to present
dangers or advantage; a continual reference of every action to the divine
will; a habitual appeal to everlasting justice; and an unvaried elevation of
the intellectual eye to the reward which perseverance only can obtain'
(*Yale* V.209). The repeated near-synonyms ('continual,' 'habitual,' 'unvaried') reinforce meaning in a manner akin to that in which the repeated
altercations of experience reinforce character. The essay, on forgiveness,
published on Christmas Eve 1751, is uncompromising: on this Christian
duty, 'eternity is suspended, and to him that refuses to practice it, the
throne of mercy is inaccessible, and the Saviour of the world has been
born in vain' (*Yale* V.210). Johnson is a kindly moralist: eternity's pendulum swings while we live, but to eschew the formation of Christian character is risky, costing us heaven. In the end, Johnson's pendulum is much
more than a literary device: it is the living of life in pursuit of virtue
and truth.

## NOTES

1. *An Account of the Life of Mr Richard Savage* was first published in 1744 and
   revised by Johnson in 1748. In 1775 it was published in a form that reverted,
   apparently by accident, to the first, uncorrected edition of 1744; some

changes were also made to the text. It is unclear whether Johnson was consulted about this edition. Because the text of the 'Life of Savage' in *Lives of the Poets* follows the 1775 edition, this chapter refers instead to Clarence Tracy, ed., *Life of Savage* (Oxford: Oxford University Press, 1971)—a collation of the early texts—on the basis that it is more likely to reflect Johnson's intentions. See *Life of Savage*, xxi–xxxvi; *Lives* III.386–7.

2. Freya Johnston, 'Savage, Richard (1697/8–1743),' *Oxford Dictionary of National Biography* (Oxford: Oxford University Press, 2004; online edn, January 2008), www.oxforddnb.com/view/article/24724, accessed 16 April 2011. See also Clarence Tracy, *The Artificial Bastard: A Biography of Richard Savage* (Cambridge, MA: Harvard University Press, 1953).

3. Johnson's anonymous 'puff' for the work in *The Gentleman's Magazine* 13 (1743), 416, ascribes it to 'a Person who was favoured with [Savage's] Confidence, and received from himself an Account of most of the Transactions which he proposes to mention.'

4. For sermons and prayers, see James Gray, *Johnson's Sermons: A Study* (Oxford: Clarendon Press, 1972), and Jane Steen, 'Samuel Johnson's Anglicanism and the Art of Translation,' *The New Rambler* (2007–8), 49–51.

5. *The Book of Common Prayer* (Edinburgh: James Watson, 1720). All psalm references cite this edition, of which Johnson owned a copy.

6. *The Holy Bible, containing the Old and New Testaments translated out of the Original Tongues,* 4 vols. (Oxford: T. Wright and W. Gill, 1769), IV, n.p. This is the folio edition of Benjamin Blayney's revision of the 1611 text, which became the basis for the Oxford standard text.

7. See *Yale* XIV.30, and also Maurice Quinlan, *Samuel Johnson: A Layman's Religion* (Madison: University of Wisconsin Press, 1964), 4.

8. Augustine, *Confessions*, ed. and trans. Henry Chadwick (Oxford and New York: Oxford University Press, 1991), Book X.

9. Augustine, *De Bono Coniugali*, in Patrick Walsh, ed. and trans. *Augustine: De Bono Coniugali; de Sancta Uirginate* (Oxford: Clarendon Press, 2001), 46.

10. *Summa Theologiae* Ia.2ae.50.5. See also Daniel Westburg, *Right Practical Reason: Aristotle, Action, and Prudence in Aquinas* (Oxford: Oxford University Press, 1994), 3.

11. Michael J. Suarez, SJ, 'Johnson's Christian Thought,' in Greg Clingham, ed., *The Cambridge Companion to Samuel Johnson* (Cambridge: Cambridge University Press, 1997), 199, 194.

12. See also *Life* I.189, n.1, on Johnson's refusal to cite Samuel Clarke in the *Dictionary* due to his unorthodox views on the Trinity.

13. Richard Hooker, *The Folger Library Edition of the Works of Richard Hooker*, general ed. W. Speed Hill, 5 vols. (Cambridge, MA, and London: Harvard University Press, 1977–90), I.79.

14. Robert DeMaria, Jr., *The Life of Samuel Johnson: A Critical Biography* (Blackwell: Oxford, 1993), 167–70.

# 11

# 'A Goose-Quill or a Gander's?': Female Writers in Johnson's *Dictionary*

*Charlotte Brewer*

In his discussion of *The Rambler* essays, Hazlitt's characterization of their author is decidedly paradoxical. On the one hand, he accuses Johnson of treating all matters with a homogeneity of style that flattens differences ('it reduces all things to the same artificial and unmeaning level [and] destroys all shades of difference'); on the other, Hazlitt's image of 'the oscillation of the pendulum' and his account of Johnson as a 'balance-master' figure him dealing with binary opposites but unable to reconcile them (*Hazlitt* VI.100–4).

To some extent, this inconsistency may be related back to Hazlitt himself. At the same time, however, it points revealingly to unresolved issues and contradictions in Johnson and his literary projects, a trait that can also be detected in Johnson's attitude towards women writers. A comparable series of paradoxes characterizes eighteenth-century attitudes to women's writing and women's education more widely. During the course of a century in which the professional woman writer became recognized as a social and economic phenomenon, female authorship and learning remained controversial—so that well into the nineteenth century Hazlitt himself declared 'I have an utter aversion to *blue-stockings*. I do not care a fig for any woman that knows even what an author means' (*Hazlitt* VIII.236).

Johnson's *Dictionary*, first published in 1755, is an illuminating focal point for some of these paradoxical positions, in relation both to Johnson himself and to his age. It has been established beyond doubt that 'Johnson…always encouraged women writers. No influential author of the century gave them more practical advice or helped them more to publish,' and his patronage was crucial in helping female writers become better accepted as respectable professionals over this period.[1] Yet he printed a proportionally tiny number of quotations from female writers in the *Dictionary*. This might initially seem unremarkable—after all, Johnson's stated 'purpose' was to 'admit no testimony of living authours' into his *Dictionary*, and he 'studiously endeavored to collect [quotations] from the writers before the restoration'—a period largely devoid of recognized female writers—whose works he regarded 'as the *wells of English undefiled*' (*Yale* XVIII.95). Notwithstanding such an objection, however, this chapter seeks to explore Johnson's under-representation of female quotation sources in his dictionary, with the aim of showing that their absence from his record of the language is more interesting and less obvious than might at first be thought.

It is clear that many of Johnson's contemporaries (and near-contemporaries) thought that women's use of language was distinctive and notable. In his letter published in *The World* on 28 November 1754, Lord Chesterfield gave some specific advice to Johnson on female diction, as an issue:

> to which perhaps he may not have given all the necessary attention. I mean the genteeler part of our language, which owes both it's rise and progress to my fair countrywomen, whose natural turn is more to the copiousness, than to the correction of diction. I would not advise him to be rash enough to proscribe any of those happy redundancies, and luxuriances of expression, with which they have enlarged our language.[2]

These comments on the profusion and redundancy of women's language are evidently something of a joke, one that Chesterfield continues to make in a second letter (5 December 1754). Here he again emphasizes the distinctiveness of female language use, in terms of praise so fulsome that they undo themselves: 'Language is indisputably the more immediate province of the fair sex: there they shine, there they excell.'[3] After enlarging on the sort of language that women write, Chesterfield comments specifically on female poetry: 'When this happy copiousness flows, as it often does, into gentle numbers, good Gods! how is the poetical diction enriched, and the poetical licence extended!'

But all this raises a ticklish question for Johnson, Chesterfield says. Should he put these distinctive female locutions ('hastily begot' and 'ow[ing]' their birth to the incontinency of female eloquence') into his dictionary or not? If he leaves them out, he will get into trouble with 'the ladies'; if he puts them in, he will get into trouble with 'the learned part of his readers,' i.e. the men. Unfortunately, Chesterfield provides no examples of the ways in which women have enlarged 'poetical diction,' and only three examples of female oral usage (in his own terms, what he hears when he sees 'a pretty mouth opening to speak'): *flirtation*, *to fuzz* ('dealing twice…with same pack of cards'), and *vastly* in the sense 'very,' as used to describe a snuffbox that is 'vastly pretty' because 'vastly small.'

How did Johnson respond to Chesterfield's advice and, in particular, to the implication that women's poetry differed from men's? Only one of the entries for Chesterfield's three words is identified in the *Dictionary* as specifically female: *flirtation* (defined as 'a quick sprightly motion'), which is said to be 'a cant word among women'—though illustrated by a quotation from Pope.[4] Johnson also ignores the sexual sense implied by Chesterfield which, as Chesterfield mentions, is found in Cibber—attributed to a female character. *Fuzz* in Chesterfield's sense is not recorded, whereas *vastly* is illustrated with quotations from male authors rather than female. The loose use of the term is not mentioned (and as it happens, elsewhere Chesterfield identifies *vastly* as typical of vulgar male speech).[5] Nevertheless, Johnson (who was later to warn in *Idler* 77 [*Yale* II.240] against 'female phrases and fashionable barbarisms,' clearly associating women with uncontrolled or inappropriate language use) does designate a number of other usages as specifically female and by implication undesirable. Examples include *horrid*, meaning 'Shocking; offensive; unpleasing,' identified as a sense occurring 'in womens cant'—again illustrated from Pope, who in the *Rape of the Lock* (1714) puts the word in the mouth of Belinda's friend Thalestris: 'Already I your tears survey, Already hear the horrid things they say'; *frightful*, 'A cant word among women for any thing unpleasing,' not supported by a quotation; *frightfully* (sense 2), 'a woman's word,' with a quotation from Swift's satiric impersonation of a woman in his 'Journal of a Modern Lady' (1729): 'Then to her glass; and Betty, pray,/Don't I look *frightfully* today?'; and *odious* (sense 4, only in the fourth edition of the *Dictionary*): 'A word expressive of disgust: used by women,' again quoted from a male poet mocking a female character ('Green fields, and shady groves, and crystal springs,/And larks, and nightingales, are *odious* things,' a view attributed to 'Fulvia' in Edward Young's *The Universal Passion*, from *Satire V. On Women* [1726]). These definitions suggest that Johnson concurs with Chesterfield's view that distinctive, and inferior, female modes of utterance exist (if not, in these instances, associated with poetry), although his actual evidence about such locutions, when supplied, is filtered through quotations from male sources ventriloquizing women, not female ones.

This linguistic failure (if it is not too harsh, and anachronistic, to judge it as such) to illustrate female locutions from female sources is an interesting one, since Johnson's extensive use of quotations is otherwise one of the most significant linguistic features of the *Dictionary*. Hazlitt conceded that Johnson was not 'a man without originality' (*Hazlitt* VI.100), but where lexicography was concerned he broke new ground, being the first monolingual English dictionary-maker to base his definitions on real examples of language use and thus playing a significant role in the evolution of English lexicography; an achievement duly recognized by his greatest successor, the chief editor of the first edition of the *OED* James Murray, who described how Johnson's method (carried over into the *OED*) 'involved and rendered possible' a much greater awareness of the range of meanings and nuances a word might convey.[6] But Johnson's quotations have more than a linguistic function in his dictionary: they also tell a cultural story that lies behind the words and the *Dictionary* itself. The content and provenance of the *Dictionary*'s quotations are significant carriers of non-linguistic information, so that the meaning of the work is constructed partly through Johnson's choice of who to quote as linguistic evidence, and partly through the views (however decontextualized from their original source) communicated by such utterances: as Johnson rightly said in the *Plan*, 'the credit of every part of this work must depend' on the 'authorities' or quotations (*Yale* XVIII.55).

Now that the *Dictionary* is searchable in electronic form (in Anne McDermott's edition for Cambridge University Press), it has been calculated that seven sources alone are responsible for nearly half the quotations in the *Dictionary*: Shakespeare, Dryden, Milton, Bacon, the Bible, Addison, and Pope; while nineteen authors account for nearly 70 per cent of the total.[7] As commentators have noted, 'By selecting the domain of research, Johnson limited both the kind of English and the kind of knowledge his book could contain,' and 'the very act of selecting a corpus such as Johnson's "wells of English undefiled" is potentially prescriptive.'[8] In explaining that the quotations were the central plank of his dictionary, Johnson justified his choice of which authors to cite by declaring that he would follow the list already drawn up by Pope. Unsurprisingly, none of these was female.[9] Although in the event Johnson spread himself much more widely, this initial list was clearly influential on him, and Pope himself, extensively quoted in the *Dictionary*, was characteristically responsible for some of its most misogynist material, for example, 'Nothing so true as what you once let fall,/Most women have no characters at all' (quoted twice, in slightly different forms, in the entries for both *at* and *character*); 'Men, some to pleasure, some to business take,/But every woman is at heart a rake' (also quoted twice, under *heart* and *rake*); 'O woman! woman! when to ill thy mind/Is bent, all hell contains no fouler *fiend*' (under *fiend*).

Such misogyny is found on a wider scale throughout the *Dictionary*'s quotations and is in line with prevailing cultural assumptions both of the time and of the centuries before and after: that women are morally and intellectually weak and certainly weaker than men, that they are fickle and have poor judgment, and so on.[10] Where language in particular is concerned, Johnson chooses some quotations that reflect standard folk-linguistic notions about women's talkativeness: under *leaky*, for example, he cites, from Roger L'Estrange, 'Women are so *leaky*, that I have hardly met with one that could not hold her breath longer than she could keep a secret'; under *taciturnity* he chooses Donne's 'Some women have some *taciturnity*, Some nunneries some grains of chastity.' Johnson also selects a number of quotations directly militating against the participation of women in public literary activity and in learned pursuits (thus qualifying as eligible quotation sources), supporting the commonplace assumption that such unnatural behavior went hand in hand with a neglect of household duties and of proper female conduct: e.g. the noun *turn* is illustrated with 'Female virtues are of a domestick *turn*. The family is the proper province for private women to shine in' (Addison), and *talkativeness* is supported by Swift's 'Learned women have lost all credit by their impertinent *talkativeness* and conceit.'

It may not seem surprising, therefore, that of the 114,000-odd quotations in the *Dictionary*, fewer than thirty, by my count, are from female authors: one each from Jane Barker, Elizabeth Carter, Hester Mulso, and Margaret Cavendish, three from Jane Collier, and a remarkable twenty from Charlotte Lennox; there is probably a handful more.[11]

But this striking imbalance can be viewed in two ways. On the one hand, as already stated, it reflects the predominant culture of the time. Much contemporary evidence indicates that both women and men felt it was not only indecorous but also immoral for women to be published authors or playwrights—and some famous published women, such as Aphra Behn or Delarivier Manley, did lead indecorous lives. Moreover, Johnson was seeking to record not 'fugitive cant'—the ephemeral colloquial language of the day, whether uttered by men or women—but (as we have seen) the '*wells…undefiled*' of pre-Restoration English (Yale XVIII.95). He wished, for the pedagogical and aesthetic reasons outlined in his *Plan*, to 'contribute to the preservation of antient, and the improvement of modern writers' (*Yale* XVIII.57), and he did this by quoting heavily from established literary masters of the past. As Chesterfield put it in his first letter to *The World*, English contrasts with French in that the French language spread over Europe as a result of military conquest: 'Whereas our language has made it's way singly by it's own weight and merit, under the conduct of those great leaders, Shakespear, Bacon, Milton, Locke, Newton, Swift, Pope, Addison, &c. A nobler sort of conquest, and a far more glorious triumph, since graced by none but willing captives!'[12] Although this may be nonsense as far as linguistic and literary history in Europe is concerned, it shows the strength of the view that great writers represent the English language—that in some way they are the English language. Similar views can be found centuries later, whether voiced by cultural commentators like J. H. Newman, or linguists like George Marsh who helped contribute to the *OED*, or indeed by the *OED* itself, whose editor James Murray identified 'all the great English writers of all ages' as the first port of call for that great dictionary's stock of over 5 million quotations.[13] Women writers almost never occur in early lists of great writers, such as Chesterfield's, and have been comparatively little treated in most literary histories up to the present day. In addition, throughout print history there have been far fewer female than male authors published (though the number rose sharply over the eighteenth century).[14]

Tracing the swing of Hazlitt's pendulum, however, one can look at the matter differently. Notwithstanding his stated intention to concentrate on pre-Restoration sources, Johnson quoted in large numbers from post-1660 writers, notably Dryden (*c.*11,400 quotations), Addison (*c.*4,400 quotations), Pope (*c.*4,000), and Swift (*c.*3,200).[15] These men were active over the very period in which women writers established a well-recognized role in public literary life—a role attested both by the growing abundance of their published work and by the ubiquitous discussions in essays, periodicals, books, collections of poetry, and other sources, by men and women alike, of the propriety and desirability of women appearing in print. The fact that female authorship was being debated so avidly means, of course, that lots of women engaged in it (as Chesterfield effectively complains). Certainly post-Restoration women had long been hailed as capable of producing writing as good as that by men, both aesthetically and intellectually—the 'matchless Orinda' Katherine Philips (1632–44), lauded by Vaughan and Cowley among others, Mary Astell (1666–1731), Anne Finch (1661–1720), Jane Barker (*c.*1652–1732), Catherine Trotter Cockburn (*c.*1674–1749), and their many contemporaries, who between them covered all the genres most liberally represented in Johnson's *Dictionary*: poetry, plays, learned and philosophical works, and translations. Repeatedly, both male and female writers maintained that equal value might be attached to writers of both genders, as typified in the Preface to *Poems by Eminent Ladies*, an anthology published the same year as the *Dictionary* by Johnson's friends George Colman and Bonnell Thornton. These volumes (reprinted in 1757 and issued in revised editions in 1773 and *c.*1785) were claimed by its editors as 'a standing proof that great abilities are not confined to the men, and that genius often glows with equal warmth, and perhaps with more delicacy, in the breast of a female,' with many of their excerpted authors having been 'particularly distinguished by the most lavish encomiums either from Cowley, Dryden, Roscommon, Creech, Pope, or Swift.'[16] Other contemporary examples of anthologies, discussions, and advocacy of women writers include Robert Dodsley's much reprinted *Collection of Poems by Several Hands* (first published 1748), which contained a number of examples of works by women, John Duncombe's poem *The Feminiad* (1754), and George Ballard, *Memoirs of Several Ladies... Celebrated for their Writings* (1752).[17]

Such contextual evidence makes the absence of female sources from Johnson's *Dictionary* more notable. When one looks at a page of Johnson— at all but a handful of pages of Johnson—one encounters a barrage of male authorities, but no female ones. For the latter part of the period treated by the *Dictionary*, this is not an accurate reflection of the use of language by culturally significant writers: both linguistically and culturally speaking, Johnson cut out a significant portion of his potential sources. In doing so, incidentally, he ignored an alternative folk-linguistic view, that women and language were not only strongly but benignly linked. Discernible in Chesterfield's satirically phrased remarks as already quoted (e.g. on language as 'indisputably the more immediate province of the fair sex'), this view is found in the epigraph to one of the most remarkable works of scholarship to have been published in the previous fifty years, Elizabeth Elstob's 1715 grammar of Anglo-Saxon, whose title page bore a letter from the learned encyclopedist George Hickes identifying the special appropriateness to women of literary and linguistic study: 'Our Earthly Possessions are truly enough called a PATRIMONY, as derived to us by the Industry of our FATHERS; but the Language that we speak is our MOTHER-TONGUE; And who so proper to play the Critick in this as the FEMALES.'[18]

Johnson's neglect of female sources is additionally striking in the light of non-dictionary evidence on his relationships with women writers and his views on their work. It is true that in 1753, while working on the *Dictionary*, he wrote in *Adventurer* 115 that 'In former times, the pen, like the sword, was considered as consigned by nature to the hands of men...the revolution of years has now produced a generation of Amazons of the pen, who with the spirit of their predecessors have set masculine tyranny at defiance,' and that *Amazon* was a double-edged term to apply to women (*Yale* II.457–8).[19] But, as noted at the start of this chapter, Johnson's personal and professional connections with female authors made an important contribution to literary history. Many of these connections (e.g. with Frances Burney and Hester Thrale) flourished after the *Dictionary* was published, but there is good evidence of Johnson's respect and regard for female writerly achievements more or less contemporary with the *Dictionary* too—notably those of Charlotte Lennox. Such regard might, one would have thought, have caused Johnson to be interested in quoting from their post-Restoration predecessors.[20] As Isobel Grundy has pointed out, the prominent writer Elizabeth Singer Rowe (d. 1737) was in 1756 publicly ranked by Johnson with Isaac Watts (who himself recognized the 'superior sweetness' of her muse), though Johnson did not repeat the pairing when he asked his publishers' permission to include Watts in the *Lives of the Poets*. In Grundy's words, 'It is tantalizing to think what might have been the effects on subsequent literary history and even on the course of literature if Johnson's *Lives* had included even one woman!'—or, one might add, if he had quoted more from female authors in his *Dictionary*. As Grundy points out, 'he made no move, however, either by direct or indirect means to revise the canon'; and the same applies to his choice of quotation sources for the *Dictionary*.[21]

Johnson's reluctance to cite texts written by women appears striking for at least one further reason, too. As in the case of Watts, who edited Rowe's work as well as admiring it, some of the post-Restoration male writers most lavishly quoted in the *Dictionary* were deeply intermeshed, in both their literary and their social lives, with female writers who were not only highly erudite, intelligent, and accomplished, but also publically influential.[22] Pope's relationship with Lady Mary Wortley Montagu, in both its benign and its vituperative phases, is an outstanding example of this phenomenon (and we may note in passing that Johnson later singled out Montagu's *Letters* as the only book he read through 'in his whole life' and 'which he did not consider as obligatory' (*Shaw-Piozzi*, 146).[23] The 'Verses to the Lady Mary Wortley Montagu,' persistently attributed to Pope in their many eighteenth-century printings, wittily exhibit the profound ambivalence with which learned male writers regarded their female colleagues, combining (in accord with Hazlitt's oscillating pendulum) admiration for their learning with a strong sense of its primal transgression:

> But if the First *Eve*,
> Hard Doom did receive,
> When only *One Apple* had she,
> What Punishment New,
> Shall be found out for You,
> Who Tasting, have rob'd the *whole Tree*[24]

In the light of Hazlitt's account, Johnson can on occasion be seen to hold himself in the center of this pendulum swing between admiration and derogation, as when (in a discussion of strife in marriage in *The Rambler*, a periodical full of depictions of women) he said he 'endeavoured to divest my heart of all partiality, and place myself as a kind of neutral being between the sexes' (*Yale* II.98). At other times, he seems to be at one end or other of the oscillating extreme. He was capable of showing exaggerated regard for women in relation to men ('Men know that women are an overmatch for them.... If they did not think so, they never could be afraid of women knowing as much as themselves,' *Life* V.226), yet he could also deny women's ability to act as intellectual equals—whether in the notorious

| Author | Designation of source in Dictionary [and work from which cited] | Word (and sense) for which quoted | Quotation [as in Johnson's Dictionary; differences of wording from the quotation's source, if identified, are noted, but not of punctuation] | In 1st /4th edition of Dictionary |
|---|---|---|---|---|
| Margaret Cavendish | Dutchess of Newcastle [work not cited or identified] | *just* (adj; sense 10 in 1st edition; sense 12 in 4th edition) | There seldom appeared a *just* army in the civil wars. | 1st and 4th |
| Jane Barker (c.1652–1732) | Mrs Barker [from *Love intrigues* (London, 1713)] | *life* (sense 5) | I'll teach my family to lead good *lives.* [from a verse lament uttered by the heroine of the novel, in which she considers the proper behaviour of a 'Vertuous Wife': 'To be a Matron, to my Houshold Good . . . Then teach my Family to lead good Lives,/ and be a Pattern unto other Wives'] | 1st and 4th |
| Elizabeth Carter (1717–1806) | Mrs Carter [from 'On Hearing Miss Lynch Sing', dated 1739 in Montagu Pennington, ed., *Memoirs of the life of Mrs. Elizabeth Carter: with a new edition of her poems*, 2 vol.s (London, 1808)] | *proportion* (sense 4) | Harmony, with ev'ry grace, Plays in the fair *proportions* of her face. | 1st and 4th |
| Hester Mulso (later Hester Chapone) (1727–1801) | Mrs Mulso [from 'To Stella', printed in *Miscellanies in Prose and Verse, by Mrs. Chapone* (London, 1755, 2nd ed.)] | *quatrain* [NB the quotation does not illustrate usage of the word but is itself a quatrain] | Say, Stella, what is love, whose fatal pow'r Robs virtue of content, and youth of joy? What nymph or goddess in a luckless hour Disclos'd to light the mischief-making boy. [The original reads: 'Say, Stella, what is Love, whose tyrant pow'r/Robs Virtue of content and Youth of Joy?/What nymph or goddess, in a fatal hour,/Gave to the world this mischief-making boy?'] | 1st and 4th |

| Author | Work | Headword | Quotation | Edition |
|---|---|---|---|---|
| Jane Collier (1714–1755) | Art of Tormenting [An Essay on the Art of Ingeniously Tormenting (London, 1753)] | *marital* | It has been determined by some unpolite professors of the law, that a husband may exercise his *marital* authority so far, as to give his wife moderate correction. [The original reads: 'It has been determined in our public courts of justice, by some unpolite professors of the law, that a husband may exercise his marital authority so far, as to give his wife moderate correction.' The text continues, 'How happy it is for English wives, that the force of custom is so much stronger than our laws! How fortunate for them, that the men, either thro' affection or indolence, have given up their legal rights; and have, by custom, placed all the power in the wife!'] | 1st and 4th |
| | | *prink* (verb) | Hold a good wager she was every day longer *prinking* in the glass than you was. | 1st and 4th (sole quotation in entry) |
| | | *termagancy* [misattributed to 'Barker'] | By a violent *termagancy* of temper, she may never suffer him to have a moment's peace. | 1st and 4th |
| | | *pique* (verb, sense 1) | The lady was *piqued* by her indifference, and began to mention going away. | 1st and 4th |
| Charlotte Lennox (c.1730–1804) | Female Quixote (variously abbreviated) [The Female Quixote: or, the adventures of Arabella (London, 1752), 2 vols.] | *simplicity* | The native elegance and *simplicity* of her manners, were accompanied with real benevolence of heart. | 1st and 4th |

(continued)

| Author | Designation of source in Dictionary [and work from which cited] | Word (and sense) for which quoted | Quotation [as in Johnson's Dictionary; differences of wording from the quotation's source, if identified, are noted, but not of punctuation] | In 1st /4th edition of Dictionary |
|---|---|---|---|---|
| | | *singular* (sense 3) | Doubtless, if you are innocent, your case is extremely hard, yet it is not *singular*. | 1st and 4th |
| | | *solemnity* (sense 7) | This speech ended with a *solemnity* of accent. | 1st and 4th |
| | | *suppose* (sense 4 in 1st edition; sense 6 in 4th edition) | One falshood always *supposes* another, and renders all you can say suspected. | 1st and 4th |
| | | *talent* (sense 2) | Persons who possess the true *talent* of raillery are like comets; they are seldom seen, and all at once admired and feared. [The original text reads '…are at once admired'] | 1st and 4th |
| | | *view* (noun, sense 4) | She was not much struck with those objects that now presented themselves to her *view*. [The original text reads 'As her Romances had long familiariz'd her Thoughts to Objects of Grandeur and Magnificence, she was not so much struck as might have been expected, with those that now presented themselves to her View'] | In 1st but not 4th (quotation from Locke substituted) |
| | | *visionary* | The lovely *visionary* gave him perpetual uneasiness. | 1st and 4th |
| | | *volubility* | She ran over the catalogue of diversions with such a *volubility* of tongue, as drew a gentle reprimand from her father. | 1st and 4th |
| | | *wildly* (sense 2) | His fever being come to a height, he grew delirious, and talked very *wildly*. | 1st and 4th |
| | *Shakespear Illustrated* (variously abbreviated) [*Shakespear Illustrated* (London, 1753), 3 vols.] | *sally* (noun) | The episodical part, made up of the extravagant *sallies* of the prince of Wales and Falstaff's humour, is of his own invention. | 1st and 4th |
| | | *starry* | Tears had dimm'd the luster of her *starry* eyes. | 1st and 4th |

| | | |
|---|---|---|
| *unravel* | Thus supernaturally is the plot brought to perfection; nor is the *unraveling* of it less happily imagined. | 1st and 4th |
| *uncle* [sole quotation in entry] | Hamlet punishes his *uncle* rather for his own death, than the murther of his father. [The original reads 'He stabs the King immediately upon the Information of his Treachery to Himself! thus his Revenge becomes interested, and he seems to punish his Uncle rather for his own Death, than the Murder of the King, his Father.'] | 1st and 4th |
| *unnecessary* | The reader can easily discover how the plot will be unravelled at last, but the *unnecessary* intricacies in unravelling it, still remain to be accounted for. | 1st only.[1] |
| *virtue* (sense 1) | The character of prince Henry is improved by Shakespear; and through the veil of his vices and irregularities, we see a dawn of greatness and *virtue*. [The original reads 'The Character of Prince *Henry*, tho' drawn after the Historians, is considerably improved by *Shakespear*; and through the Veil of his Vices and Irregularities, we see a Dawn of Greatness and Virtue, that promises the future Splendor of his Life and Reign.'] | 1st and 4th |
| *wherever* | *Wherever* Shakespeare has invented, he is greatly below the novelist; since the incidents he has added are neither necessary nor probable. | 1st and 4th |
| *whetstone* | A *whetstone* is not an instrument to carve with; but it sharpens those that do. | 1st and 4th |

[1] Of the seven 1st edition quotations for this word—from Hooker, Shakespeare, Bacon, Dryden (twice), Addison, and Lennox—Lennox's alone is dropped from the 4th edition.

*(continued)*

| Author | Designation of source in *Dictionary* [and work from which cited] | Word (and sense) for which quoted | Quotation [as in Johnson's *Dictionary*; differences of wording from the quotation's source, if identified, are noted, but not of punctuation] | In 1st /4th edition of *Dictionary* |
|---|---|---|---|---|
| | | *wreath* (noun, sense 2) | To prince Henry the laurels of his rival are transferred, with the additional *wreath* of having conquered that rival. [The original reads 'for the Lawrels of his Rival are all transferred to him, with the additional Wreath of having conquered that Rival'.] | 1st only.[2] |
| | | *wonderful* | All this is very *wonderful*, Shakespeare multiplies miracle upon miracle to bring about the same event in the play, which chance with more propriety performs in the novel. | 1st only.[3] |

[2] Of the five 1st edition quotations for this word—from Shakespeare, Roscommon, Dryden, Prior, and Lennox—Lennox's alone is dropped from the 4th edition.

[3] Of the three 1st edition quotations for this word—from the Bible, Milton, and Lennox—Lennox's alone is dropped from the 4th edition.

remark on women's preaching ('like a dog's walking on his hinder legs' [*Life* I.463]) or in admitting them as sources for his *Dictionary.*

All this makes one turn with some interest to the female-authored quotations Johnson actually did print (see the accompanying Table). The first question, evidently, is why he should so strikingly have favored Lennox. Johnson himself explained that that he quoted from living authors only 'when some performance of uncommon excellence excited my veneration, when my memory supplied me, from late books, with an example that was wanting, or when my heart, in the tenderness of friendship, solicited admission for a favourite name' (*Yale* XVIII.95).[25] Friendship must have counted for something where Lennox, Carter, and Mulso were concerned—and so perhaps did Lennox's praise of Johnson in the *Female Quixote* as 'the greatest genius in the present age,' in a chapter once suggested to have been written by Johnson himself.[26] Looking at the quotations themselves, however, one sees that eight of those from *Shakespear Illustrated* are distinctive for their content, and may therefore have additionally qualified as a 'performance of uncommon excellence.' Under *sally, virtue*, and *wreath*, Johnson picks three quotations, only two pages apart, from Lennox's discussion of Shakespeare's originality and ingenuity in presenting the character of Prince Henry; under *unravel* and *unnecessary* we learn about Shakespeare's handling of plot; under *wherever* and *wonderful*, Shakespeare's art is compared with that of the novelist; while under *uncle*—for which Lennox provides the only quotation—Johnson chooses a striking remark on Hamlet's motivation in killing Claudius. All this sheds a new light on his views of *Shakespear Illustrated*, a work for which (as for the *Female Quixote*) he wrote the Dedication.[27]

'Uncommon excellence' may also explain the origin of the Mulso quotation. An anonymous reviewer tells us that:

> Dr Johnson, on reading this ode ['To Stella', which Johnson imperfectly quotes] several years ago in MS. declared that 'he never before had any opinion of female poetry'; and, though a copy was refused him, having retained great part of it by memory, soon after quoted the fourth stanza in his Dictionary, to exemplify the meaning of the word *Quatrain*, with the name of *Mrs. Mulso* annexed to it, a name then unknown to the literary world.[28]

This anecdote is reinforced by Samuel Richardson's report to Elizabeth Carter, on 2 October 1753, that Johnson had '*rambled* thither [to Richardson's house in Fulham] principally on her [Mulso's] account. He is in love with her. And extremely fond of her verses to Stella. Most magnificently does he express himself of them.'[29] Johnson similarly admired Carter (quoted s.v. *proportion*): while exchanging Greek epigrams with her in 1738 he told Edward Cave, 'She ought to be celebrated in as many different Languages as Lewis le Grand' (*Letters* 1.17).

Biographical details aside, none of Johnson's quotations from female authors (other than those from Lennox already discussed) appears particularly remarkable either for use of language or for sentiments expressed. This is true even of the five or six that touch on issues of gender: it is difficult to see anything distinctive, for the period, about the notion that women should be angels of the household (s.v. *life*) or direct fury against their husbands (s.v. *termagancy*), that a female face might be well proportioned (s.v. *proportion*), that husbands may in some ironically nuanced way correct their wives (*marital*), that a woman may *prink* in front of the glass, or (in the only quotation to mention language, under *volubility*) be loquacious enough to draw 'a gentle reprimand' from a father. More significant may be the fact that none of the entries concerned begins with a letter occurring in the early part of the alphabet: it is only from *j* onwards, and predominantly from *p*, that Johnson cites female authors. Given the dates of publication of the Lennox and Collier works concerned, it is tempting to think that Johnson had these texts to hand when he was working on the relevant parts of the *Dictionary*.

One can speculate why Johnson should have changed his citation policy (however minimally) halfway through the alphabet, what it was about *The Female Quixote* and *Shakespear Illustrated* that especially took his fancy—perhaps that both, in their different ways, constitute works of literary criticism?—or indeed why Collier and Lennox should have been cited by the titles of their works rather than their names (though both were published without their authors' names on the title pages).

We can also ask whether the *Dictionary* would have been significantly different if Johnson had quoted from female sources more extensively. Both he and Chesterfield believed that women's use of language was demonstrably different from that of men, and it is not difficult to find the same view expressed by others too, for example, Robert Gould: 'Succeeding Times will see the Difference plain,/And wonder at a Style so loose and vain.'[30] Taking 'Style' to include content, we can conjecture that the views communicated by the quotations—the *Dictionary*'s cultural hinterland— might have been more varied and less misogynistic if Johnson had quoted texts written by women. For instance, under *stickler*, to mean 'An obstinate contender about any thing,' Johnson quotes Addison: 'The inferior tribe of common women have, in most reigns, been the professed *sticklers* for such as have acted against the true interest of the nation.' Instead, Johnson could have quoted from the *Essay in Defence of the Female Sex*, written by a woman, probably Judith Drake, in 1696: 'Our Company [i.e. women] is generally by our Adversaries represented as unprofitable and irksome to Men of Sense, and by some of the more vehement Sticklers against us, as Criminal.'[31] As its title implies, this essay is full of sentiments arguing women's equality with men, and Johnson could have drawn widely on such remarks in many other female-authored texts.

At first glance, it might seem that quoting female-authored texts would have affected Johnson's record of vocabulary too. Drake provides several examples of words or senses not included in the *Dictionary*: for instance, *stinkpot* to mean 'naval bomb,' not treated by Johnson, and a figurative sense of 'artillery' where Johnson has only literal illustrations ('we have a sort of ungenerous Adversaries [i.e. men], that deal more in Scandal than Argument, and when they can't hurt us with their Weapons, endeavour to annoy us with Stink-Pots. Let us see therefore, Madam, whether we can't beat them from their own Ammunition, and turn their own Artillery upon them').[32] Johnson's single quotation for *stinkpot* is from Gabriel Harvey (1665), referring to a disinfectant with an unpleasant smell ('The air may be purified by fires of pitch-barrels, especially in close places, by burning of *stinkpots*')—but, given her martial imagery, Drake's meaning is clearly that of *OED* sense 2, dated to 1669: 'A hand-missile charged with combustibles emitting a suffocating smoke, used in boarding a ship for effecting a diversion while the assailants gain the deck.' As it happens, Drake's figurative use of *stinkpot* antedates by forty-two years the first instance recorded in *OED* (from Warburton), and it is easy to find many more such examples of words and senses, missed both by Johnson and the *OED*, in other texts written by women (Jane Barker is a good source).[33]

But a moment's reflection, together with further reading in both dictionaries and primary texts, will confirm what is self-evident in the cases of *stinkpot* and *artillery*: one cannot assume that words and senses found in female authors, but unrecorded by Johnson, constitute a specific female vocabulary that women used and men didn't. Thus *stinkpot* is in Swift, and *artillery* is used metaphorically by Cowley (characterizing Katherine Philips's reworking of male poetic traditions, as it happens).[34] One cannot therefore say that by limiting himself to male sources, Johnson omitted a distinctive category of language that he might otherwise have included: it is just as easy to find words and senses, missing from both Johnson and the *OED*, in male-authored texts too. Drake herself discusses this point, and was almost certainly correct to respond as she did, to detractors such as Gould, that 'they will no more be able to discern a Man's Style from a Woman's, than they can tell whether this was written with a Goose-Quill or a Gander's.'[35]

So in confining himself to male quotation sources Johnson did not necessarily, by that act alone, reduce the lexical scope of his *Dictionary*. He did, however, limit its cultural perspective. He misrepresented the ratio, male to female, of linguistic and cultural endeavor from 1660 onwards, when the number of women writing and publishing began to rise steeply, and in doing so he may be thought to be guilty of the 'timidity' of which Hazlitt accuses him ('no advance is made by his writings in any sentiment, or mode of reasoning' [*Hazlitt* VI.102]).

Over the nineteenth century the productivity, visibility, and respectability of women writers continued to increase (if not their eligibility to be considered great writers, on a par with men), and the next great English dictionary, the *OED*, admitted a number of them into its ranks, including some from the seventeenth and early eighteenth centuries: notably Behn, Manley, and Centlivre, each cited around two hundred times (the *OED* favored female dramatists and prose writers over poets, despite Chesterfield's testimony on the abundance of female poetic diction). But the imbalance between male and female sources in the *OED*, though less absolute than in Johnson, remains stark. Many female authors, though well-known in their day, are quoted in tiny numbers or not at all, whereas Pope, Johnson, Dickens, Tennyson, and other major male authors of the past are each cited in thousands of entries.[36]

Owing to the *OED*'s infinitely more comprehensive and authoritative treatment of the history of the language—and its lack of a specified single author, working over an identifiable period in time—this later dictionary gives the misleading impression that its quotation sources fairly represent literary and linguistic culture as far as gender is concerned. By contrast, any student of the eighteenth century will or should be aware that Johnson's *Dictionary*, magnificent as it is, constitutes a very partial record. This is not least because we know, from critics such as Hazlitt, that it is the work of a complex individual driven by many contrary influences.

## NOTES

1. Lawrence Lipking, *Samuel Johnson: The Life of an Author* (Cambridge, MA: Harvard University Press, 1998), 60, citing Isobel Grundy, 'Samuel Johnson as Patron of Women,' *Age of Johnson* 1 (1987), 59–77, and James Basker, 'Myth upon Myth: Johnson, Gender, and the Misogyny Question,' *Age of Johnson* 8 (1997), 175–87. I am grateful to the Leverhulme Trust for funding the research on the *OED* of which this essay is a by-product, to Robert De-Maria for advice on various matters, including invaluable help in identifying quotations in Johnson's *Dictionary* relating to women, and to Elizabeth Scott-Baumann for information on Cowley and Katherine Philips.
2. *The World* 100 (28 November 1754), 603.The letter is reprinted in James T. Boulton, ed., *Samuel Johnson: The Critical Heritage* (London: Routledge, 1971), 95–8.
3. *The World* 101 (5 December 1754), 606. Reprinted in Boulton, *Johnson: The Critical Heritage*, 98–102.

4. Unless otherwise noted, all definitions and quotations discussed are in both the first and fourth editions of Johnson's *Dictionary*.

5. David Roberts, ed., *Lord Chesterfield's Letters* (Oxford: Oxford University Press, 1992), 27 September o.s. 1749, 161–5.

6. James A. H. Murray, *The Evolution of Lexicography* (Oxford: Clarendon Press, 1900), 38–9. For the use of quotations in earlier dictionaries, see Paul Korshin, 'Johnson and the Renaissance Dictionary,' *Journal of the History of Ideas* 35 (1974), 300–12.

7. Rüdiger Schreyer, 'Illustrations of Authority: Quotations in Samuel Johnson's *Dictionary of the English Language*,' *Lexicographica* 16 (2010), 67.

8. Robert DeMaria, Jr., 'Johnson's Dictionary,' in Greg Clingham, ed., *The Cambridge Companion to Samuel Johnson* (Cambridge: Cambridge University Press, 1997), 90; Geoffrey Barnbrook, 'Johnson the Prescriptivist?,' in Jack Lynch and Anne McDermott, eds., *Anniversary Essays on Johnson's Dictionary* (Cambridge: Cambridge University Press, 2005), 96.

9. They include Bacon, Hooker, Dryden, L'Estrange, Locke, Addison, Swift, Spenser, Shakespeare, and Milton, all among Johnson's most quoted authors. See Joseph Spence, *Observations, Anecdotes, and Characters of Books and Men*, ed. James Marshall Osborn, 2 vols. (Oxford: Clarendon Press, 1996), I.389–90.

10. See e.g. Felicity Nussbaum, *The Brink of All We Hate: English Satires on Women, 1660–1750* (Lexington: University Press of Kentucky, 1984), Robert Shoemaker, *Gender in English Society, 1650–1850* (London: Longman, 1998), and Jennifer Coates, *Women, Men and Language* (Harlow: Longman, 2004), Chapter 1; also Giovanni Iammartino, 'Words by Women, Words on Women in Samuel Johnson's *Dictionary of the English Language*,' in *Adventuring in Dictionaries: New Studies in the History of Lexicography*, ed. John Considine (Newcastle upon Tyne: Cambridge Scholars Publishing, 2010), 94–125.

11. Anne McDermott ('Johnson's "Dictionary" and the Canon: Authors and Authority,' *The Yearbook of English Studies* 28 [1998], 62 n.64) states that Johnson includes quotations from Catherine Cockburn too; I have been unable to identify these in electronic searches of her edition but am most grateful to Catherine Dille for drawing my attention to three further quotations.

12. *The World* 100, 602–3. See also Boulton, *Johnson: The Critical Heritage*, 97.

13. See further Charlotte Brewer, 'The Use of Literary Quotations in the *OED*,' *Review of English Studies* 61 (2010), 93–125.

14. See Charlotte Brewer, '"Happy Copiousness"? *OED*'s Recording of Female Authors of the Eighteenth Century,' *Review of English Studies* (forthcoming).

15. Figures derived from Schreyer, 'Illustrations,' 67.

16. 'Preface,' iii; the first edition anthologizes eighteen well-known female poets, including Elizabeth Carter (cited by Johnson in his *Dictionary*).

17. Dodsley anthologized a total of 130 writers of whom 10 were women; figures drawn from Robert Dodsley, *A Collection of Poems. By Several Hands*, ed. Michael J. Suarez (London: Routledge/Thoemmes Press, 1997), 1.

18. Elizabeth Elstob, *The Rudiments of Grammar for the English-Saxon Tongue* (London: W. Bowyer, 1715).

19. As documented by Nussbaum, *Brink of All We Hate*, 44–50.

20. See Grundy, 'Johnson as Patron of Women,' 62ff; Duncan Isles, 'The Lennox Collection,' *Harvard Library Bulletin* 18 (1970), 317–44; 19 (1971) 36–60, 165–86, 416–35; and *Hawkins*, 172 (for the account of the party Johnson threw for Lennox on publication of her first novel).

21. Grundy, 'Johnson as Patron of Women,' 66; Isaac Watts, 'To Mrs Elizabeth Singer, on her divine poems,' in Elizabeth Singer Rowe, *The Miscellaneous Works...of Mrs Elizabeth Rowe,* 2 vols. (London: R. Hett and R. Dodsley, 1739), I.cxviii.

22. Schreyer's figures indicate that Watts is quoted just under one thousand times in the *Dictionary*.

23. Johnson similarly distinguished 'Don Quixote, Robinson Crusoe, and the Pilgrim's Progress' (*Shaw-Piozzi*, 152), as well as Burton's *Anatomy* and Fielding's *Amelia*; see Robert DeMaria, *Samuel Johnson and the Life of Reading* (Baltimore and London: Johns Hopkins University Press, 1997), 181–2.

24. Quoted from A. Hammond, ed., *A New Miscellany of Original Poems* (London, T. Jauncy, 1720), 274; see *Pope* VI. 423. For their rightful attribution to Thomas Burnet, see Harold Williams's untitled review of this volume, *Review of English Studies* n.s. 7 (1956), 83–6; for Pope's relationship with Wortley Montagu, see Isobel Grundy, *Lady Mary Wortley Montagu* (Oxford: Oxford University Press, 1999).

25. Allen Walker Read, 'The Contemporary Quotations in Johnson's Dictionary,' *English Literary History* 2 (1935), 246–51, identifies the Mulso quotation (and its discussion in *The Gentleman's Magazine*), five of the Lennox ones, and provides information on a number of others (all male).

26. See Charlotte Lennox, *The Female Quixote*, ed. Margaret Anne Doody (Oxford: Oxford World's Classics, 1989), 414–15, 419–22.

27. Allen T. Hazen, ed., *Samuel Johnson's Prefaces & Dedications* (New Haven and London: Yale University Press, Oxford University Press, 1937), 104–10, 94–8.

28. 'List of Books,—with Remarks,' *Gentleman's Magazine* 45 (1775), 88; author unidentified in James M. Kuist's *The Nichols File of the Gentleman's Magazine: Attributions of Authorship and other Documentation in Editorial Papers at the Folger Library* (Madison: University of Wisconsin Press, 1982).

29. Quoted in James L. Clifford, *Dictionary Johnson* (London: Heinemann, 1980), 121.

30. Robert Gould, *A Satyrical Epistle to the Female Author of a Poem, call'd Silvia's Revenge* (London: R. Bentley, 1691), 22.

31. *An Essay in Defence of the Female Sex* (London: A. Roper, E. Wilkinson, and R. Clavel, 1696), 8; see Hannah Smith, 'English "Feminist" Writings and Judith Drake's "An Essay in Defence of the Female Sex" (1696),' *The Historical Journal* 44 (2001), 727–47.

32. *Essay in Defence*, 58–9.

33. Brewer, ' "Happy Copiousness?" '

34. 'To the most excellently accomplish'd, Mrs K. P. upon her Poems,' in Katherine Philips, *Poems* (London: R. Marriott, 1664), sig. A3v. *OED* records the figurative use of *artillery* (in male-authored texts) from 1592 onwards.

35. *Essay in Defence* (London, 1697 [3rd edn]). These remarks occur in a letter (unpaginated) added to the third edition at the front of the volume entitled 'The Lady's Answer'; the text is reproduced in subsequent editions.
36. See Brewer, 'Happy Copiousness?' and, for some comparative figures, 'The *OED*'s Treatment of Female-Authored Sources of the Eighteenth Century,' in *Current Issues in Late Modern English*, eds. Ingrid Tieken Boone van Ostade and Wim van der Wurff (Bern: Peter Lang, 2009), 209–38.

# 12

# The Battle of the Word-Books: Competition, the 'Common Reader,' and Johnson's *Dictionary*

*Lynda Mugglestone*

'No expectation is more fallacious than that which authors form of the reception which their labours will find among mankind,' stated Johnson in 1756.[1] The reception of the *Dictionary* would, in this, prove no exception. Too mundane for honors and too insignificant to warrant attack, dictionary-making, as envisaged by Johnson in 1747, was a task that 'would awaken no passion, engage me in no contention, nor throw in my way any temptation to disturb the quiet of others by censure, or my own by flattery' (*Yale* XVIII.27). Merely the 'slave of science' in Johnson's 1755 'Preface' (*Yale* XVIII.73), the lexicographer was, as in the often-quoted definition that appears within the *Dictionary* itself, seen as a 'harmless drudge, that busies himself in tracing the original, and detailing the signification of words.'

The publication of Johnson's *Dictionary* in April 1755 challenged a number of these conceptions. Flattery could, for instance, seem inseparable from the abundant praise the dictionary received. David Garrick's poem 'On Johnson's *Dictionary*' displaced drudgery by the transcendent images of triumph and national conquest. Johnson, Garrick contended, had not merely written a dictionary but 'like a hero of yore/Has beat forty *French* and will beat forty more.'[2] Adam Smith, reviewing the *Dictionary* in the *Edinburgh Review*, stressed 'the merit of its author' which, he added, 'appears very extraordinary,' while, in the *Gentleman's Magazine*, it was the 'utmost purity and relevance' of Johnson's 'Preface' that attracted commendation.[3] Johnson's private correspondents offered more opportunity for 'quiet' to be disturbed. The *Dictionary*, wrote Thomas Birch, was a 'Work long wanted, and now executed with an Industry, accuracy, and Judgement equal to the Importance of the Subject' (*Letters* I.102n).

Revealing the breadth that the critical pendulum in this respect might span, Johnson's *Dictionary* was, however, also to find itself located in a variety of oppositional discourses in which 'contention' was conspicuous while even 'passion' could, at times, be all too plain. Critical commendation here stood at odds with the 'considerable discomfort' experienced, as Gwin Kolb and James Sledd long ago noted, by competing lexicographers.[4] Yet, as this chapter will explore, discomfort can seem a marked understatement for the images of challenge and combat that come to the fore. Confirming the fallibility of assumptions that reduce the dictionary-maker to the passive and harmless drudge, Johnson's work would be criticized in competing lexicographic works as too small or too big, too expensive, too difficult, too detailed, as well as out of step with the 'common reader,' and what the common reader should desire in a work of this kind.

Ink—a highly 'malignant Liquor' and the 'great missive Weapon, in all Battels of the *Learned*' (as Swift observed in his own *Battel of the Books* in 1704)[5]—repeatedly proved its utility in the kinds of conflict that emerge. Title pages, prefaces, dedications, as well as the contents of competing lexicographic works could all be recruited into a discourse of targeted attack. Offering apt illustration of the kind of 'intestine hostilities' that, as Johnson noted in *Rambler* 145 (*Yale* V.10), so often marked 'manufacturers of literature' and 'drudges of the pen,' mid-eighteenth century lexicography can appear a markedly adversarial space, characterized by verbal sniping as well as outright attack, by resistance as well as defense.

Popular accounts of eighteenth-century lexicography often suggest a seamless synecdoche with Johnson's own work, with perhaps a cursory mention of Nathan Bailey's popular *Universal Etymological English Dictionary* (first published in 1721, and in print in various editions throughout the century). The reality of publishing history here offers a sharp corrective. Published either in entirety (as Johnson's *Dictionary* was in April 1755) or by means of serial publication (like the weekly numbers in which Johnson's second edition appeared from June 1755), contemporary lexicography confirmed the existence of what Johnson described—here in a letter to Samuel Richardson—as 'an age of dictionaries' (*Letters* I.79). 'The importance of *Dictionaries* being so great, the public, instead of wondering at their variety, should rather wonder that their variety is not greater,' as Daniel Fenning argued in the introduction to his *Royal English Dictionary* in 1761.[6] Over eighty monolingual English dictionaries—new works such as those by Fenning or Johnson, as well as new editions of older texts, such as the seventh edition of John Kersey's *New English Dictionary* (1759)—appeared between 1755 and 1775. Each endeavored to secure a share in a highly competitive marketplace, claiming particular qualities by which prospective users might be tempted into purchase.

As Fenning illustrates, contemporary lexicographers could assume a markedly comparative diction by which, as in Johnson's definition of *compare* ('To make one thing the measure of another; to estimate the relative goodness or badness…of any one thing, by observing how it differs from others'), newly published texts are placed in oppositional relationships to those already extant. If Fenning emphasizes variety within the dictionary as genre, he also, for example, deftly presents his own work as one of valuable synthesis, able 'to unite these scattered rays, as it were, into one focus' (and at an affordable price of six shillings too).[7] Any reader in possession of this 'treasury,' he pointedly observed, will surely 'congratulate himself in having met with a dictionary on a more extensive plan than any that have already been published.'[8]

In a similar way, John Wesley, constructing himself on the title page of his *Complete English Dictionary* (1764) as a 'Lover of *Good English* and *Common Sense*,' simply assures prospective readers that 'he thinks this the best *English* DICTIONARY in the World'—a statement which includes, and intentionally transcends, that published by Johnson five years earlier. As Wesley's 'Preface' makes clear, he has read Johnson, incorporating what he deemed to be necessary and omitting the rest.[9] Anne Fisher, a rare female lexicographer, deploys other comparative tactics in her *Accurate New Spelling Dictionary* (1773). Her dictionary, she stresses, contains a 'much larger COLLECTION of Modern WORDS than any Book of the Kind and Price extant' as well as 'more modern, primitive, or original conversation words, than any other larger Dictionary.'[10] Here it is lexical currency (and obsolescence) that serve as the chosen line of attack—not least, as Chapter 11 has discussed, given Johnson's well-established engagement with earlier rather than contemporaneous language use. The orthographical conservatism of other dictionaries—again including Johnson—which fail to separate U and V (and I and J) as alphabetic divisions, offered further ammunition. As Fisher contended, '*I* and *J,* and also the *U* and *V* are four distinct and different letters…yet they have been ever blended and confounded in Dictionaries, to the great entanglement of youth.'[11] Here too her practice would be deliberately 'more modern.'

As such territorial strategies suggest, the dictionary as commodity plays a significantly different role from, say, that of the novel as commodity. Serious novel readers, for example, might greet with enthusiasm newly published works—such as Tobias Smollett's *The Adventures of Ferdinand Count Fathom* (1753), or *The Invisible Spy* (1755) by Eliza Haywood—reading, and indeed, should finances permit, buying one or both, along with other contemporary and earlier works. In contrast, the decision to invest in a new dictionary, as contemporary lexicographers were well aware, tended to mean the purchase of a single work, selected in preference– to—and, critically, at the expense of—other coexisting texts. In terms of the 'battle of the word-books,' this alone renders both challenge and competition much sharper. As John Maxwell, one of a range of aggrieved mid-eighteenth-century lexicographers, complained in October 1755, '*Johnson's* work coming out first will hinder the sale' of other texts. More particularly, he realized, it would impact on his projected *Treasure of the English Tongue*, which, though advertised, was yet to appear.[12] 'People will not consider, which is the best Plan, or best executed, but will be ready to take up with the first,' Maxwell warned. Yet, as he pointed out in a counterattack that aimed to reverse this process, 'Under the particle AS, [Johnson] has but thirty heads...whereas I have above ninety.'[13]

Marketing for Joseph Nicol Scott's edition of Bailey's *New Universal Etymological Dictionary* (1755) provides a further apposite example. Advertisements for both Scott and Johnson enacted a head-to-head confrontation on facing pages of *Jackson's Oxford Journal* in June 1755.[14] The former proclaimed its use of visual as well as verbal illustration ('Copper Plates...explain those Figures which cannot be so well understood from verbal Description only'). Against Johnson's single-handed act of composition, it foregrounded too the image of superior expertise derived from specialist contributors in domains such as mathematics and botany. Advertising for Johnson's *Dictionary* meanwhile stressed 'the acknowledged Utility of this Work' as well as 'the Desire that many have expressed to be possessed of it.' The contest for the reader's allegiance was plain, as was the conflict in terms of contents, price, and value. Johnson's *Dictionary* was to be 'elegantly printed' in 165 parts, spanning 580 sheets, with a total cost of over £4. 'The Whole not to exceed Two Guineas,' prospective purchasers of Scott's edition of Bailey were instead assured. Long the most popular as well as the largest dictionary, Bailey's *Dictionary* would not cede territory without a fight. As Philip Gove has confirmed, Scott's edition was deliberately instituted as a 'rival dictionary...prepared for the purpose of holding the field against Johnson.'[15]

As such strategies indicate, advertising (in a variety of guises) was seized as a potentially effective weapon, whether in the attempt to secure territorial advantage or to challenge the claims of others. Maxwell's *Plan* for his dictionary had, as he admitted, been deployed in precisely this way, being spurred, in particular, by the appearance of Johnson's *Plan of a Dictionary* in 1747: 'When I found that [Johnson] began to advertise, I thought it was proper for me to advertise also, that I was upon such a work, and that with this view, viz. to hinder as many as I could thereby influence, from buying [Johnson's] work, when it should come out, in expectation that mine might prove a much better one.'[16] Such strategies of retaliation and response are by no means rare. The consortium of publishers who supported Johnson's own work, for instance, deftly kept his dictionary in the public eye long before its formal appearance, either by means of straightforward advertisement or by what we might today call 'advertorials.' The targeted article headed 'The Signification of Words now Varied,' included in the *Gentleman's Magazine* in 1749 and signed 'W. S.,'[17] can, in this light, be seen as a form of pre-emptive strike, here against Benjamin Martin's *Lingua Britannica Reformata* which appeared in the same year. Lest prospective purchasers be tempted by Martin's claims ('what a most defective and imperfect State our Dictionaries have hitherto been...how necessary a Work of this kind becomes to remove the *Opprobrium* under which this Branch of English Philology has so long laboured'),[18] the article tactically—if erroneously—assured readers that Johnson's *Dictionary* was already in a state of 'great forwardness.' 'It is hoped, that our language will be more fixed, and better established, when the publick is favoured with a new dictionary, undertaken with that view,' it stressed.[19] It was Johnson's 'new dictionary,' not that of Martin, which readers should desire. Delayed gratification would, in this context, bring its own rewards.

Chesterfield's 'puffs' in the *World* in late 1754 enact similar patterns of combat and intended dominance. Whereas Johnson is assigned a role as would-be dictator, existing dictionaries are depicted in terms that foreground both weakness and inadequacy. Denied even the status of dictionaries in Chesterfield's critical gaze, they are 'at present...more properly what our neighbours the Dutch and the Germans call theirs, WORD-BOOKS, than dictionaries in the superior sense of that title.' Johnson's claims to rule the field, in both commercial and scholarly terms, are forcefully advanced:

> I think the public in general, and the republic of letters in particular, greatly obliged to Mr. Johnson, for having undertaken and executed so great and desireable a work. Perfection is not to be expected from man; but if we are to judge by the various works of Mr. Johnson, already published, we have good reason to believe that he will bring this as near to perfection as any one man could do....I therefore recommend the previous perusal of it to all those who intend to buy the dictionary, and who, I suppose, are all those who can afford it.[20]

As Johnson observed two years later in his preface to Rolt's *Dictionary of Trade and Commerce*, 'There was never from the earliest ages a time in which trade so much engaged the attention of mankind, or commercial gain was fought with such general emulation.'[21] Though Chesterfield's role as putative patron was rejected by Johnson (a decision regretted by Robert Dodsley who, 'with the true feelings of trade,' pointed out that 'he had a property in the Dictionary, to which his Lordship's patronage might have been of consequence,' *Life* I.264), the diction of competition and conquest that Chesterfield had deployed remained significant. Maxwell, for example, swiftly challenged Chesterfield's convictions about the inferior status of other lexicographical works. His 1755 *Letter from a Friend in England* (a work which amply supports Johnson's sense that 'when we think our excellencies overlooked by the world, or desire to recall the attention of the publick to some particular performance, we sit down with great composure and write a letter to ourselves,' *Yale* V.247), deliberately changes the direction of both attack and intended defeat. It is now Maxwell's projected dictionary that will be 'so superior' upon completion as to leave no pretence for any rivalship or competition' with 'Mr *Johnson.*'[22] Other elements of Chesterfield's evaluative hierarchies are also reversed. While readers can, Maxwell points out, 'take up with Johnson's work, if they choose it, and...they care not to wait any longer,' a 'much better' work lies in prospect, one in which the 'material Faults' he has observed (e.g. in Johnson's etymologies and the ordering of senses) will be unequivocally redressed.

Johnson is by no means entirely innocent within oppositional discourses of this kind. Maxwell clearly recognized the way in which Johnson's *Plan* operated as an advertisement. Johnson's targeted criticism of the 'very miscellaneous idea' that had hitherto informed English dictionaries was, for example, carefully set against his own 'idea of an English dictionary' (*Yale* XVIII.30)—one in which the 'miscarriage' of previous attempts to engage with meaning would be remedied (*Yale* XVIII.46) alongside other weaknesses. 'The terminations of the English are few, but those few have hitherto remained unregarded by the writers of our dictionaries,' as Johnson also contended (*Yale* XVIII.43). Syntax ('which I do not know that any regard has been yet shewn in English dictionaries' (*Yale* XVIII.44)) formed another target. As Johnson later confessed, his strategy had been one of intended usurpation in the hope that 'my book might be in place of all other dictionaries whether appellative or technical' (*Yale* XVIII.100). Maxwell had indeed been right to be on his guard (even if, in the end, he simply admitted defeat, abandoning his own work before publication took place).

Lexicography—fought in a public arena in which words can be weapons as well as the fundamental components of dictionary entries—can therefore be a highly partisan process. The writer of dictionaries, here precisely in accord with Johnson's observations on writers in general in *Rambler* 93, acts as a 'kind of general challenger' who 'quits the common rank of life, steps forward beyond the lists, and offers his merit to the publick judgment' (*Yale* IV.134). Johnson himself can be placed within the same mould, facing the same consequences, for good or ill. As he had reminded readers of the *Rambler*, the 'challenger' is one 'whom every one has a right to attack' (*Yale* IV.133–4). Nevertheless, for the dictionary-maker as critic, it is the language of vested interests that often frames both attack and intended victory, revealing in the process the presence of what Johnson had early identified as that 'partiality that almost every man indulges with regard to himself' (*Life of Savage*, 49). Maxwell's combative response to Johnson's work in his 1755 *Letter* again provides apt illustration. Particular battle lines are drawn up by which Johnson is to be defeated in terms of size (Maxwell's forthcoming dictionary, we are told, will be bigger, occupying four volumes rather than Johnson's two), as well as vanquished in both clarity and contents—Maxwell's diachronic range is greater, he claims, while his work will also redress Johnson's deficits in the treatment of regional words and proverbial idioms.

Other dictionary-makers, writing smaller and cheaper dictionaries, can conversely declare conquest in ways which confirm Johnson's conviction that criticism 'has not yet attained the certainty and stability of science' (*Yale* V.76). Size—and the ideal size of the good dictionary—triggers attack on two fronts. Johnson found his work convicted as too small (as by Maxwell), and far too large (as by competing lexicographers such as Daniel Fenning, John Baskerville, and James Buchanan). Johnson's pride in the material scale of what he had accomplished was clear; the *Dictionary* was 'vasta mole superbus' ('proud in its prodigious bulk'), he wrote to Thomas Warton (*Letters* I.100). *Bulk* for Johnson was 'greatness, largeness'; it signified 'magnitude, size, quantity.' His admission that 'bulk' might also daunt prospective readers ('the bulk of my volumes would fright away the student,' *Yale* XVIII.94) was nevertheless readily seized upon by other dictionary-makers. *Bulk*, as Buchanan's *New English Dictionary* (1757) confirmed, could all too easily be allied with the *bulky*, a term occupying a somewhat different semantic territory: 'It is certain, that the best English dictionaries hitherto published are too bulky and unhandy,' Buchanan now contended.[23] Johnson—along with Bailey—was simultaneously commended and trounced. *Bulky*: 'large, big, fat, heavy,' Buchanan's dictionary explained.

The economy of a work that could easily be carried was, as Buchanan pointed out, also able to provide 'immediate recourse' in any moment of linguistic indecision.[24] Signally unlike the two compendious folios of Johnson's first edition (with their combined weight of twenty pounds), Buchanan's dictionary was, he suggested, quite literally, handy ('Ingenious, ready at doing any thing'; 'Convenient, near at hand'), a quality secured by a design 'purged of all obsolete and despicable words.' It also, again unlike that of Johnson, 'suppressed the figurative and metaphorical,' which, as Buchanan argued, were 'too apt to mislead and perplex youth.' Dictionaries were, after all, texts to be actively used (and, ideally, as often as possible). As another dictionary-maker, Francis Allen, stressed in 1765: 'Foreigners and natives, who stand in need of a work of this kind, must acknowledge it necessary to have it always at hand, that they might recur to it either when reading, or writing, or speaking.'[25] Convenience intentionally triumphed over size: 'this they could not possibly do if the book itself were too large to be portable,' as Allen continued. Occupying a single volume, his dictionary was deliberately 'printed...in a size which will render it fit for the pocket.'[26]

Johnson's sense of achievement in the scale of his work ('I have much augmented the vocabulary,' *Yale* XVIII, 84) could therefore be subject to some highly critical rereading by contemporary lexicographers. Even if not mentioned by name, Johnson lurks intertextually behind John Marchant's comments (in the 'Preface' to his *New Complete English Dictionary* of 1760) that those who write '*large Dictionaries in Folio*' disregard the real needs of ordinary readers '*who have not always Leisure for the Perusal of such voluminous Works.*' Challenge and a legitimate sense of competition construct expansiveness as demerit and extensive detail as potential deficit. Like Allen, Marchant instead persuasively presents a '*Volume of much less Compass, yet big enough to contain Instruction for the Generality of Readers.*'[27]

What readers are assumed to want—or indeed need—could be markedly contentious. Johnson had decided to provide a detailed engagement with 'ordinary' as well as 'hard' words (here deliberately transcending Bailey)—as in the eighteen senses Johnson gives for *at*, or the twenty-two under *by*. Yet, for other lexicographers, a preferential restraint is made to counter the kind of redundancy that such wide-ranging policies of inclusion can suggest. John Baskerville's *Vocabulary, or Pocket Dictionary* of 1765 is, for example, as he deftly points out, 'not crowded with the common Words of the Language, such as every Person must be supposed to understand.'[28] As Marchant likewise argued: '*Another Compiler is so very explicit in the Meaning of every trifling Word, that, sometimes, he gives it three or fourscore different Significations, which might very well be expressed, with equal Clearness, in one Third of that Variety of his Explanations.*'[29] The question of how many senses the ordinary user of dictionaries needed was important. Johnson, for instance, carefully discriminated between sixty-six different senses in his entry for *put* as 'verb active'—with a further fourteen under 'verb neuter.' *Put* in Marchant's text occupies a compact paragraph. Marchant's 'Preface'—and the choice of pronouns he deploys—carefully confirms both distance and division in this matter: '*Our Definitions of Words and Things, tho' concise, are sufficient for their*

*Explanation in their fullest Latitude.*' In contrast, Marchant adds: '*His Terms being so very synonymous... they contain only a Turn of Words, without the least Difference in their Sense.*' As in Fenning's *Royal English Dictionary*, a 'succinct manner' and 'comprehensive brevity' intentionally claim the field, uniting 'profit with amusement, improvement with delight, and worth with frugality.'[30]

The virtues of economy—lexical, semantic, and financial—can overtly triumph in such discourses. As the targeted advertising for Scott's folio edition of Bailey confirmed, value in pragmatic as well as qualitative senses also formed a topic of clear lexicographic concern. Marchant's negative appraisal of '*large Dictionaries in Folio*' was, for instance, given still more momentum by his observation that such works 'are too dear for *the Purchase of most People in private Life.*'[31] Johnson's 1755 folios cost £4 10s, here easily winning the contest for the most expensive monolingual English dictionary; Marchant's 'small Performance' was, in contrast, published in parts at sixpence per issue across a relatively short span of time. Even when Johnson's publishers adopted sixpenny parts, as for his second edition, he arguably won—or lost—this battle too. Across three years and nine weeks of publication, the real price was £4 2s 6d (unbound). Nicol Scott's Bailey meanwhile cost less than 'Two Guineas.'

Cost, as this indicates, was an effective weapon, and it clearly prompted the decision to produce a condensed octavo edition of Johnson's *Dictionary* in 1756, priced at ten shillings. 'A small dictionary appeared yet to be wanting,' its 'Preface' combatively asserted: 'Many dictionaries have been written, and with different degrees of skill; but none of them have yet fallen into my hands by which even the lowest expectations could be satisfied.' This new dictionary ('as opposed to others,' the 'Preface' states) would have words 'more diligently collected, more accurately spelled, more faithfully explained, and more authentically explained.'[32] Intentionally trading on Johnson as 'brand,'[33] the shortened definitions and omitted citations of this 'abstract or epitome' presented a text that both was—and was not—'Johnson.' It arguably, however, merely served to spur on other lexicographers who had engaged with this readership from the outset. As Allen pointed out four years later, his dictionary had been carefully designed to be 'fit for the pocket' in both size and price. Yet, as prospective readers were assured, even at a price of six shillings, 'the purchaser will find that nothing necessary has been omitted; and that works of larger dimensions may contain more useless articles, but cannot contain any that are more useful.' As here, economy could be made to embody lexicographical virtues that determinedly excluded lexicographers such as Johnson, allying him with the negatively connoted values of expense, excess, and extravagance. Even Johnson's octavo edition had two volumes, as well as entries such as *abarticulation* ('That species of articulation which has manifest motion'). Allen's dictionary, as his title page affirmed, instead gave prominence to 'all the Words made Use of in the Common Occurrences of Life.' *Abarticulation* was not included.

Such charges, in effect, repeatedly distance Johnson from the 'common reader' who, at least in his *Plan*, had been depicted as critically important to the dictionary's formation: 'Since it will be required by common readers…the explications should be sufficient for common use' (*Yale* XVIII.47); 'It is not enough that a dictionary delights the critic, unless at the same time if instructs the learner; as it is to little purpose, than an engine amuses the philosopher by the subtilty of its mechanism, if it requires so much knowledge in its application, as to be of no advantage to the common workman' (*Yale* XVIII.29). Nevertheless, if Johnson's 'common reader' is later identified as one who delights in the poetry of Gray (*Lives* IV.184) as well as one familiar, his dictionary suggests, with writers such as Shakespeare, Milton, and Dryden (and, indeed, able to combat the occasional example given in Greek), then the 'common readers' of other dictionaries habitually assume rather different social and cultural locations. Marchant's readers, as he stresses on his title page, are those who have not '*had the Benefit of a learned or liberal Education.*' As such, they prize clarity and transparency, ease and accessibility in the demands they make of the good dictionary. As Marchant therefore indicates in another targeted assault on Johnsonian verbal excess, the social reality of '*most People in private Life*' meant that they '*have not always…Capacity to comprehend these learned and abstruse Speculations.*' Nor, as his title page indicates, do they necessarily have '*leisure for reading a multitude of books.*' Indeed, as Baskerville states in his own 'Preface,' what is, in reality, commonly read may be far removed from the '*wells of English undefiled*' (*Yale* XVIII.95), which inspired many of Johnson's entries. Instead, it is the language of popular novels that Baskerville aims to provide—the words occurring in 'those Authors' preferred by 'Ladies who have a Turn for Reading'—as well as the 'more difficult Words which occur in sensible genteel Company.'

The demands of the common reader here divide the field. Like Allen, Buchanan and Fenning are, for example, careful to point out their own priorities in writing dictionaries that record 'every word made use of the common occurrences of life.'[34] Their work stresses the reality of ordinary use, and of ordinary users. In these terms, the 'common reader,' as for James Thomson Callender, could be constructed as the real casualty of Johnson's work. 'What is a common reader the wiser for hearing that the Oak has male flowers; that the leaves are sinuated, and that the species are five?' Callender demanded. Indeed, 'that the leaves are sinuated is a most trifling circumstance, for who but a botanist or a fool is interested in the projections of a leaf?[35] As in Johnson's decision to explain *fire* as 'the igneous element' (and *hair* as one of the 'common teguments of the body'), his definitions can be 'oenigmatical' such that, as Callender argued, 'the greater part convey no meaning to the common reader.'[36] Not a lexicographer himself, he accorded victory for the benefit of his own readers to Johnson's competitors: 'There are other books of the same kind, and of half the price too, which find room for copious and useful definitions. Pardon's dictionary is not much less than the Doctor's octavo, though it is only six shillings.'[37] Even Johnson's octavo edition, with its address to 'common readers' of a more pedestrian kind, was cast aside.

Callender, challenging conventional collections of 'beauties'[38] by his deliberately adversative *Deformities of Dr Johnson*, can be seen as the kind of 'publick foe' aptly delineated by Johnson's definition of *enemy* (whose 'charge,' as *Rambler* 28 explains, is 'often totally false, and commonly . . . mingled with falsehood,' *Yale* III.155). As Callender's own reviewers noted, the *Deformities* was indeed 'a monument of . . . malignity,' intentionally cutting Johnson down to size out of 'personal provocation' rather than judicious and critical appraisal.[39] Callender's work remains, however, effective testimony to the conflicts that Johnson could generate, and the striking absence of neutrality that dictionary-making as enterprise reveals. Other dictionary-makers, as we have seen, can trenchantly assert the status and value of their own works while deflecting Johnson's assumed strengths—his breadth of inclusion, his detailed interpretations of semantic nuance, or his careful anatomization of phrasal verbs, as under *put*—into critical weakness (even when, from critics perhaps less 'misled by interest,' *Yale* IV.132, the same features attract unequivocal praise). The swing of opinion is marked. 'Johnson's *Dictionary* will . . . leave the reader equally astonished at the acuteness of the lexicographer, and at the complex nature and use of certain minute parts of human speech,' wrote James Beattie in a rather different mode: 'Even of our prepositions . . . one has upwards of twelve, one more than twenty, and one no fewer than thirty different meanings.'[40]

A consideration of these contemporary debates confirms the flux and diversity that continued to characterize English lexicography, revealing too its identity as wide-ranging genre rather than a domain that can, in any sense, be dominated by a single emblematic text.[41] The criticisms raised by competing writers against Johnson, for example, clearly also contained a measure of truth. 'The first two editions were really too expensive for many potential users,' as Allen Reddick confirms: 'readers found them cumbersome and difficult to use, with too much extraneous material cluttering up what they considered to be the essential information—the most common definitions and the orthography.'[42] Even Johnson's condensed 1756 edition—the 'Preface' of which, as we have seen, issued its own challenges in strikingly comparative diction—scarcely served to counterbalance the forces of dissent and detraction in subsequent works.

Johnson's discussion of the proper response of writer to critic in *Rambler* 23, in this respect, offers an interesting point of resolution. Critics, he wrote, can all too easily confront the writer with the 'boundless variety of irreconcilable judgments.' Yet to endeavor to respond to all such criticism merely leads to 'the hopeless labour of uniting heterogeneous ideas,' harassing the mind 'in vain' by the attempt to '[collect] into one point the several rays of borrowed light, emitted often with contrary directions' (*Yale* III.126). Here too metaphors of conflict recur, rendering even Mr Rambler like 'a ship in a poetical tempest, impelled at the same time by opposite winds...but held uptight by the contrariety of the assailants' (*Yale* III.130). Yet remedy comes not from submitting to such attacks but from adhering to one's own principles and aims. After all, 'if we make the praise or blame of others the rule of our conduct, we shall...be held in perpetual suspense between contrary impulses.' Rather than being, as it were, caught in the critical pendulum, the writer should strive to 'place some confidence in his own skill, and to satisfy himself in the knowledge that he has not deviated from the established law of composition' (*Yale* III.126).

Competing lexicographers could therefore continue to advance their claims in the language of critical attack. Advertisements for Frederick Barlow's *Complete English Dictionary* in June 1773, for instance, stressed the fact that all preceding dictionaries have been 'either too voluminous or too concise,' while also capitalizing on the image of financial excess which was, by that point, firmly associated with Johnson's work (the large dictionary 'renders the work too expensive for those who are in most need of it, and are incapable of procuring it for the want of pockets of opulence').[43] The first part of Barlow's dictionary was, in contrast, to be free. Meanwhile, Johnson's fourth edition of his dictionary, published in the same year, remained true to the principles of his first. As *Rambler* 23 presciently concluded, 'Had the opinion of my censurers been unanimous, it might, perhaps, have overset my resolution; but since I find them at variance with each other, I can, without scruple, neglect them, and endeavour to gain the favour of the publick, by following the direction of my own reason' (*Yale* III.130).

NOTES

1. 'Preface' to Richard Rolt, *A New Dictionary of Trade and Commerce* (London: T. Osborne and J. Shipton, 1756), A1r.

2. David Garrick, 'On Johnson's *Dictionary*,' *The Gentleman's Magazine* 25 (1755), 190.

3. Adam Smith '*A Dictionary of the English Language*,' *The Edinburgh Review* 1 (1755), 61; [John Hawkesworth], 'Some Account of a Dictionary of the ENGLISH LANGUAGE,' *The Gentleman's Magazine* 25 (1755), 150.

4. Gwin Kolb and James Sledd, 'Johnson's "Dictionary" and Lexicographical Tradition,' *Modern Philology* 50 (1953), 171.

5. Jonathan Swift, *The Cambridge Edition of the Works of Jonathan Swift*, general eds. Claude Rawson, Ian Higgins, and David Womersley, I: *A Tale of a Tub and Other Works*, ed. Marcus Walsh (Cambridge: Cambridge University Press, 2010), 145.

6. Daniel Fenning, *The Royal English Dictionary: or, a Treasury of the English Language* (London: S. Crowder, 1761), vii.

7. Ibid., vii.

8. Ibid., viii.

9. [John Wesley], *The Complete English Dictionary*, 2nd edn (Bristol: William Pine, 1764).

10. Anne Fisher, *An Accurate New Spelling Dictionary, and Expositor of the English Language*, 2nd edn (London: Hawes, Clarke, and Collins, 1773), title page, ii.

11. Ibid., iii.

12. John Maxwell, *A Letter from a Friend in England To Mr Maxwell, Complaining of his Dilatoriness in the Publication of his So-Long-Promised Work* (Dublin: S. Powell, 1755), 3.

13. Ibid., 5.

14. See Philip Gove, 'Notes on Serialization and Competitive Publishing: Johnson's and Bailey's Dictionaries, 1755,' *Proceedings of the Oxford Bibliographical Society* 5, (1938), 308.

15. Ibid., 305.

16. Maxwell, *Letter*, 5.

17. As Clifford notes, it 'seems likely' that 'W. S. was William Strahan, or someone writing for him.' See James L. Clifford, *Dictionary Johnson: The Middle Years of Samuel Johnson* (London: Heinemann, 1979), 54.

18. Benjamin Martin, *Lingua Britannica Reformata: or, a New English Dictionary* (London: J. Hodges, 1749), viii.

19. W. S., 'The Signification of Words now Varied,' *The Gentleman's Magazine* 19 (1749), 66.

20. [Philip Dormer Stanhope], *The World* 100 (28 November 1754), 599. Reprinted in James, T. Boulton (ed.), *Samuel Johnson: The Critical Heritage* (London: Routledge, 1971), 95–8.

21. Rolt, *Dictionary of Trade*, A1r.

22. Maxwell, *Letter*, 6.

23. James Buchanan, *Linguæ Britannicæ vera Pronunciatio: or, a New English Dictionary* (London: A. Millar, 1757), iv.
24. Ibid.
25. Francis Allen, *A Complete English Dictionary* (London: J. Wilson and J. Fell, 1765), iv.
26. Ibid.
27. John Marchant, *A New Complete, English Dictionary, Peculiarly Adapted to the Instruction and Improvement of those who have not had the Benefit of a Learned or Liberal Education* (London: J. Fuller, 1760), 'Preface.'
28. [John Baskerville], *A Vocabulary, or Pocket Dictionary* (Birmingham: Dod, Rivington, 1765), 'Preface.'
29. Marchant, *Dictionary*, 'Preface.'
30. Fenning, *English Dictionary*, viii.
31. Marchant, *Dictionary*, 'Preface.'
32. S. Johnson, *A Dictionary of the English Language…Abstracted from the Folio Edition*, 2 vols. (London: J. Knapton, 1756).
33. See further Chapter 14.
34. Fenning, *English Dictionary*, viii.
35. James Thomson Callender, *A Critical Review of the Works of Dr Samuel Johnson* (London: T. Cadell, 1783), 59.
36. James Thomson Callender, *Deformities of Dr Samuel Johnson. Selected from his Works* (Edinburgh: W. Creech, T. Longman, 1782), 27.
37. Ibid., 47.
38. See Arthur T. Hazen, 'The Beauties of Johnson,' *Modern Philology* 35 (1938), 289–9, and also Chapter 7 (this volume).
39. See *The Monthly Review* (1783), 185–6.
40. James Beattie, *Dissertations Moral and Critical* (Dublin: Exshaw, Walker, 1783), I.329.
41. See Lynda Mugglestone, 'Registering the Language—Dictionaries, Diction, and the Art of Elocution,' in *Eighteenth-Century English: Ideology and Change*, ed. Raymond Hickey (Cambridge: Cambridge University Press, 2010), 309–38.
42. Allen Reddick, *The Making of Johnson's Dictionary, 1746–1773*, rev. edn (Cambridge: Cambridge University Press, 1996), 86.
43. See *The York Chronicle and Weekly Advertiser* 34 (1772–3), 272.

# 13

# Fixity and Instability in the Text of Johnson's Poems

*James McLaverty*

The impression conveyed by accounts of Johnson's composition of poetry, both in Boswell's *Life* and in the recollections of other contemporaries, is that his poems arrived as fixed single things. When they were not improvised on the spot, they were composed rapidly in the head and dashed down on paper in half lines.[1] But, although Boswell and Johnson were proud of this combination of rapidity and finish, the accounts of composition in the *Lives of the Poets* showed the critical pendulum swinging in the opposite direction, with admiration for the slow progress of texts towards perfection. In particular, Alexander Pope's artistic diligence was praised, and over one hundred lines of his draft *Iliad* translation were transcribed with enthusiasm: 'Of these specimens every man who has cultivated poetry, or who delights to trace the mind from the rudeness of its first conceptions to the elegance of its last, will naturally desire a greater number' (*Lives* IV.23).[2] Yet these very materials are those that Johnson's own practice was valued for eliminating. In the *Lives of the Poets* Johnson acknowledged these contrasting practices and balanced them as different paths to poetic achievement:

> Of composition there are different methods. Some employ at once memory and invention, and, with little intermediate use of the pen, form and polish large masses by continued meditation, and write their productions only when, in their own opinion, they have completed them. It is related of Virgil, that his custom was to pour out a great number of verses in the morning, and pass the day in retrenching exuberances and correcting inaccuracies. The method of Pope, as may be collected from his translation, was to write his first thoughts in his first words, and gradually to amplify, decorate, rectify, and refine them.   (*Lives* IV.63)

Virgil, Pope, and possibly Milton exemplified the second method, Johnson himself the first.

Johnson's establishment of an easy movement between these two positions on poetic composition, deciding he could praise both the immediate and the deliberately progressive, had the advantage for him of simplifying this new field of investigation. Both positions depended on an idealization that imposed order on processes of literary production that are often irregular and haphazard. Many questions consequently remained neglected. What of works that were incomplete? Or that were resumed after an initial completion and then redeveloped over a period of time? Or that were the product of collaboration? The two poles of composition served to exclude these questions and to present a satisfyingly stable view of literary texts. Textual stability was something Johnson valued. When Edmond Malone was considering correcting Pope's works, Johnson warned him off, telling him: 'An author's disposition of his own works is sacred, and an editor has no right to vary it.'[3] Those who were to play Malone to Johnson's Pope, his twentieth-century editors, would have been untroubled by this edict. They would gladly have followed his prescription, but, both in the evaluation of modes of composition and in the disposition of his own works, Johnson betrayed expectations, neglecting to provide either exemplary evaluations or a sacred text.[4] In their attempts to remedy this deficiency, his editors displayed impressive erudition and powers of analysis in order to fix a reading text of each poem and thereby to attain the stability Johnson would have wanted. But this chapter, while acknowledging a profound indebtedness to the achievements of these editions, aims to unpick their work and to return to the field of Johnson's own composition unlimited by his idealizations, highlighting instead the way an emphasis on singularity and completion coexists with a plurality of readings and a variety of textual histories. It takes the view that the poems live most intensely in a variety of attempts to arrive at a best self.

Early in his career, Johnson seemed willing to take on the responsibility of editing his collected works. His contracts for both *The Vanity of Human Wishes* (1749) and *Irene* (1749) show he sold the copyright while reserving to himself the right to print one edition; but these editions never matured into being.[5] That the idea of an authorized edition persisted is clear from a conversation with John Nichols, when Johnson, contemplating his own death, said that he had power from the booksellers to print 'a regular edition of his own Works' but had no power to assign the right to anyone else, unless he wrote notes to create new works.[6] Even in the absence of this collected edition, Johnson's neglect of his poems is surprising and at odds with his concern with stability in language and in the texts of others. Of the roughly 114 poems that now appear in his collected works, only thirty-five were printed in his lifetime. A mere four were printed individually (*London* in 1738, the 'Drury-Lane Prologue' in 1747, *The*

*Vanity of Human Wishes* in 1749, and the 'New Prologue to Comus' in 1750), and there were only two collections (Dodsley's *Collection of Poems by Several Hands* in 1748 and subsequent editions, and Anna Williams's *Miscellanies in Prose and Verse* in 1766) in which his poems appeared with his clear approval. The rest were printings in magazines or in independent collections. Of the seventy-nine poems not published in his lifetime, twenty-four first appeared in print in the *Works* of 1787, thirteen in Boswell's *Life* or *Journal*, twenty-four in other collections (mainly Hester Piozzi's), and eighteen in the twentieth century. A survey of the printings of Johnson's poems up to 1850 reveals that they were disseminated freely, without authorial or editorial control, up until Johnson's death in 1784, when George Kearsley's *Poetical Works* of 1785 marked the beginning of an editorial attempt to draw his work together.[7] It also points up how Johnson's professionalism made for an unshaped career. He responded to publishing opportunities, suggestions from others, or to immediate financial need; he was not concerned, as Pope, for example, had been, to develop an impressive narrative. Alert to others' self-fashioning, he would have been less Johnsonian if he had taken a similar care over himself.

Many of Johnson's poems were composed very rapidly. Some, of course, are very short; there is not a very substantial body of work. This rapidity of composition figures as an essential aspect of Johnson's poetic achievement. In the Oxford edition, twenty-four poems are said to be 'impromptu' or produced 'extempore,' or were dashed off for a particular purpose. And the sense that the poems were the product of a single creative process pervades accounts of their composition. The emphasis is always on facility, with the poem committed to paper only as a final stage. That might be expected of an occasional poem, such as 'To Mrs Thrale, on Her Completing Her Thirty-Fifth Birthday' (*Poems* 204–5), when, according to her *Anecdotes*, 'he burst out suddenly, for so he did without the least previous hesitation whatsoever, and without having entertained the smallest intention towards it half a minute before' (*Shaw-Piozzi*, 115), but a similar rapidity is claimed for more substantial poems. The impressive lines on Claudy Philips (*Poems* 89–91), now engraved in stone in St. Peter's Collegiate Church, Wolverhampton, were produced in conversation as a response to Richard Wilkes's epitaph: 'stirring about his tea for a little while, in a state of meditation, he almost extempore produced the following verses, "Philips whose touch" etc.' (*Life* I.148–9). Of the poems that took somewhat longer, the Latin verses on Pope's grotto were 'the casual amusement of half an hour' (*Poems* 92), while 'Skia' seems to have been composed in one day (5 September 1773) and the companion 'Oda' to Hester Thrale the following day, after Johnson had retired to his chamber (*Poems* 192–5).

The accounts of two of Johnson's most important poems convey a similar impression of rapid composition. Of *The Vanity of Human Wishes*, Johnson told George Steevens, 'I wrote...the first seventy lines...in the course of one morning....The whole number was composed before I threw a single couplet on paper' (*Johnsonian Miscellanies* II.313–14). Johnson told Boswell this was his general practice in making verses: 'I have generally had them in my mind, perhaps fifty at a time, walking up and down in my room; and then I have written them down, and often, from laziness, have written only half lines. I remember I wrote a hundred lines of "The Vanity of Human Wishes" in a day' (*Life* II.15). Such accounts, if they presented the whole truth, would make the task of the textual editor easy but, on examination, the picture proves more complex.

The first problem arises with the little impromptu poems. They might be expected to be single, but in some cases the differences between versions are striking. Hester Thrale reports that Johnson translated some lines from his friend Joseph Baretti's *Small Talk for the Use of Young Ladies* (1773), 'Long may live my lovely Hetty!' (*Poems* 201–2), 'very elegantly and all in a Minute' (*Thraliana*, I.210). But there are widely different versions recorded by Hester Thrale and by Baretti himself, one of six and one of seven lines, with only the second line strictly the same. Although I should be surprised to find that the final line of Baretti's version ('Huzza! Huzza! Huzza!') was Johnson's, it is probable that on different occasions Johnson dictated different versions of the poem; a choice between them was never made. That certainly seems to be the case with the epitaph on Hogarth (*Poems* 181–2) which is a revision of a three-stanza draft originally written by David Garrick (and sent to Johnson, by Garrick, for his opinion and advice). Thrale's version of the epitaph (in *Thraliana* 41) is surely Johnson's memorial reconstruction of the revised text that he had sent to Garrick in reply; Johnson's letter to Garrick (*Letters* I.384 n.3) itself presents an undecided reading in line 2, 'traced/wav'd.' More complex variation appears in the case of a poem that on the surface looks perfectly simple, the parody of Thomas Warton, 'Hermit hoar, in solemn cell' (*Poems* 206–8). Boswell gives a complete, two-stanza version of the poem in his account of his discussions with Johnson on 18 September 1777:

> Hermit hoar, in solemn cell,
>   Wearing out life's evening gray;
> Smite thy bosom, sage, and tell,
>   What is bliss? and which the way?
>
> This I spoke; and speaking sigh'd;
>   —Scarce repress'd the starting tear;—

> When the smiling sage reply'd—
> —Come, my lad, and drink some beer.
>                                    (*Life* III.159)

Boswell insists on the impromptu nature of the first stanza but leaves the status of the second unclear ('He at an after period added the following stanza'). In a note, he explains a somewhat complicated process. The first stanza belonged to 18 September 1777, but when Boswell and Johnson met eight months later, on 9 May 1778, Johnson said 'Where is bliss?' would be better than 'What is bliss?' He also composed the second stanza then, but Boswell was not allowed to write it down. Boswell did not get a copy of the second stanza until spring 1779, and still later Johnson accepted his suggestion of changing 'hoary' to 'smiling' in the second stanza. So what seems in Boswell to be an instantaneous poem in fact evolved in at least three stages over eighteen months or more. The twentieth-century editions adopt Boswell's text, but once again authority is unclear. They substitute 'Where is bliss?' for 'What is bliss?' with the justification that at that point Boswell is being faithful to 18 September 1777 rather than to the complete poem, but should they also accept Boswell's substitution of 'smiling' for 'hoary' in the second stanza, a change made in order to avoid repetition? Johnson was repeating the identifying adjective in a pseudo-medieval way; Boswell not only spoils that effect, he anticipates the comic reversal of the final line and thereby weakens it. Johnson might well have preferred, as I do, the versions he gave to Hester Thrale (*Thraliana* I.209 n.1, 398; *Shaw-Piozzi* 82). Once again, there is no single authoritative text.

Poems published by Johnson in his lifetime show similar complexities, including the involvement of other writers. The clearest examples are the prologues, which make up a significant part of this publication history. Prologues tend to be examples of divided textual authority, because they belong to the playhouse and an actual performance as well as to the author at his desk. They could be printed in the newspapers (usually the day after performance), or as separate pamphlets (probably days later), or as part of the play. Granted sufficient information, editors might deliberately choose to print either a text that represents the performance or a text that represents the author's script. Johnson himself reluctantly recognized the collaborative nature of prologue writing. He told Steevens that, following his usual practice, he had composed the lines of the 'Prologue and Epilogue, Spoken at the Opening of the Theater in Drury-Lane 1747' (*Poems* 105–9) in his head before writing them down, adding, 'I did not afterwards change more than a word of it, and that was done at the remonstrance of Garrick. I did not think his criticism just; but it was necessary he should be satisfied with what he was to utter' (*Johnsonian Miscellanies* II.314). This is a clear example of reluctant collaboration, but it is not known what the agreed change was. In the case of the prologue to Hugh Kelly's *A Word to the Wise*, performed for the benefit of Kelly's widow at Covent Garden on 29 May 1777 (*Poems* 209–11), Johnson complained about an unauthorized change. The first night, seven years earlier, had been a disaster, and Johnson's prologue celebrates the capacity of moral purpose to transform an audience's response on a night 'When pleasure fired her torch at Virtue's flame.' In lines 9–10, the version in the *Public Advertiser* reads:

> Let no resentful petulance invade
> Th'oblivious grave's inviolable shade.

But the other newspapers (the *General Evening Post*, for example) read:

> For no renew'd hostilities invade…

The Reverend John Hussey recorded Johnson's objection in his copy of Boswell's *Life*: 'On reading over this Prologue to Dr Johnson, the morning after it was spoken, the Doctor told me instead of *renew'd hostilities* he wrote *revengeful petulance*, and did not seem pleased with the alteration.'[8] In an earlier memorandum to Boswell, Hussey gave the *Public Advertiser*'s reading 'resentful petulance,' which was probably Johnson's. The reading 'renew'd hostilities' must derive from the playhouse; it probably alludes to the political nature of the first hostile reception of the play, which sprang from Kelly's support for the government. Editors of Johnson's collected works would want the reading 'resentful petulance,' but a modern editor compiling a collection of dramatic pieces, the equivalent of *The Theatrical Bouquet* (1778), would want to print the reading from the majority of the newspapers.

A similar distinction might be made in the more complex case of the prologue to Goldsmith's *The Good Natur'd Man* (*Poems* 179), first performed at Covent Garden on 29 January 1768. The version of the prologue printed with the play on 5 February differs from the one that had appeared earlier in the newspapers. The parallel texts below embolden the variants, including the letters around changes in punctuation but not changes in capitalization. The first major variation comes in the first six/eight lines when Johnson introduces the parallel between the playwright seeking applause and the politician seeking election.

| Newspapers | Play |
|---|---|
| From *St James's Chronicle*, 30 January 1768 | From *Good Natur'd Man* (1768) |
| Prest by the Load of Life, the weary Mind | Prest by the load of life, the weary mind |
| Surveys the general Toil of human Kind; | Surveys the general toil of human kind; |
| With cool Submission joins the labouring Train, | With cool submission joins the labouring train, |

*(continued)*

And social Sorrow loses half its Pai**n.**
**Amidst the Toils of this returning Year,**
**When Senators and Nobles learn to fear;**
Our **little** Bard, without Complaint, may share
**The** bustling Season's epidemic Care.

And social sorro**w, l**oses half **it's** pai**n:**
5
Our **anxious** Bard, without complaint, may share
**This** bustling season's epidemic care.

There was to be a general election in 1768, and David Fleeman believed Johnson's friendship with Henry Thrale, MP for Southwark, led him to take a hand in drafting his election addresses immediately after this, in February and March of that year.[9] Allusion to the coming election runs through the prologue, but the additional couplet in the newspapers might have been thought too narrowly tied to its time, and too bold in its treatment of parliamentarians, for the published play. There seems no reason, however, to doubt its authenticity as an authorial version of the prologue. The other significant reading of the newspapers, 'little' rather than 'anxious' bard, touches on Goldsmith's sensitivity about his height, but I am not persuaded Johnson could not have written it. If it was a variation introduced by Robert Bensley, who spoke the prologue, it is surprising Goldsmith allowed it, and it seems more likely that 'anxious' was a revision made in the printing of the play, which Goldsmith would have supervised himself.

The second major variant passage (beginning l.15/17) develops the idea of the power that has become possessed by the many, whether electorate or audience:

Uncheck'**d, on bot**h **Caprice may vent its** Rage,
As **Children fret** the Lion in a Cage**;**
**The** offended Burgess hoards his angry Tale,
For that blest Year when all that vot**e,** may rail;
**The Poet's Foes their Schemes of Spite dismiss,**
Till that glad Nigh**t** when all that hat**e,** may hiss**;**

Uncheck'**d on bot**h**, loud rabbles vent their** rage,
As **mongrels bay** the lion in a cag**e.**
**Th'**offended burgess hoards his angry tale,
For that blest year when all that vot**e** may rail; 20
**Their schemes of spite the poet's foes dismiss,**
Till that glad night**,** when all that hat**e** may hiss**.**
**This day the powder'd curls and golden coat,**
**Says swelling Crispin, begg'd a cobler's vote.**
**This night, our wit, the pert apprentice cries, 25**
**Lies at my feet, I hiss him, and he dies.**

The play text here is very aggressive. The audience is a rabble, mongrels baying. In the newspapers, there is no rabble, just 'Caprice,' and the dogs are children. The four extra lines in the play continue an alternation of couplets on the election and on the play, but they do not strike me as Johnsonian. The contempt and fear expressed towards the lower orders is atypical; the elaborate particularity of the cobbler adds little to the argument; and the couplet on the apprentice repeats the opportunity to hiss. The two texts might represent Johnson's oscillating attitude to the audience, but I am attracted to the hypothesis that the play text represents Goldsmith's reworking of the poem in order to express his disappointment at the play's reception. If it did, the adjustment of the final line to transfer credit from the audience ('Trusts without fear, to **candour**, and to you') to the author ('Trusts without fear, to **merit**, and to you') might also be his. Johnson's editors unanimously choose the play version (Oxford says 'it must be taken to be what Johnson wrote'), presumably because its source is more respectable, but the newspaper text is more persuasively Johnsonian. Both should be printed in an edition, but if I were allowed only one text, I would choose that in the newspapers.

Surprisingly, the poems for which Johnson was solely responsible show little more stability than these play texts, as two of his most successful poems, 'On the Death of Dr Robert Levet' and *The Vanity of Human Wishes*, reveal. Johnson's poem on Levet, his friend and housemate (*Poems* 232–5), was popular, being printed in the *Gentleman's Magazine*, the *British Magazine and Review*, and the *Universal Magazine* in August 1783, and rapidly reprinted in the leading journals in the months afterwards. There are also several transcripts by friends. Many of the variants are just mistakes, such as Hawkins's 'letter'd ignorance' for 'letter'd arrogance' in his *Life* (*Hawkins*, 335), but two periodicals stand out for the quality of their texts. One is the *Gentleman's Magazine*, which traditionally provides the copy text; the other is the *London Magazine*. The *London Magazine* prints the poem a month later than the *Gentleman's Magazine*, but it runs an advertising campaign in which it makes a point of claiming that its version is authentic. That September number also offers an account of Levet, his failed marriage, and his fostering by Johnson that precedes the appearance of that information in the *Gentleman's Magazine* by eighteen months. The differences between the two versions are not great, and in the parallel text below I have been selective about the punctuation changes included.

| *Gentleman's Magazine* | *London Magazine* | |
| --- | --- | --- |
| | ELEGY | |
| *On the Death of Dr* ROBERT LEVET | On the DEATH of Mr LEVET. | |
| *By Dr* JOHNSON | By Dr SAMUEL JOHNSON. | |
| See LEVET to the grave descen**d;** | See LEVET to the grave descen**d!** | 2 |
| No**r,** letter'd arroganc**e,** deny | No**r** letter'd arroganc**e** deny | 11 |
| In **m**isery's darkest cavern's known | In **M**isery's darkest caverns known, | 17 |
| His useful **care** was ever nigh, | His useful **aid** was ever nigh, | |
| **Where** hopeless anguish pour'd **his** groan, | **When** hopeless Anguish pour'd **the** groan, | |
| And lonely **w**ant retir'd to die. | And lonely **W**ant retir'd to die. | |
| Then with no **throbbing fiery** pain**,** | Then with no **throbs of fiery** pain**:** | 33 |
| And **forc'd** his soul the nearest way. | And **free'd** his soul the nearest way. | 36 |

Both are impressive texts, and it seems unlikely they are witnesses to the same original. Possibly they present different stages in composition, with the *Gentleman's Magazine* later and more polished. The *Gentleman's Magazine*'s 'Dr' in the title is preferable to 'Mr' because it accentuates the poem's central irony. The commas around 'letter'd arrogance' are clearly right, and the full personification of 'pour'd his groan' is preferable to the neutral but unidiomatic 'pour'd the groan'; the presence of 'her groan' in Hester Piozzi's transcription suggests 'pour'd the groan' might have been Johnson's attempt at gender-neutral language. 'Useful aid' in the *London* version is surely tinged with tautology. 'Throbbing fiery pain' is characteristic of Johnson's aim at concision in revision and removes what is perhaps too straightforward a parallel with 'cold gradations of decay' in the following line. So I would regard the *Gentleman's Magazine* version as representing the completion of a period of composition, an earlier stage of which is represented by the *London Magazine*, which was entitled to boast the authenticity of its document.

However, this preference for the *Gentleman's Magazine* version leaves a problematic conclusion. Editors say they have taken their text from the *Gentleman's Magazine*, but they do not print its conclusion ('Death broke at once the vital chain,/And forc'd his soul the nearest way'), reading 'free'd' instead. I think they are right to do so, because for once the one is hiding in the many, and all versions are witnesses, direct or indirect, to 'free'd.' The key is the apostrophe in 'free'd,' which is characteristic of Johnson's practice in the *Dictionary*, and links the two readings. An amanuensis or compositor trying to interpret difficult writing would look for a word with an obvious missing letter, and 'freed' would not come to mind. An examination of *The Vanity of*

*Human Wishes* manuscript shows the other letters (*r, o, e, c*) are easily confused. It is probable that in this case there was only one version of the poem designed for print, but the others were drafts or records given to friends. What we have is a witness to a form of manuscript publication.

In the account Johnson gave Boswell of the composition of *The Vanity of Human Wishes* (*Poems* 110), the emphasis was on rapidity, with one hundred lines written in a day and only half lines recorded. Its full textual history, however, shows an awkward pattern of revision, and its twentieth-century editors struggled to create a satisfactory reading text. First published in 1749, the poem was revised both in accidentals and in substantives for inclusion in Dodsley's *Collection* in 1755, but James Boswell, Jr., reported other manuscript variants entered onto a copy of the first edition. As these changes do not include the *Collection* revisions, it seems plausible to assume that, if they are by Johnson, they preceded them.[10] These revisions pose two problems. Which version should be chosen for reading text? Should there be an attempt, on the lines suggested by Fredson Bowers and adopted by David Fleeman, to create one definitive text from the existing variants by taking accidentals and substantives from different texts and by incorporating James Boswell's substantive reading as well as those from 1755?[11]

Although the two versions of *The Vanity of Human Wishes* are separated by only six years, some variations are responsive to historical developments. A famous revision replaces the word 'Garret' by 'patron' in l.160:

| | | |
|---|---|---|
| There mark what Ills the Scholar's Life assail, | There mark what ills the scholar's life assail, | 159 |
| Toil, Envy, Want, the **Garret**, and the Jail. | Toil, envy, want, the **patron**, and the jail. | |

The change of that one word marks, even if proleptically, a turning point in literary history, with the rejection of the system of patronage.[12] The revision strengthens the poem, but it responds to an event in Johnson's life with wider significance; it does not restate an original conception. Johnson's letter rejecting Chesterfield's patronage of the *Dictionary* was dated by Boswell 7 February 1755; Dodsley's *Collection* appeared about a month later, on 18 March, with this revision. A revision earlier in the poems shows another time-dependent development:

| | | |
|---|---|---|
| And leaves the ***bonny*** *Traytor* in the Tow'r, | And leaves the **wealthy** traytor in the Tow'r, | 34 |

The allusion was originally not to Prince Charles Edward Stuart, but to the Scottish Lords who had supported him in the rebellion of 1745. By 1755 the allusion was obscure and unsuited to the generality of the poem, and it was omitted. Not all changes, it is true, represent personal or historical developments. For example, the move to firmer personification and concision in:

| | |
|---|---|
| And **Sloth's bland Opiates shed their** Fumes in vain; | And **Sloth effuse her opiate** fumes in vain; 150 |

And the increased hopelessness of man in this couplet:

| | |
|---|---|
| Must helpless Man, in Ignorance sedate, **Swim** darkling down the **Current** of his Fate? | Must helpless man, in ignorance sedate, 345 **Roll** darkling down the **torrent** of his fate? |

These and similar passages make the claims of 1755 as the version for printing in an edition very strong. But I think the choice is based on an evaluation, not on a commitment to the progressive view of literary composition. The problems with that view can be shown by a brief glance at the manuscript. At the end of the passage on Wolsey we are confronted in line 124 with the choice of Wolsey's wealth and fall or being content to be:

| | |
|---|---|
| The **Wisest Justice** on the Bank of Trent | The **wealthiest Landlord** on the Bank 124 of Trent |

'Wisest Justice' is crossed out and 'wealthiest Landlord' is substituted. The reading of 1749 is a development of that: 'richest Landlord.' But when we get to 1755, Johnson restores his initial manuscript reading. This uncertainty about which reading to choose (like the 'traced/wav'd' dilemma in the Hogarth epitaph) shows the inadequacy of both the 'completed before writing' and the 'slowly developing' theories of composition. The passage of the poem, like the person, through time makes evaluation more difficult than that.

If the picture is complex when substantives are being interpreted, it grows more so when accidentals are taken into account. There are, of course, changes in punctuation between editions, but more strikingly there are changes in capitals. In the first edition of *London* all nouns have initial capitals; in Dodsley's *Collection* in 1748 only those that are proper nouns or might count as personifications do. Capitalization in *The Vanity of Human Wishes* is more perplexing. In 1749 all nouns have initial capitals, but in the *Collection* in 1755, some do and some don't. On the first page the capitals are taken down ('Then say how hope and fear, desire and hate,' l.5); but later the capitals start to

appear in cases of personification ('Preferment's gate,' 'Delusive Fortune hears,' ll.73, 75), and after the 'young enthusiast' reaches the
'throne of Truth' (l.142), capitals start to invade the poem more and
more thoroughly. They are still reserved for abstract nouns, but words
that would not have had capitals at the beginning of the poem do so
towards the end:

> Where then shall Hope and Fear their objects find?
> Must dull Suspence corrupt the stagnant mind?   (ll.343–4)

Only at the very end of the poem does the earlier practice reassert itself:

> With these celestial wisdom calms the mind,
> And makes the happiness she does not find.   (ll.367–8)

Were it not for this reassertion, I would assume the compositor had simply
forgotten his task of restyling. As it is, I must confess I do not understand
the capitalization of 1755. Perhaps Johnson wanted to intensify the emotional anxiety of his poem as it progressed, only to quiet it at the end.

Different editors have tackled the problem of revised accidentals in different ways. The Oxford editors in 1941 simply followed 1755; the Yale
editors in 1964 followed 1755 but lowered these capitals in line with edition policy; Fleeman in his Penguin in 1971 and in his revision of the
Oxford edition in 1974 based his text on 1755 but, following the recommendations of Fredson Bowers, introduced capitals from 1749.[13] Fleeman also included the James Boswell revisions in his text. One of these
('New,' l.41) may correct a misreading of the manuscript; another ('scapes,'
l.167) is superseded by 1755, which restores the manuscript reading;
three more are possible improvements. Fleeman, therefore, bravely attempted to forge the one text from the several strands left by Johnson.
The resulting text is the authoritative one for quotation, standing in place
of the author's sacred 'disposition of his own work,' but I think there are
many reasons for wishing to move beyond it. The first problem with the
fusion of these three texts is that it provides no text that Johnson saw or
approved. The modern literary critic or philologist says penetratingly to
the textual critic, 'Excuse me. When was this text written? What stage in
the author's career does it belong to? Which readers was it available to?
Where can I find the manuscript or printed book it represents?' To this
eclectic editors, unless they are recovering a document, have no satisfactory answer: the accidentals belong to 1749, most substantives to 1755,
and other substantives to an unknown date. A fundamental claim for the
eclectic edition, that the accidentals represent Johnson's own preferences,
is unsustainable in the light of the manuscript. In 1749 all nouns were
capitalized in the first paragraph, but in 1755 only 'China' and 'Peru'

were. In the manuscript, the picture is mixed as these abbreviated quotations from the first ten lines show: 'Observation with extensive view'; 'anxious toil... eager Strife'; 'busy Scenes of Crouded Life'; 'hot desire and raging Hate'; 'snares... Maze of Fate'; 'paths without a Guide'; 'Phantoms in the mist'; 'fancied ills... airy Good.' The capitals are difficult to interpret: in doublets the second noun is more likely to attract a capital; nouns expressing positive value also attract capitals; but nouns in prepositional phrases tend to be in lower case. I cannot observe any consistency in Johnson's practice. The capital for 'Crouded,' for example, may stem from the word's closeness to its noun, or it may be emphatic, or it may be a fluke. However, it does not appear in the first edition, and these irregular capitals are much more like those of 1755 than those of 1749. Without any evidence that Johnson approved the capitalization of the first edition, it is difficult to claim that imposing them on 1755 represents his preferences.

The struggle of Johnson's editors to supply the gap he left by providing an authoritative text of his poems was admirable. At its most ambitious it tried to unite respect for the immediate (for accidentals) and for the developing (for substantives) text. But such editing, like the theories of composition that underlie it, tends to disguise the realities of literary creation. Composition is irregular, its conclusion difficult to determine; collaboration cannot always be controlled; transmission of texts is hazardous; revision is often discontinuous. Future editors will, I suspect, be more accepting of this instability and aim to make access to it easier. Space is not so limited that print editions could not provide more than one text of a work, making their origins clear; perhaps future electronic editions, more friendly to literary users than their predecessors, might show one text mutating into another. Most desirable at present is an edition of Johnson's manuscripts, with a companion enquiry into his orthography and methods of composition. There are many stories of Johnson's habits of composition, but few studies of the evidence that remains of it.

## NOTES

1. Accounts of composition are to be found in the head notes of *The Poems of Samuel Johnson*, eds. David Nichol Smith and Edward L. McAdam, 2nd edn, rev. J. D. Fleeman (Oxford: Clarendon Press, 1974), henceforward *Poems*. This chapter is based on the J. D. Fleeman Memorial Lecture, given at the Johnson Tercentenary Conference at Pembroke College in September 2009, and is deeply indebted to Fleeman's work throughout.
2. Similar sentiments are expressed over the plan of *Paradise Lost* (*Lives* I.261).
3. James M. Osborn, 'Johnson on the Sanctity of an Author's Text,' *PMLA* 50 (1935), 928–9. I have expanded Malone's contractions.

4. The major twentieth-century editions, in addition to the Oxford edition in n.1, are *Yale* VI and J. D. Fleeman's *Samuel Johnson: The Complete English Poems* (Harmondsworth: Penguin, 1971).

5. The topic is surveyed in the Oxford edition of the *Poems*, xi, with *The Vanity of Human Wishes* receipt quoted, 110; for *Irene*, see *Life* I.98.

6. *The Gentleman's Magazine* 61 (1791), 499; *Life* IV.409.

7. A chronological list, deriving mainly from *Poems* (1974), is to be found at the end of the addenda and corrigenda to J. D. Fleeman, *A Bibliography of the Works of Samuel Johnson*, 2 vols. (Oxford: Clarendon Press, 2000), on the American Bibliographical Society's Bibsite: http://www.bibsocamer.org/Bib-Site/bibsite.htm.

8. Hussey's copy is in the National Library of Australia (*Poems* 209).

9. See entry 68.2TE in Fleeman's *Bibliography* II.1167.

10. The copy Boswell recorded has disappeared. The variants were incorporated in Hawkins's *Works*; see *Poems* 64, and in the Oxford, Yale, and Penguin editions, but A. D. Moody, 'Johnson's Poems: Textual Problems and Critical Readings,' *The Library*, 5th ser., 26 (1971), 22–38, thinks the corrections likely to be Hawkins's. I suspect they are Johnson's but unremarkable.

11. Fleeman's aim was to realize Johnson's 'definitive intentions' (*Poems* [1971], 11). He was influenced by Fredson Bowers's review essay, 'The Text of Johnson,' *Modern Philology* 61 (1964), 298–309.

12. Of course, such a view represents a simplification, as Dustin Griffin insists in 'The Rise of the Professional Author?,' in *The Cambridge History of the Book in Britain*, eds. John Barnard, D. F. Mokenzie, David McKitterick and I. R. Wilson, V: 1695–1830, eds. Michael J. Suarez, S.J, and Michael L. Turner (Cambridge: Cambridge University Press, 2009), 132–45, summarizing some of his *Literary Patronage in England* (Cambridge: Cambridge University Press, 1996).

13. Fleeman's keenness to respect his predecessors got him into some difficulties in his revision of the Oxford edition. In the first paragraph, for example, Fleeman prints 'guide,' thus making it the only noun without a capital, when both the first edition and the manuscript have a capital. In capitalization, the lemmata in his collation often fail to correspond to his text.

# 14

# What Is It About Johnson?

*Isobel Grundy*

This chapter addresses the phenomenon that is Samuel Johnson, his particular appeal, and the curious disjunctions between his writings, his life, and his fame. Johnson hungered for fame from very early in his career (as he makes abundantly clear with his constant attention, in the *Rambler* essays, to literary ambition). Well before the end of his life, he achieved what today is called celebrity—albeit, as time has proved, in a more enduring form than the modern idea of 'celebrity' tends to suggest. This chapter investigates what it is about Johnson that makes him so much studied, so much quoted, so much appealed to as an authority, yet so personally valued by his admirers, and on such various grounds. What is it about him that speaks to a whole range of different public conceptions of what a great writer should be?

Johnson embodies contradictory energies, which may explain why he continues to be read. What the reading public (that is, posterity) needs or desires or demands of those it elects as great writers consists of diverse, perhaps incompatible, elements. The first requirement must be pleasure from reading: 'That book is good in vain, which the reader throws away,' as Johnson argues in the 'Life of Dryden.' 'He only is the master, who keeps the mind in pleasing captivity; whose pages are perused with eagerness, and in hope of new pleasure perused again' (*Lives* II.147). But then a second—and absolute—requirement is that of meaning or value: the sense that a book has given something besides pleasure, that time reading is time invested as well as spent. Perhaps this corresponds with what Johnson, in the context of his love of and delight in poetry, mentioned as reading '*solidly*' or studying ancient poets, an activity that he gauged only by its later effects (*Life* I.70). Many books give pleasure without leaving any precious residue, which in any case depends on the reader's capacity for retention. Yet no matter how imperfect the average or even the highly trained reader's recall of books, there is no lack of testimony to the way that writers such as Johnson can become a continuing part of their readers' thinking.

A third requirement (not new, but going back to the professionalization of authorship in Johnson's own day) is that the great writer must be a 'brand': that is, an identifiable, marketable commodity. The one-to-one relation of isolated writer with isolated reader, if it ever existed, has been largely subsumed in the relation of writer as producer to reader as consumer, that marketplace relationship which Johnson constantly acknowledges and with which he grapples from the very first number of the *Rambler*. Noting that periodical writers do not think it a 'deviation from modesty to recommend their own labours,' he avoids condemning their 'ostentatious and haughty display of themselves' (*Yale* III.4–5, 6). Steele and Addison met the desire for brand recognition with the personae of Mr Bickerstaff and Mr Spectator. Steele shut up shop when Mr Bickerstaff was unmasked, feeling no longer able to attack vice 'with a Freedom of Spirit that would have lost both its Beauty and Efficacy, had it been pretended to by Mr *Steele*.' Addison delineated Mr Spectator in order to satisfy the kind of reader who 'seldom peruses a Book with Pleasure 'till he knows whether the Writer of it be a black or a fair Man, of a mild or cholerick Disposition, Married or a Batchelor.'[1]

Johnson perfectly understood the modern concept of the brand (even if, as his *Dictionary* confirms, his sense of the word itself was somewhat different). In *Idler* 40, he memorably mocks advertising campaigns for 'The True Flower of Mustard' and 'Daffy's Elixir,' pointing out the gap between perceptions and truth, and between rhetoric and reality (*Yale* II.126–7). His own continuing pre-eminence as a brand owes much to Boswell, as well as something to others who wrote about him (though other writers identified as great, such as Shakespeare and Jane Austen, have become brand champions without the services of a Boswell). Johnson nevertheless achieved brand status well before anyone was keeping notes about him—but from the first there were competing versions. 'Mr Rambler' and 'Dictionary Johnson' were two very different identities, though acquired from concurrent projects.[2]

Johnson is now not merely a brand but, arguably, an icon and an institution. Like Shakespeare, Austen, or Burns, he stands in the public mind for more than an individual, emblematizing a particular environment, historical, social, and local. Icons have been marketable brands at least since the time of David Garrick's Stratford Jubilee of 1769 and the brisk sale of wood from Shakespeare's mulberry tree.[3] Garrick himself sold well during his lifetime, on fans, wineglasses, and china; Johnson was depicted on tradesman's tokens and a Wedgwood portrait profile.[4] With the Jubilee, literary tourism definitively succeeded to the earlier cultural practice of pilgrimage. Johnson's birthplace in Lichfield, Staffordshire, and his house in Gough Square (the most presentable of all his London residences), at least for some visitors, are now something close to shrines.

If the dead writer 'be[comes] his admirers,' as Auden wrote of Yeats,[5] then Johnson is now subject to the vagaries of individual appropriation and the personal taste that expresses itself in brand loyalty. Readers tend to feel a strong sense of proprietorship about him, as if each has fashioned an ideal version of this complex icon to the exclusion of the often remarkably different versions fashioned by others. The deeply personal nature of response to Johnson can be gauged from the sense of outraged ownership that can grip his readers. It is ridiculous to suppose that one can police his reputation, when it is a non-physical entity and is, by innumerable orders of magnitude, bigger than any single individual, affected every day by dozens of published and hundreds of unpublished voices. But every reader with a personal admiration for a many-sided author is subject to feelings of possessiveness—as if each wishes to protect his or her own writer from other admirers. A kind of emotional triangle subsists between Johnson, each separate individual among his readers and admirers, and the mass of his public—as can be seen from the outrage as well as mere disagreement that greeted J. C. D. Clark's account of Johnson's alleged Jacobitism, or, less recently, Donald Greene's account of his alleged radicalism.[6]

So a fourth reader requirement is that an author should somehow belong or relate to the reader personally. To the requisites of pleasure in reading, meaningful reading, and brand identity, this adds the desire to get acquainted with an author, to meet with a person, a mind, through the medium of the work. For an author to offer personal contact, mind to mind, with a reader, is not a matter of writing personally or confessionally (confessional writing, indeed, often seems fairly oblivious of its readers). Nor is it a matter of how much is known about an author outside their writings. Shakespeare and Austen each offer a sense of personal contact, mind to mind, but they achieve this rather through fictional characters and stories than through their sonnets or letters respectively. Though Johnson's writing is seldom ostensibly personal, I would argue that he makes himself personally available through his writing every bit as much as through his conversation. The man who substitutes 'patience' for 'hope' in the Christian triad 'faith, hope, love' (*The Vanity of Human Wishes*, ll.361–4; *Yale* VI.108), the man who casts himself as 'the Idler' and then goes on to produce excoriating pictures of various kinds of idleness, is putting his own character on the line. His epistolary joking with Hester Thrale—'To sit down so often with nothing to say, to say something so often, almost without consciousness of saying, and without any remembrance of having said, is a power of which I will not violate my modesty by boasting, but I do not believe that every body has it' (*Letters* III.89), where the reader could easily be wrong-footed in tracing the twists, the assumptions, and the implications of what is said—does indeed unite

souls, not by the kind of innate sympathy that Johnson mocks in this passage, but by the reader's capacity to follow the writer through the twists
and turns of his thought.

So Johnson is pre-eminent in these four qualities: in giving pleasure, in
offering important meaning, in his power as an icon, and in the sense of
his presence—the accessibility of the mind that Hester Piozzi called
'indeed expanded beyond the common limits of human nature' (*Shaw-
Piozzi* 160). To feel one has been made familiarly free to roam in such a
mind (and Piozzi moves on from this phrase to her image of Johnson's
mind as a richly explorable 'royal pleasure-ground,' *Shaw-Piozzi* 160) is
perhaps the greatest source of exhilaration in reading Johnson. Thus the
fourth reader desideratum circles round like the snake of eternity to con-
nect with the first, which was pleasure. These four desiderata converge on
the idea of a personal relationship. In the 'Life of Milton' Johnson figures
demanding books as teachers and easier books as youthful companions
(*Lives* I.290), but these two contrasted categories of person are alike in
ranking often among an individual's most influential relationships. The
memory of learning is as pleasurable as the memory of companionship.

Each of these aspects of Johnson is colored by his contrarieties. The
pleasure of reading him is the pleasure of tracking his thought sentence by
sentence, paragraph by paragraph through twists and turns and victories
over internal opposition. Johnson seldom offers a word without hard
thinking behind it that unfolds, expands, changes shape in the reader's
mind; he seldom offers a sentence or a paragraph or a whole essay whose
direction can be foreseen. Objections raised en route sometimes redirect
the entire argument. The effort one puts into reading him makes it, ex-
hilaratingly, a collaborative enterprise.

For instance, in *The Vanity of Human Wishes*, the famous couplet 'He
left the name, at which the world grew pale,/To point a moral, or adorn a
tale' sounds, at first hearing, simple, predictable, with the air of recounting something that is just as it ought to be (ll.221–2; *Yale* VI.102). Only
slowly does the punch register. When Charles XII passes from frightening
the world to pointing a moral, that is no easy or regular transition but a
sudden shock, a bathetic reversal. Part of the pleasure of reading Johnson
is, as here, his power to throw the reader off-balance, to produce mental
realignments. The fictional correspondent Florentulus in *Rambler* 109
imagines the grave and sympathetic Mr Rambler 'snuffing his candle,
rubbing his spectacles, stirring his fire, locking out interruption, and set-
tling himself in his easy chair,' gleefully to *enjoy* a new species of human
misery (*Yale* IV.215). This enforced re-evaluation of the author whom one
is reading as a moralist delivers a moral shock. Johnson gives pleasure by
provoking (unsettling) laughter, not excluding laughter at himself. So one

can identify aspects of this pleasure by fastening onto small details, a couplet or a sentence, but the pleasure itself springs from keeping pace with the questing, the surging forward, the doubling back, with which Johnson's mind moves in its pursuit of complex and sometimes inconsistent truth. As Imlac says, 'Inconsistencies...cannot both be right, but, imputed to man, they may both be true' (*Yale* XVI.330).

The mental realignments induced by following Johnson's thought meet the reader requirement of meaning as well as the requirement of pleasure. His meaning resides less in the oft-cited aphorisms than in the process that produces them, the way that aphorism-worthy truths emerge from a specific situation or argument.[7] They lead the reader through mental struggle to a moment of equilibrium. In *Rambler* 33, one woman tells another who is in despair over her ruined beauty to consider herself 'as a being born to know, to reason, and to act' (*Yale* IV.345). This now much-quoted aphorism has a particular argumentative force in its original fictional context, where it is a new proposition, sweeping away the concerns of the story so far. In *Rambler* 161, Johnson's history of a room in a lodging-house concludes with two sisters: one dying, the other caring for her. At the end, the survivor 'wiped away the tears of useless sorrow, and return[ed] to the business of common life' (*Yale* V.94). This pronouncement, not exactly an aphorism, realigns the implications of the anecdote, and might seem at odds with Johnson's usual opinion, in seeing death not as part of common life, but as set against it.

The discursive as well as the fictional essays make the reader work to extract their meaning. *Rambler* 58, for instance, about the moral commonplace that money is the root of all evil, begins by suggesting that preachers against wealth might not, given the chance, be averse to amassing some of it. The essay then confronts the fact that, after centuries of moralizing against it, the love of money is not a jot the weaker. But perhaps, says Johnson, the moralizers are not quite useless: while failing to make a dent in acquisitiveness, they may have provided some comfort for the great majority whose experience of money is the lack of it. Having thus challenged the whole project of moralizing about money, he finally introduces some fairly stock ideas (*Yale* III.309–13). This essay, like many *Ramblers*, shifts the terms of its own debate. Johnson seems to suggest that we already know how we ought to behave around money; what we do not know is how best to use our moral knowledge. He forces readers to track not only his meaning but also his process of searching out meaning.

So demands for enjoyment and for meaning, pleasure and instruction, the old familiar *dulce et utile*, blend together. Modern readers may seek these things from old and new texts, whether such texts are circulated in tweets and consumer reviews or through syllabuses and reading lists. But the reader's power of choice over the new is not matched by choice among the canonical (into which category, irrevocably, Johnson has passed). Despite the jeremiads of some, the canon is still being widely taught, and the majority of those who read Johnson do so for the first time under compulsion. Like every one of his contemporaries, he has readers-by-duty and runs the risk of being like his own Milton, a master or teacher to readers who would prefer an equal.[8]

A reader may be drawn to a known name yet at the same time repelled by its canonical authority. The status of the generic dead white male (literary) stands lower than ever today—though before now, as Great Writer, it carried high market value. 'Dr Johnson' is often seen as bugbear (dictionary-maker, moralist, therefore by implication pedant and fault-finder). This kind of label promises not so much pleasure, interaction, and discovery, as institutionalized tedium. Yet most of those who read Johnson remember him, and even entertain a personal devotion to him, having encountered him first as a task.

Johnson, I believe, differs from his syllabus peers Pope, Swift, Henry Fielding, or Richardson in that his role as teacher often turns out, after the first introduction, to be an attraction rather than a barrier. Our personal relationship with him is no less personal for being that of mentor and disciple. Readers are drawn to his seriousness, which is inextricably blended with the pleasure of reading him. The blend is seldom comfortable and can be very uncomfortable, as in his 1757 review of Soame Jenyns for *The Literary Magazine*, whose readers may feel that to take pleasure in such anger as Johnson reveals is hardly justifiable. Here the paradoxes begin from the first sentence, where Johnson asserts that Jenyns cannot dispel the perplexity indissolubly linked with his subject (that of a just and loving creator of a creation full of evil and cruelty): 'This is a treatise consisting of six letters upon a very difficult and important question, which I am afraid this author's endeavours will not free from the perplexity, which has intangled the speculatists of all ages, and which must always continue while *we see* but *in part*' (*Yale* XVII.397). The phrasing alludes to St. Paul's First Epistle to the Corinthians, to verses that form part of the well-known passage on charity, or love. 'For we know in part.... For now we see through a glass, darkly; but then face to face: now I know in part; but then shall I know even as also I am known' (13:9, 12). The whole passage (often read at weddings and funerals) is normally felt to be joyful or comforting; yet in his review Johnson makes it the gateway to deeply disturbing thoughts. He does nothing to dissipate Jenyns's, and humanity's, perplexity in the face of evil, and from the idea of being seen and known by a superior being he generates not comfort but dread.

Typically, Johnson's review of Jenyns does not dissolve the moral problem that has been posed, but leaves it intact and threatening even after lessons have been drawn from it. Even when Johnson himself offers a moral lesson, he does so after a gradual approach to it which produces an experience of discovery rather than instruction, and which can even produce anxiety and bewilderment preceding resolution. His teachings are remembered more for his presenting of problems (love of procrastination, unwillingness to scrutinize one's own heart, the malign power of habit) than for his presenting of solutions.

These aspects of his seriousness, or what we might term 'teacherliness' (a word not in the *OED*) deeply involve his own humanity, and thus imply a personal involvement, inviting too a personal response. Indeed, the varying personal responses among readers of Johnson throw light on his own variousness. Often quoted on title pages and in chapter headings, he has also stood godfather to a remarkable tally of diaries and personal confidences composed by people drawn precisely to his variousness and personal openness. He is, for such a strongly marked personality, extraordinarily open (more than Swift, more than Richardson) for readers to relate themselves to him, if not actually to reshape him in their own image. He has lent himself alternately to feminism and to sexism, to British nationalism and to internationalism, to Toryism and to radicalism. This seems to be a strange outcome for an author of such fierce opinions and personal force, and its causes invite exploration.

In 1785, the year after Johnson's death, the conservative Anglican educationalist Sarah Trimmer was so deeply affected by his prayers and meditations that she at once adopted them as pattern for a spiritual journal of her own (a choice that her early nineteenth-century editor felt some need to defend).[9] In the next generation Mary Ann Kelty, an evangelical religious seeker and an admirer of the Society of Friends, set out by titling her first novel *The Favourite of Nature* (1821) from *Rambler* 160 (which says that the power of arousing friendship is 'a felicity granted only to the favourites of nature,' *Yale* V.88). She ended her career in 1866 with the last of several variously titled diary volumes which she opens by invoking Johnson, 'our great moralist,' to justify both her writing and publishing. Both her early, pious bluestocking heroine and her aged self are called to the bar of Johnson's judgment, in confidence that he will judge sternly, but not according to rigid codes.[10]

This kind of spiritual response to Johnson is still vigorous, expressed not only in scholarly books about his religion but in contexts of personal self-scrutiny. In the mid and the late twentieth century two novelists successively turned to him in diaries kept to confront old age and loss of productivity. Then approaching ninety, the Irish novelist Edith Somerville (best known for highly un-Johnsonian comedy, even slapstick, and for yet more un-Johnsonian spiritualist beliefs) closed a year's record in her unpublished diary with a rewritten couplet from *The Vanity of Human Wishes*: 'Superfluous lags the Veteran on the stage/in vain defiance of relentless age.'[11] Approaching eighty, the crime novelist P. D. James (known for the literary and philosophic inclinations of her detective-hero Adam Dalgleish) took from Johnson a title, *Time to Be in Earnest*.[12] For these varied individuals, his writings represent strength and seriousness in the face of human mortality.

Hugo Dyson, fellow of Merton College, Oxford (and member of the Inklings), used to tell his students how he feared what might have happened if he could have met Johnson face to face. Johnson, he suspected, might have dismissed him as a lightweight, a gadfly, or jester rather than a constructive thinker. He never wondered, he said, what other canonical authors would think of him, only Johnson.[13] In this equally personal response Johnson's *gravitas* and his mentoring role make him not a guide through darkness but a potentially severe judge.

Another group of Johnson's readers found in him not earnestness but iconoclasm. Among the radicals of the 1790s, Mary Wollstonecraft turned to him (as she might have turned to Mary Astell if she had known her writings as closely) for his appreciation that the life of the mind belongs to both sexes.[14] Wollstonecraft invoked Johnson in personal distress or difficulty, but she also incorporated him into her thinking and writing. She anthologized him in *The Female Reader* (1789), reprinting the pair of essays that end with the lesson about knowing, reasoning, and acting. She echoes that lesson in closing her introduction to this anthology ('As we are created accountable creatures we must run the race ourselves'),[15] and again and again throughout her writings.

Other gender radicals, too, enlisted Johnson both as friend or personal counselor and as political ally. Mary Hays quotes him on the title page of her *Appeal to the Men of Great Britain in Behalf of Women*, begun in the early 1790s but not published until 1798. 'Let it be remembered, that the efficacy of ignorance has been long tried, and has not produced the consequences expected. Let knowledge therefore take its turn, and let the patrons of privation stand awhile aside, and admit the operation of positive principles.' (Johnson was writing of Gaelic speakers, not of women; it is Hays who implicitly parallels these as two deprived groups.)[16] Eliza Fenwick, too, frequently suggests Johnson in her radical novel *Secresy* (1795), most often in the words of her rational feminist heroine, Caroline Ashburn, but also in those of the quintessentially romantic secondary heroine, Sibella Valmont, who strongly asserts her right to think and reason. For these proto-feminists Johnson offered the kind of approach to women that stems, for a man, from 'an act of the imagination' which places us for a time in someone else's condition (*Yale* III.318). Inés Joyes y Blake, the first Spanish translator of *Rasselas*, published her *El principe de Abisinia* (1798) between the same covers as a Wollstonecraftian treatise in defense of women, as if she saw a natural concatenation between these two responses to recent texts in English—a concatenation no longer surprising since James Basker and others have investigated Johnson as an Enlightenment patron of radical women.[17]

In the generations immediately following Johnson, it was obvious to those of his readers who thought about these things that he was a champion of women: not of their abstract equality, let alone liberty, or any agenda for improving their status, but of them as beings born or created to think and act for themselves, enmeshed in the same web of responsibilities, obligations, and likelihood of failure as men. This made him useful to women pronouncing on moral issues in public, or approaching mainstream politics from a humanitarian angle. Elizabeth Heyrick, who addressed herself not to gender issues but to those of race and class, the penal code, and especially abolition of slavery, turned to Johnson as a reformist leader precisely for these issues. After quoting him in a Trimmer-like context (on the title page of an early educational work), she went on to quote Johnson in highly controversial texts. In *Observations on the Offensive and Injurious Effect of Corporal Punishment* (1827), for instance (a trenchant polemic that reaches beyond its immediate subject into discussing the social causes of crime, the way that the penal system actually increases crime, the effects of specific pieces of legislation, and the terrible state of Ireland), 'our great moralist Johnson' helps Heyrick to speak truth to power.[18] She associates Johnson with the pioneering reformers John Howard and Elizabeth Fry.

So from the 1790s well into the nineteenth century, Johnson's name promised powerful support for moral challengers of the status quo. Those moved by acts of the imagination to campaign for various oppressed groups claimed him as an authority whose general moral propositions supported their public platforms for change. This Johnson is glaringly, obviously different from the iconic Johnson who emerged during the Victorian period, created by writers like Hazlitt (Johnson reverenced authority and offered no new thoughts) and Thomas Babington Macaulay (Johnson's understanding was 'strong but enslaved').[19] In this case it is not so much that the pendulum swung as that contradictory views of Johnson lay side by side without mixing.

It is telling that Macaulay (writing of the *Rambler*) found Johnson generally sound 'on the education of children, on marriage, on the economy of families, on the rules of society'[20]—as if he ranked the domestic Johnson as more sane and acceptable than the political Johnson. Macaulay seems prepared to admire Johnson's writing on those topics about which he himself had no desire to write. He rejects Johnson the master or model, but has less trouble with Johnson the traveler on a different road from his own.

Thomas Carlyle, though not a detractor of Johnson but an adulator, put forward a version yet more at odds with those of the 1790s radicals. Carlyle presents Johnson as icon: one of a 'sacred band' of almost super-human Fathers or Great Men. 'They are the chosen of the world: they had this rare faculty not only of "supposing" and "inclining to think," but of knowing and believing.' 'Aloft, conspicuous, on his enduring basis, he stands there, serene, unaltering.'[21] In *On Heroes* he goes further, arguing the highly un-Johnsonian idea that the Great Man is no quirky individual but 'ever the same kind of thing: Odin, Luther, Johnson, Burns...these are all originally of one stuff.'[22] The ordinary person, Carlyle claims, willingly prostrates himself or herself before greatness, feels all the better and wiser for such prostration. This in no way describes the responses of the Johnson disciples mentioned above, who saw him not as infallible superman but as a fellow enquirer or a comrade in arms against oppression and injustice.

Of all the varying Johnsons considered here, Carlyle's monolithic version is least reconcilable with the views put forward in this volume, but it has cast a long shadow over the progress of Johnson's reputation. It sends one back to the experience of reading Johnson the moralist. *Rambler* 58 on the love of money, for instance, moves towards moral propositions expressed without uncertainty or qualification: does this exemplify Carlyle's 'knowing' rather than 'inclining to think'? Johnson holds back to the end his assertion of what money cannot do, preceding it with suggestions about the inadequacy of moralists and their project. Rather than standing serene and unaltering on an enduring basis, he stands in tension, poised between opposing forces, and with explicit recognition of the weakness of his own position.

Carlyle's picture may have been affected by historical context, filling a need on the academic or theoretical side to correspond with the tavern sage, the clubbable, intensely English dogmatizer, the Tory bulwark, of Johnson the popular Victorian icon. That public Johnson, too, was perhaps shaped by his admirers' need to find him not like themselves but different: higher, greater, more masculine and more patriarchal. The pendulum has swung since then towards a version of Johnson that Howard Weinbrot has anatomized, as shaken almost to breaking point by psychological weakness and contradictions—and Weinbrot himself has, in this volume, helped to swing the pendulum back again.[23]

With all the variety of historical and personal Johnsons, any attempt to appropriate him has to reckon with his contradictoriness. Johnson as guide in spiritual darkness, as social reformer, as pedestaled hero, can prove salutary only in full understanding of his variety or contrarieties. While I cannot see him as 'the same kind of thing' as Luther or Burns or (God save the mark!) Odin, I see him as possessing a perhaps surprising affinity with writers known as the opposite of serene or unfaltering: with Blake ('Without Contraries is no progression. Attraction and Repulsion, Reason and Energy, Love and Hate, are necessary to Human existence') and Whitman ('Do I contradict myself?/Very well then...I contradict myself;/I am large...I contain multitudes').[24]

Mercifully, Carlyle's brand of oracular pronouncement is now un-fashionable. Critics and teachers of literature today are rightly loth to narrow down so complex and contradictory a presence as Johnson. They are happy to see opinions about him differ, even opposing positions being fortified. Johnson is available to all his readers, according to their intelligence and imagination. His admirers of every stripe are primed to rush into the lists to combat perverse or mistaken images of him, while believing that their own image is complex and embracing. But nobody is disinterested; no one can claim impartiality or objectivity; one can only hope to shape one's personal relationship with Johnson through abandoning critical or social ideology, and individual prejudices or preconceptions.

Johnson's continuing street currency in journalism and in popular cul-ture is almost entirely filtered through Boswell: 'When a man is tired of London he is tired of life' (*Life* III.178); 'Patriotism is the last refuge of a scoundrel' (*Life* II.348); and so on. These spoken words, while they share the punchiness of Johnson's writings, naturally cannot share the unset-tling structure, the back-and-forth arguments, or the gradual, paradoxical effects of those. The popular Johnson is shadowed by ignorance—when journalists mention concentrating the mind through the prospect of being hanged (*Life* III.167), how many allude to the complex equivoca-tion surrounding those words as they were originally spoken?

Nevertheless this street currency—robust if not exact—represents the liveliest immortality that Johnson enjoys. The fame of Johnson the man of maxims needs no help from those who like to read him. But his readers (who owe him a debt of gratitude for pleasure enjoyed, for a sense of meaning in the maze of life, and for the sense of connection with which he honors them) need to keep reading him: honestly, carefully, through thickets and rough places in his always effortful and often paradoxical thinking.

NOTES

1. *Tatler* 271 (1711), in Donald F. Bond, ed., *The Tatler*, 3 vols. (Oxford: Clarendon Press, 1987), III.363; *Spectator* 1 (1711), in Donald F. Bond, ed., *The Spectator*, 5 vols. (Oxford: Clarendon Press, 1965), I.1.
2. 'Mr Rambler' was first used by the journal's fictional correspondents; 'Dictionary Johnson' was, Boswell says, in general use by 1763 (*Life* I.384–5).
3. Three books appeared in 1964 on the Jubilee: Christian Deelman, *The Great Shakespeare Jubilee* (London: Michael Joseph); Johanne Magdalene Stochholm, *Garrick's Folly; The Shakespeare Jubilee of 1769 at Stratford and Drury Lane* (London: Methuen); Martha Winburn England, *Garrick's Jubilee* (Columbus: Ohio State University Press).
4. John Overholt and Thomas A. Horrocks, *A Monument More Durable Than Brass, The Donald & Mary Hyde Collection of Dr. Samuel Johnson: An Exhibition* (Houghton Library: Harvard University, 2009), 118–19.
5. W. H. Auden, 'In Memory of W. B. Yeats,' in *Collected Shorter Poems 1927–1957* (London: Faber and Faber, 1966), 141.
6. See Donald Greene, *The Politics of Samuel Johnson*, 2nd edn (Athens, GA, and London: University of Georgia Press, 1990).
7. See Isobel Grundy, 'Johnson: Man of Maxims?' in Isobel Grundy, ed., *Samuel Johnson: New Critical Essays* (London: Vision; Totowa, NJ: Barnes & Noble, 1984), 13–30.
8. On the 'duty' of reading Milton, see *Lives* I.290.
9. Trimmer, Sarah, *Some Account of the Life and Writings of Mrs Trimmer, with Original Letters, and Meditations and Prayers, Selected from Her Journal* (London: F. C. and J. Rivington, J. Johnson, and J. Hatchard, 1814), I.75.
10. Mary Ann Kelty, *Loneliness and Leisure: A Record of the Thoughts and Feelings of Advanced Life* (London: Hamilton, Adams, 1866), 3.
11. Maurice Collis, *Somerville and Ross: A Biography* (London: Faber and Faber, 1968), 271. Collis does not recognize the allusion: 'New forms arise, and diff'rent views engage,/Superfluous lags the vet'ran on the stage,/Till pitying Nature signs the last release' (*The Vanity of Human Wishes*, ll.307–9, *Yale* VI.106).
12. P. D. James, *Time to Be in Earnest: A Fragment of Autobiography* (London: Faber and Faber, 1999).
13. Personal knowledge.
14. James Basker, 'Radical Affinities: Mary Wollstonecraft and Samuel Johnson,' in Alvaro Ribeiro and James G. Basker, eds., *Tradition in Transition: Women Writers, Marginal Texts, and the Eighteenth-Century Canon* (Oxford: Clarendon, 1996), 41–55.
15. Mary Wollstonecraft [as Mr Cresswick, Teacher of Elocution], ed., *The Female Reader, or Miscellaneous Pieces in Prose and Verse, selected from the best writers and disposed under proper heads, for the improvement of young women* (London: Joseph Johnson, 1789), xv.

16. Quoting letter from Johnson to William Drummond, 13 August 1766 (*Letters* I.271). Boswell included the letter in *Life* II.29–30. Hays must on this evidence have been an early reader.

17. Basker, 'Radical Affinities,' 41–55.

18. Elizabeth Heyrick, *Observations on the Offensive and Injurious Effect of Corporal Punishment* (London: Hatchard and Son; Hurst, Chance, 1827), 21.

19. James T. Boulton ed., *Samuel Johnson: The Critical Heritage* (London: Routledge, 1971), 86–7, 89, 424.

20. Ibid., 426.

21. Ibid., 433.

22. Thomas Carlyle, *Works of Thomas Carlyle* (*Centenary Edition*), 30 vols. (London: Chapman and Hall, 1896–9), V: *On Heroes, Hero-Worship and the Heroic in History* (1897), 43.

23. See Chapter 16.

24. 'The Marriage of Heaven and Hell' (1790–93), Plate 3, in *The Complete Writings of William Blake. With Variant Readings*, ed. Geoffrey Keynes (London, New York, and Toronto: Oxford University Press, 1966), 149; *Walt Whitman's Leaves of Grass: The First (1855) Edition*, ed. Malcolm Coelwy (New York: Penguin, 2005), 62 (ellipses in original text).

# 15

# Johnson and the Warton Brothers

## David Fairer

The story of Johnson's relations over more than three decades with the 'learned brothers,' Joseph and Thomas Warton, has been told as one of intimate friendship, followed by growing strains, and final rupture.[1] But, as any biographer knows, tracing a satisfying narrative shape from scattered evidence can mean tidying up things that are mixed and ambiguous. It is clear that the appearance of Johnson's *Lives of the Poets* (1779–81) was a crucial juncture when the Wartons took offence at their friend's rough handling of Collins, Gray, and the youthful Milton, and determined to rebut his views.[2] But this only exposed publicly a critical divide that had long been evident, while Thomas's election to The Club in 1782 hardly suggests a permanent breakdown had occurred. From the 1750s onwards there are expressions of warmth and intimacy, but also hints of uneasiness and suspicion; there are amicable encounters, compliments, and gestures of assistance and encouragement; critical tensions bubble up to the surface, unkind things are said, and yet probably the mix of genial conversation, amusement, disagreement, raillery, and gossip went on much as before.

Rather than attempt to retrace a biographical narrative, this chapter will find its focus in elements of mutual stimulus and fruitful provocation, both critical and creative. The Warton brothers never considered themselves part of the Johnsonian 'circle'—far from it—and it is this uneasy distance that makes their interactions revealing. Placing Johnson in Wartonian contexts, and vice versa, helps to highlight contrasting aspects of the man and his work. There is friction and resistance, but also geniality and laughter. Within this force field Johnson is less a figure of entrenched opposition than an alert, even playful mind aware of ironies and nuances. As poets and critics of poetry, Johnson and the Wartons struck off each other. The two brothers represented an amicable critical opposition that Johnson enjoyed baiting, parodying, and shocking; while the Wartons found in Johnson a figure of stubborn resistance who helped them articulate their poetic enthusiasms.

For the Wartons to sit in a circle with Johnson could be an uncomfortable experience. There is an eloquent image of this in the painting by James Doyle, *A Literary Party at Sir Joshua Reynolds's* (1848), which became a popular engraving (fig. 15.1).[3] It shows the Doctor holding court and expressing with emphasis some opinion or principle. Far left, seated behind the great man, Boswell looks on, observing, as we do, the whole scene. Around the table from Johnson, Reynolds's ear trumpet is catching every syllable, while poor Garrick's eyes appear to be glazing over; but Burke, General Paoli, and Dr Burney are all attention. The scene is focused on the great man and what he is saying. Until, that is, we glance to the other end of the table, where we find Thomas Warton turning round to Goldsmith and making a whispered remark behind his hand. The disturbance is also an aesthetic one, with the Wartonian presence transforming what is otherwise a static formal group into a more fluid, interesting, and lively 'conversation piece.' Somehow our eye is always being drawn to Warton, and we long to know not only what Johnson is saying but what Tom is, most impolitely, interjecting.

A scene that may have been in the painter's mind is the one recalled by Joseph Warton's biographer, John Wooll, who describes an incident at

**Fig. 15.1.** William Walker (engraver), after James E. Doyle, *A Literary Party at Sir Joshua Reynolds's*, 1848. Courtesy of The Lewis Walpole Library, Yale University.

Reynolds's house when the following sharp exchange was overheard between Johnson and Joseph: '*Johnson*. "Sir, I am not used to be contradicted." *Warton*. "Better for yourself and friends, Sir, if you were; our
admiration could not be encreased, but our love might."' 'The party inter-
fered,' continues Wooll, 'and the conversation was stopped.'[4] Wooll suggests, and others have followed him, that the altercation marked a turning
point in the two men's relations, and a 'coolness' set in. Coolness, however, was not in Joseph Warton's repertoire. In Wooll's account the riposte
has hardened into a 'dispute,' but the dialogue as recorded is a more nuanced one. After all, Joseph includes himself as one of the 'friends' whose
admiration is not in doubt: 'our admiration *could not* be encreased, but
our love *might*.' He is urging Johnson towards friendship and love. The
terms of Joseph's response are not to contradict, but to mollify, to soften
him into a more congenial friend. The clash has this ironic aspect: it is
Johnson's words that sound like an ultimatum ('Sir, I am not used to be
contradicted'), whereas Joseph's are conditional, leaving room for concili-
ation, opening up possibilities ('*if* you *were*,' 'our love *might*,' my
emphases).

The exchange does have the ring of truth, and his friend's assuasive
language has a critical implication that Johnson well understood. In the
'Life of Pope' he characterizes Joseph Warton's *Essay on the Writings and
Genius of Pope* (1756) as 'a book which teaches how the brow of Criticism
may be smoothed, and how she may be enabled, with all her severity, to
attract and to delight' (*Lives* IV.72). Johnson's words are carefully chosen,
and have been taken as complimentary; but coming from him they have
an extra kick. His use of the word 'teaches' acknowledges Joseph's reputation as a genial schoolmaster (and it has to be said, a lax disciplinarian);
but the image that follows, though couched in positive terms, hints at
satiric incongruity with its picture of the 'severe' goddess of Criticism
striving 'to attract and to delight.' We suspect some enhancement, a hint
of the dressing table, in the phrase 'the brow of Criticism may be
smoothed.' There is amusement at the way the lady's natural 'severity' is
being compromised by alluring arts, in a cosmetic desire to please.

Johnson may have liked 'smooth' versification, but he knew the difference between smoothness and strength: Waller, for him, is 'rather smooth
than strong' (*Lives* II.54), and he was as suspicious of botox criticism as
he was of smoothing out life. Imlac, we recall, says to Rasselas: 'The world,
which you figure to yourself smooth and quiet as the lake in the valley,
you will find a sea foaming with tempests, and boiling with whirlpools'
(*Yale* XVI.56). At the heart of criticism, for Johnson, is a degree of con-
*front*ation (standing forehead to furrowed forehead), which is a function
of critical responsibility, applying pressure to test worth. Glancing back at

the incident at Reynolds's house, it is clear that years previously Mr Rambler himself had described a critical confrontation of a similar kind. There he made it quite clear whose side he was on:

> The critick's purpose is to conquer, the author only hopes to escape; the critick therefore knits his brow, and raises his voice, and rejoices whenever he perceives any tokens of pain excited by the pressure of his assertions, or the point of his sarcasms. The author, whose endeavour is at once to mollify and elude his persecutor, composes his features, and softens his accent, breaks the force of assault by retreat, and rather steps aside than flies or advances. (*Rambler* 176; *Yale* V.165)

The critic 'knits his brow': there's no smoothing here. What is being choreographed in this little scene is what can be thought of as the Wartonian sidestep, the ability to turn aside, which here for Johnson is a token of softness. Annoyingly, thanks to the deft arts of politeness, the critic's knife sinks into folds of elegant drapery. There is a hint of frustration behind Johnson's gleeful provocation. Rather than his opponent squaring up to him and the pendulum of argument swinging between them, there is the turn, the softening of accent, the eluding of the 'point' (which in Johnson is intended to be a sharp one). We are back for a moment with the Wartonian 'turn' pictured in Doyle's conversation piece, aware of how a gesture of disengagement can be satiric, too.

A similar maneuver is evident in the Wartons' public reaction to Johnsonian severity. In them, what might appear critically evasive or indecisive is recast as a capacity for moving on and taking a fresh view, finding a different angle on the scene (the hint of picturesque response is appropriate here).[5] Their indignation is channeled into innocent enthusiasm, and their tactical sidestep becomes a strategic widening of readerly sympathies. The most striking instance of this is Thomas's reaction to Johnson's harsh judgment on Milton's *Lycidas* (1638), which took the form of a two-page reply in his scholarly edition of the early poems (1785). Warton found the attack personally hurtful, given the degree to which his own poetry had drawn inspiration from the youthful Milton, and Johnson's memorable dismissal of the elegy still has outrageous force: 'It is not to be considered as the effusion of real passion.... Passion plucks no berries from the myrtle and ivy, nor calls upon Arethuse and Mincius.... Its form is that of a pastoral, easy, vulgar, and therefore disgusting' (*Lives* I.278–9). After quoting directly the terms of Johnson's criticism, Thomas acknowledges and accepts them, only to turn them aside and make his appeal elsewhere:

> It is objected, that its pastoral form is disgusting. But this was the age of pastoral; and yet *Lycidas* has but little of the bucolic cant, now so fashionable.

The Satyrs and Fauns are but just mentioned. If any trite rural topics occur, how are they heightened!

> Together both, ere the high lawns appear'd
> Under the opening eye-lids of the morn,
> We drove afield, and both together heard
> What time the gray-fly winds her sultry horn,
> Batt'ning our flocks with the fresh dews of night.

Here the day-break is described by the faint appearance of the upland lawns under the first gleams of light: the sunset, by the buzzing of the chaffer, and the night sheds her *fresh dews* on their flocks. We cannot blame pastoral imagery, and pastoral allegory, which carry with them so much natural painting. In this piece there is perhaps more poetry than sorrow. But let us read it for its poetry. It is true, that passion plucks no berries from the myrtle and ivy, nor calls upon Arethuse and Mincius.... But poetry does this; and in the hands of Milton, does it with a peculiar and irresistible charm.[6]

Warton deflects Johnson's statements rather than rebuts them; he concedes 'truth' and turns away. To use the *Rambler's* terms, he eludes his persecutor, softens his accent, and 'rather steps aside than flies or advances.' Thomas's repeated *but*s work not to make an objection or enter a caveat, but to open out another perspective on the poem. '*But* me no *buts*,' we can almost hear Johnson protest. But here it is the Wartonian critic who is making an appeal to the common reader and to our own experience of the lines. That is what lies behind his turn toward us: 'let us read it.'

Of the two brothers, it was Joseph who specialized in the enthusiastic appeal to shared experience; he was after all the author of *The Enthusiast: Or, The Lover of Nature* (1744) ('an enthusiast by rule,' Johnson called him, *Life* IV.33). It was evidently something that Johnson found hilariously funny. His friend's legendary warmth was a character trait that Johnson enjoyed imitating. Frances Burney gives an account of how he '[a]t times, when in gay spirits...would take off Dr Warton with the strongest humour; describing, almost convulsively, the ecstasy with which he would seize upon the person nearest to him, to hug in his arms, lest his grasp should be eluded, while he displayed some picture, or some prospect' (*Life* II.41).

His brother Thomas, displaying the prospect of *Lycidas*, is practicing a kind of restrained version of this 'turn' of delight, and it is Johnson who has stimulated the response. It is as if Johnson's grudging coolness has to be countered, and the imaginative sympathy he refuses supplied in fuller measure.

There is creative antagonism here for both sides, something that must have been a regular feature of encounters between Johnson and the Wartons over the years. William Hayley, in dedicating his *Life of Milton* (1796) to Joseph (a critical gesture in itself), reminds him of the Johnsonian provocations he used to experience, and no doubt had often recounted to sympathetic friends. Hayley tells him:

> You, my dear friend, have heard the harsh critic advance in conversation an opinion against Milton, even more severe than the many detractive sarcasms with which his life of the great poet abounds; you have heard him declaim against the admiration excited by the poetry of Milton, and affirm it to be nothing more than the cant (to use his own favourite phrase) of affected sensibility.[7]

In contrasting the 'dear friend' with the 'harsh critic,' Hayley uses the Rambler's opposing terms, but to very different ends. 'You have heard him,' Hayley says, recalling the Wartonian audience before whom Johnson could sharpen his points and toy with the predictable responses of admiration. It has always been recognized that Johnson's rough handling of Shakespeare, Milton, and Gray is aimed at their enthusiasts. Indeed his critical strategy at certain points in the *Lives* has this covert dramatic quality, and some of the phrases honed for the *Lives* may have had their first try-out when Joseph and Thomas Warton were listening. Johnson's critical tactic of consciously withholding the expected imaginative sympathy, refusing the concession to taste, or the generous appeal to history, is that of someone who knows those responses intimately, and finds them too easy. He seems at times to be playing his own affective game, holding to the steady composure of his judgments while he senses the sharp intakes of breath from his surrounding friends. We can almost hear them punctuating his prose: '[Gray's] odes are marked by glittering accumulations of ungraceful ornaments; they strike, rather than please; the images are magnified by affectation; the language is laboured into harshness. The mind of the writer seems to work with unnatural violence. *Double, double, toil and trouble*. He has a kind of strutting dignity, and is tall by walking on tiptoe' (*Lives* IV.183).

These bullet-point judgments gave Joseph Warton the impetus to react in just the way Johnson might have predicted: he would expect nothing less of his rapturous friend. It is as if Johnson has thoughtfully supplied the cold, worldly, blocking figure that the sentimental text often exploits in order to heighten by contrast the flow of feeling. Johnson is playing his part in the sentimental scenario. Once again he stands in the way, and so the Wartonian critic is forced to turn and find his own imaginative ground. When he revised his *Essay on Pope* the year after the 'Life of Gray' appeared, Joseph rallied to the defense of 'The Bard' (1757), the ode whose climactic final couplet he had criticized in his first edition for being too cold and precise ('He spoke, and headlong from the mountain's height/Deep in the roaring tide he plung'd to endless night'). Now in 1782 Joseph announces that he has altered his earlier opinion (an interesting Wartonian turn), and in a two-page note added for the revised edition he warms to his task:

> Imagine then that you see this wretched old man, starting up suddenly on the top of a rocky eminence, in full view of the English army; wild with despair, and animated with the thoughts of vengeance: with haggard eyes; his beard loose; and his hoary hair streaming like a meteor in a dark and troubled sky... after soothing his despair by a survey of happier times and more merciful princes, [he] throws himself from the rock, with a kind of sullen satisfaction, into the flood below.

Thanks to this ending, Joseph now concludes, 'the horrors of the poem... affect the imagination of the reader, more deeply and more irresistibly.'[8] Johnson's seemingly cold common sense, his detecting of Gray's false elevation and heavy breathing, has brought the enthusiast out of Joseph, who proceeds in his own irresistible way to swamp judgment with feeling and stir up the reader's emotions. Johnson is not answered so much as swept aside. As Joseph evokes the poem's climax, Gray's phrases merge into his own, and the critic brings the scene imaginatively to life with the *gusto* of a poet-painter (we can detect the Wartons' influence on Hazlitt here).

Contemporaries of Johnson and the Wartons appreciated that between them the men marked out a gap between critical judgment and aesthetic response, across which an unresolvable argument might swing. The picture specifically of Johnson and Joseph as critical antagonists was encouraged by the publication of Robert Potter's *A Dream* in 1789, a vision in which the two men argue head to head. By that date their opposition had become representative of a broader clash of ideas.[9] Potter has been reading both Joseph's *Essay* and Johnson's *Lives*, when he falls asleep. The dream's dialogue opens cordially enough, with Joseph congratulating his fellow critic on the publication of the *Lives*; but things soon deteriorate:

> *Warton.* And yet, like other doctors, we differ. You want taste, Sir.
> *Johnson.* Sir, you want sense.
> *Warton.* Pardon me, Sir, I did not mean to offend you: indeed you have too much sense;—I mean too little fancy, and no sublimity of imagination.[10]

'Taste' and 'sense' are batted between them in this duel of critical positions. But as Johnson rushes to the net with his capping reply, Warton draws back, turning the argument by a gracious apology and concession that at once modulate into a wider, all-embracing accusation. In this dramatized exchange it is tempting to see only binaries: sensibility versus reason, aesthetics versus judgment, subjective versus objective, taste versus sense. But the closer picture, as always, is more complicated. The Wartonian approach comes across not as a refutation of Johnson, but an outflanking move that shifts the emphasis from direct judgment to a more fluid responsiveness, from critical opposition to imaginative engagement.

If Johnson supposedly had 'too little fancy,' the Wartons repeatedly exploited its workings in ways that opened up aesthetic effect and emotional affect as essential impulses behind poetry and criticism. In doing so, they drew criticism itself into the ambit of the poetic. In Joseph's 'Z' papers for *The Adventurer* (1753), the critic is frequently subsumed into the reader, as happens in his ecstatic reaction to the language of Shakespeare's Caliban: 'The poet is a more powerful magician than his own PROSPERO: we are transported into fairy-land; we are wrapt in a delicious dream, from which it is misery to be disturbed; all around is enchantment!'[11] All the elements for Johnsonian parody, even the physical gestures, seem in place; and it is clear that in Johnson's eyes, his friends' fondness for emotional maneuverings, their submission to pleasure and imaginative stimulus, their general willingness to be transported, must compromise their judgments. In the Wartons' critical appreciation, judgmental criteria might shade into more flexible and modulated subjectivities. For Thomas as a critic of Spenser, *The Faerie Queene* 'engages the affection of the heart, rather than the applause of the head'; it is a poem 'where the faculties of creative imagination delight us, because they are unassisted and unrestrained by those of deliberate judgment.' He concludes: 'tho' in the FAERIE QUEENE we are not satisfied as critics, yet we are transported as readers.'[12] For Johnson, 'there is always an appeal open from criticism to nature' ('Preface' to Shakespeare, *Yale* VII.67); for the Warton brothers, however, there was always an appeal open from criticism to imagination.

This licensing of an unchallenged imaginative space is inimical to the Johnsonian critic-moralist, who prefers to negotiate the difficult terrains of human experience. What for the Wartons is a potential world of responsive delight calls forth Johnsonian circumspection and apprehension. The contrast shows itself in the way Johnson's early allegorical story, *The Vision of Theodore, the Hermit of Teneriffe* (1748), and Thomas Warton's *The Pleasures of Melancholy* (1747) share the same geographical location, yet offer very different views of it. Thomas's essentially poetic eminence is established in the opening lines:

> Mother of musings, Contemplation sage,
> Whose grotto stands upon the topmost rock
> Of Teneriff…
> There oft thou listen'st to the wild uproar
> Of fleets encount'ring, that in whispers low
> Ascends the rocky summit, where thou dwell'st
> Remote from man, conversing with the spheres![13]

This removed figure, who becomes Warton's guide in his imaginative excursion, has the identical vantage point sought by Johnson's hermit: 'I conceived a wish to view the summit of the mountain, at the foot of which I had so long resided' (*Yale* XVI.196);[14] but before the old man has made much headway ('the declivities grew more precipitous, and the sand slided from beneath my feet'), he is favored with an admonitory dream in which the path ahead becomes the challenge of life itself, 'the Mountain of Existence,' with all its obstacles, distractions, and dangers. While Warton's teenage visionary blithely occupies the summit for an indulgence in the pleasures of poetic melancholy, Johnson's old hermit finds his dream also terminating in melancholy, but in her true home: a gloomy labyrinth in whose depths 'the hopeless wanderer is delivered up to Melancholy…[who] having tortured her prisoner for a time, consigns him at last to the cruelty of Despair' (*Yale* XVI.212). Chastened by his uncomfortable vision, Johnson's hermit never makes the ascent. There will be no imagined flight there either.

The two scholarly young men whom Johnson came to know in the early 1750s were already prominent poets specializing in indulgence of the fancy. In 1746 Joseph Warton advertised his *Odes* to the public in just those terms, disingenuously conceding 'that any work where the imagination is much indulged, will perhaps not be relished or regarded.' His odes are written, he says, in defiance of 'certain austere critics' who might 'think them too fanciful and descriptive.'[15] 'Fancy' is appropriately the volume's presiding genius, and she is addressed in the opening ode as a magical power who can transport the mind instantly to any location it chooses. Carried along by this acquiescent deity, the poet is granted a succession of scenes for vicarious experience: 'Me, Goddess, by the right-hand lead…/…Or sometimes in thy fiery car/Transport me…/…Then guide me from this horrid scene…/…For thou can'st place me near my love,/Can'st fold in visionary bliss….'[16] This is the fluid emotional language of the youthful initiate, a mental traveler who finds no barrier to his desires. In *The Enthusiast* Joseph's lover of nature indulges his adventurous spirit to the full, and again the transport is free: 'O who will bear me then to western climes,/…that I may hunt/The boar and tiger thro' Savannah's wild,/Thro' fragrant desarts, and thro' citron-groves.'[17] In *The Pleasures of Melancholy*

(1747) brother Thomas's obliging genie is the figure of Contemplation ('Lead me, queen sublime'), who conducts him through a succession of atmospheric scenes in which *let* becomes the password to unlock every door, remove every barrier: 'Oft let me sit' (this occurs three times), 'Or let me tread' (twice), 'let me watch,' 'Then let my thought contemplative explore.'[18] Again and again the mere wish brings the desired landscape into view, and scenes are promptly realized on the wings of thought:

> Mid hollow charnel let me watch the flame
> Of taper dim, shedding a livid glare
> O'er the wan heaps; while airy voices talk
> Along the glimm'ring walls; or ghostly shape
> At distance seen, invites with beck'ning hand
> My lonesome steps...[19]

These two longer meditative poems, of established popularity by the mid-1750s,[20] are a 'choice of life'—but in the Wartonian, not Johnsonian sense. They offer an attractive selection rather than a willed choice. Their varied poetic scenes, fluid and pageant-like, are unhindered realizations of desire. Both texts thus speak the poetry of the Happy Valley, the place where 'every desire was immediately granted' (*Yale* XVI.10). Within imagination, each successive wish slips effortlessly into fulfillment, and the brothers' poetic texts are in this way a series of *velleities,* i.e. they represent 'no more than an idle, un-operative complacency in, and desire of the end, without any consideration of the means.'[21] In its entry for *velleity* sense 1, the *OED* appropriately includes Richard Baxter's admonition (1662): 'We must distinguish... Between the simple Velleity of the Will, and the choice that followeth.'

Johnson's *Rasselas* (1759) finds its most serious, and humorous, moments in that difficult space between wish and will; it determinedly resists the unproblematic elisions of Wartonian fancy. Although wishes set the agenda, they are at every turn wrong-footed by actual events, by a need to question and test. To read the tale alongside the kind of mid-century poetry of sensibility that the Wartons made their own highlights the degree to which Johnson responds satirically to the poetic mechanisms they loved.[22] To a reader of *The Enthusiast* and *The Pleasures of Melancholy* Rasselas's persistent problems of transportation out of the Happy Valley are delightfully funny: ' "I am afraid," said he to the artist, "that your imagination prevails over your skill, and that you now tell me rather what you wish than what you know" ' (*Yale* XVI.24). *Touché.* Johnson finds great amusement throughout his tale in materializing the scenes of poetic fancy that were the Wartons' speciality. In their world, imagined caves are places of whispered revelation; their poetic flights are sublimely independent of machinery; their pyramids produce atmospheric background sounds; their shepherds are acutely sensitive to their surroundings; their rapt visionaries contemplate the skies; their hermits nurture exquisite feelings ('Yet feels the hoary Hermit truer joys,/As from the cliff that o'er his cavern hangs,/He views the piles of fall'n Persepolis').[23] In *Rasselas*, however, the Wartonian avatars of fancy are interrogated and their lives assessed. Meditative scenarios become sites for interviews. What is happily licensed by Wartonian poetry is brought in for narrative questioning. In *The Enthusiast* and *The Pleasures of Melancholy*, for example, the various Wartonian shepherds are rapt innocents, silent vehicles for a heightened sensibility ('Still the shepherds shew/The sacred place, whence with religious awe/They hear, returning from the field at eve,/Strange whisp'ring of sweet musick thro' the air').[24] In *Rasselas* the prince and his friends settle them down for a bad-tempered discussion about the class struggle (*Yale* XVI.76–7).

Its flirtation with poetic scenarios, especially those of which the Warton brothers were fond, is characteristic of the mischievous satire that runs through Johnson's book. In particular the imagination is repeatedly challenged by a moral imperative, as Johnson conceives it, of pushing each poetic impulse towards realization, however awkward, and each desire towards a choice. All wishes in his story are in this way predicates: they presuppose an object, and thus can be tested and judged—and humorously frustrated. For Johnson, the ultimate question, which poetry should not evade, is the one posed in line 343 at the climax of *The Vanity of Human Wishes* (1749): 'Where then shall Hope and Fear their *objects* find?' (*Yale* VI.107; my emphasis). In the Happy Valley, Rasselas realizes that an unimpeded ease of gratification disallows genuine desire. If everything is available, nothing is wanting, so that individual will and effort are never exercised: 'if I had any known want,' the prince declares, 'I should have a certain wish; that wish would excite endeavour' (*Yale* XVI.15–16). In these early chapters Rasselas hesitates between Wartonian and Johnsonian impulses. He is at one moment the complacent self-elegist pleased with the delicacy of his own melancholy ('His chief amusement was to picture to himself that world which he had never seen; to place himself in various conditions,' *Yale* XVI.17–18), and at another he is the dissatisfied aspirant for whom all experience should have an object and poetic meditation is not enough. The prince might appropriately echo the words of Shakespeare's Orlando in *As You Like It*: 'I can live no longer by thinking.'[25] This unsettled youth (who in chapters 8–12 requires a lesson from an older poet who has lived in the world and has seen it all) declares, with an exasperated sense of the limitations of Wartonian fancy: 'I fly from pleasure...because pleasure has ceased to please' (*Yale* XVI.15). Ironically similar on this score is Imlac, who has 'a mind replete with images, which [he] can vary and combine at pleasure'; but in the Happy Valley they have become mere tantalizing memories ('none of my pleasures can be again enjoyed,' *Yale* XVI.54–5).

The book generates much of its subtle humor by teasing any readers who think they might be about to wander in a Wartonian poetic realm where 'airy voices' and 'beckoning hand' combine to grant their desires.[26] In the tale's admonitory opening Johnson disabuses them at once: 'Ye who listen with credulity to the whispers of fancy, and pursue with eagerness the phantoms of hope...attend' (*Yale* XVI.7). This sounds as if it might be directly aimed at the Wartons, who repeatedly celebrate the intense visionary inwardness of the whisper ('At every season let my ear/Thy solemn whispers, FANCY, hear').[27] The invitation, and its frustration, is a comic thread running through Johnson's tale, which plays ironically with an assumed language of the poetic, and a reader willing to be 'transported.' The idea takes a more menacing turn when we encounter the astronomer, whose mind has come to resemble a Wartonian text, which 'dances from scene to scene, unites all pleasures in all combinations.' 'This, Sir,' concludes Imlac, 'is one of the dangers of solitude' (*Yale* XVI.152–3). It is as if Johnson in these powerful chapters on the delusions of 'the man of learning' is supplying the sequel to Joseph Warton's *Odes* volume, which having opened with an ode to Fancy closes with one to Solitude: 'O let me calmly dwell with thee,/From noisy mirth and bus'ness free,/With meditation seek the skies,/This folly-fetter'd world despise!'[28] The book ends with those words. The young poet's imaginative quest may be harmless enough, but Johnson's astronomer learns the dangers of a mental world where 'fictions begin to operate as realities' (*Yale* XVI.152). Curiously, that neat phrase sums up the satiric tactics of Johnson's tale, in which imagined situations are realized, and the pleasing fictions of mid-century poetry are pressed to give a sober account of themselves.

There is thus an element of incongruity in bringing Johnson into company with the Wartons, and perhaps that is a good reason for making the attempt. Their respective texts, rather than interlocking, seem to wrong-foot each other, and in so doing to ask questions that neither is fully prepared to answer. In both cases an element of the disingenuous is detectable. If the Wartons in their poetic criticism found ways of deflecting the Johnsonian challenge by making their appeal to imaginative response, Johnson in his turn could press hard on the precise letter and attempt to bring the elusive fancy to book. Viewing one phenomenon through the lens of the other highlights an argumentative element in their work, and suggests a long-standing difference in temperament and principle. The men's critical disagreements of the 1780s were not a game-changing break in their friendship, but the continuation of a mutual provocation that had existed for decades, and which had been creatively stimulating on both sides.

## NOTES

1. The emotional dynamics of Johnson's friendship with Thomas Warton are traced by John Vance, 'Samuel Johnson and Thomas Warton,' *Biography* 9 (1986), 95–111. See also his essay, 'The Samuel Johnson—Joseph Warton Friendship,' *Johnson Society Transactions* (1982), 44–55; and Hugh Reid, ' "The Want of a Closer Union…": The Friendship of Samuel Johnson and Joseph Warton,' *The Age of Johnson* 9 (1998), 133–43.

2. Joseph Warton wrote to Thomas Balguy, 25 April 1781: 'Dr Johnson's Prefaces and Lives a[re I] suppose good Bath-reading. We are very angry about what he has said of Gray; tho I always knew that Johnson had not a grain of true Taste' (Bodleian MS Eng.Lett.*c.*590, ff.188–9). On Joseph's relations with Johnson, see *Lives* IV.238–40.

3. It does not show a meeting of The Club, given its anachronisms (e.g. Thomas Warton was elected eight years after Goldsmith died).

4. John Wooll, *Biographical Memoirs of the Late Revd. Joseph Warton, D.D.* (London: Cadell and Davies, 1806), 98.

5. On angled 'looking,' Johnson, and the picturesque, see David Fairer, ' "Fishes in His Water": Shenstone, Sensibility, and the Ethics of Looking,' *The Age of Johnson* 19 (2009), 129–48.

6. *Poems upon Several Occasions … by John Milton*, ed. Thomas Warton (London: J. Dodsley, 1785), 34.

7. William Hayley, *The Life of Milton, in Three Parts* (London: Cadell and Davies, 1796), 12.

8. Joseph Warton, *An Essay on the Genius and Writings of Pope … The Fourth Edition, Corrected*, 2 vols. (London: J. Dodsley, 1782), I.394–5.

9. Describing a divided critical scene in 1782, Vicesimus Knox contrasted the two 'parties:' 'On one side, are the lovers and imitators of Spenser and Milton; and on the other, those of Dryden, Boileau, and Pope,' *Essays Moral and Literary*, 2 vols. (London: Charles Dilly), II.186, no. CXXIX ('On the Prevailing Taste in Poetry').

10. Robert Potter, *The Art of Criticism; as Exemplified in Dr. Johnson's Lives of the Most Eminent English Poets* (London: T. Hookham, 1789), 199.

11. *Adventurer* 93 (1753), reprinted in *Shakespeare: The Critical Heritage*, 6 vols. ed. Brian Vickers (London: Routledge & Kegan Paul, 1774–81), IV.64. Joseph's *Essay on Pope* judged the poet by the principle that 'it is a creative and glowing IMAGINATION … and that alone, that can stamp a writer with this exalted and very uncommon character' (*Essay on Pope* (1782), I.v).

12. Thomas Warton, *Observations on the Faerie Queene of Spenser* (London: R. and J. Dodsley, 1754), 13.

13. Thomas Warton, *The Pleasures of Melancholy*, ll.1–16 (1755 text: see note 20).

14. The 12,200 ft. summit of El Piton was once thought to be the world's highest point (cf. *Paradise Lost*, IV.987). It is said to cast the longest shadow on earth.

15. Joseph Warton, *Odes on Various Subjects* (London: R. Dodsley, 1746), sig. A2ʳ.

16. 'Ode I. To Fancy,' ll.8–9, 49, 59–60, 69, 74–5.

17. Joseph Warton, *The Enthusiast*, ll.233–41 (1748 text: see note 20).

18. On Johnson's use of *let*, see further Chapter 3 and Chapter 9.

19. Thomas Warton, *The Pleasures of Melancholy*, ll.44–9 (1755 text: see note 20).

20. *The Enthusiast: Or, The Lover of Nature. A Poem* (London: R. Dodsley, 1744); *The Pleasures of Melancholy. A Poem* (London: R. Dodsley, 1747). Both poems were revised for inclusion in Dodsley's *A Collection of Poems. By Several Hands*, 3 vols. (London: R. Dodsley, 1748; 4th edn, 4 vols., 1755): *The Enthusiast* (1748 edn, III.68–78, followed by 'Ode to Fancy'), and *The Pleasures of Melancholy* (1755 edn, IV.214–25).

21. *Dictionary*, s.n. *velleity*, quoting Robert South.

22. Also relevant here is Mark Akenside's *The Pleasures of Imagination* (London: R. Dodsley, 1744).

23. *The Pleasures of Melancholy*, ll.259–61. See also ll.16, 49, 205, 247, 281, and *The Enthusiast*, ll.2, 21, 66, 172, 199, 209, 247.

24. *The Enthusiast*, ll.172–5.

25. *As You Like It*, V.ii.50.

26. Cf. the quotation from *The Pleasures of Melancholy*, p.190 above.

27. 'Ode I. To Fancy,' ll.87–8. Cf. also *The Enthusiast*, ll.23, 175, and *The Pleasures of Melancholy*, l.14.

28. 'Ode XIV. To Solitude,' ll.21–4.

# 16

# Johnson Rebalanced: The Happy Man, The Supportive Family, and his Social Religion

*Howard D. Weinbrot*

Johnsonian studies, of course, long have flourished. They also have long reflected the relevant critical fashions and standards of their ages and, in the nature of things, they have often conflicted with one another. Johnson, for example, has been called a political 'liberal' and a 'conservative' believer in the divine right of kings, a loyal Hanoverian and a principled, seditious, Jacobite supporter of the exiled House of Stuart. The conflict set off a decade-long paper war that, for some, still festers.[1] There nonetheless have been certain common denominators in criticism and biography from Boswell in 1791 to Jeffrey Meyers in 2008.[2] In this chapter I will consider three of these that I think distort Johnson's personal, intellectual, and spiritual views. Such persistence embodies what Johnson called 'This fatal slumber of treacherous tranquillity' (Sermon 8; *Yale* XIV.86). I do not seek to awaken posterity by nailing my theses to Lichfield Cathedral's doors. After all, predicting the past is even more difficult than predicting the future. In rebalancing rather than revolutionizing, I hope to urge a more rounded version of Johnson. Namely, Johnson was neither somber Sam forever tottering on the edge of insanity, nor foolishly miserable in his created London family of Francis Barber, Anna Williams, and others. Nor was he an intolerant High Church Anglican hostile or indifferent to all but the Established Church. I hope that these rebalancing acts can spur other efforts to reconsider what I think are other misrepresentations of Johnson's complex realities.

Boswell memorably characterized Johnson's apparent combat with his internal enemies:

His mind resembled the vast amphitheatre, the Colisaeum at Rome. In the centre stood his judgement, which, like a mighty gladiator, combated those apprehensions that, like the wild beasts of the Arena, were all around in

cells, ready to be let out upon him. After a conflict, he drives them back into
their dens; but not killing them, they were still assailing him.   (*Life* II.106)

A cottage industry has grown up around these remarks. We read about
Johnson the enchained masochist; Johnson's 'long and desperate struggle';
Johnson 'haunted by dread' and 'oppressed by bugbears'; Johnson 'always
at war with himself'; Johnson 'lacerated' by 'his mental illness' and thus
'poised dangerously between control and madness.'[3] For such commentators, whether Johnson was in Lichfield, London, or the dark lodgings of
his dark mind, his reason seemed like a flickering candle in the wind. This
Samuel Johnson behaved like an August Strindberg who flunked out of
Freudian psychoanalysis and changed his name to Samuel Beckett.

Not quite. I stipulate that Johnson often suffered from what probably
was severe agitated depression, perhaps from Tourette's syndrome, and
perhaps from the mood changes attributable to frequent opium use.[4] Yet
I also argue that his personal achievement is the greater because he over-
came such obstacles. Such overcoming and consequent long periods of
normalcy require further emphasis. Johnson found, for example, that vigorous physical and intellectual exercise were reasonably effective anti-
depressants. He used both benign medications with the good sense that
allowed him to produce a great body of great work. One novelist nonetheless has said that he behaved like 'a chained and tormented bear.'[5] This
view suggests that even after three hundred years we should approach
Johnson as if he were a restrained but dangerous animal rather than as a
complex human being of extraordinary literary and human merit.

Johnson's merit was based, in part, on his role as guide to the guide-
less. He at once leads us and is at our side as he engages in what *Rambler*
8 calls the 'moral discipline of the mind' (*Yale* III.42). This association
encourages what Johnson's early biographer Arthur Murphy movingly
called a 'posthumous friendship' with Johnson (*Johnsonian Miscellanies*
I.355). Murphy's remark defines an essential aspect of Johnson's character as an urban *beatus ille*,[6] as a happy man who enjoyed company and
friendships, kept them in repair, and repaid his friends' acts of kindness.
George Birkbeck Hill's 1878 corrective essay on 'Lord Macaulay and
Johnson' wants rereading in this respect. Birkbeck Hill's Johnson is a
smiling convivial man.[7] A good laugh and communal pleasures were
such regular parts of his regular behavior that they were among the defining traits of his character. Johnson knew that laughter was physically and
psychologically healthy, good in itself, and essentially social and bonding for
individuals and the group. As Richard Cumberland reports, on the opening
night of Oliver Goldsmith's *She Stoops to Conquer* (1773), 'All eyes were upon
Johnson' in a side box: 'when he laughed every body thought themselves war-
ranted to roar.'[8] Cumberland understood that Johnson was happiest 'when

animated by the cheering attention' of friends. Mrs Elizabeth Cumberland, to whom 'he was kind and cheerful,' was among these: 'my wife would have made tea for him as long as the New River could have supplied her with water.'[9]

Frances Burney also was well aware of Johnson's kind and cheerful mode. Her diaries are less artful than Boswell's biography, in which Boswell is puzzled by a laughter so apparently inconsistent with Johnson's *gravitas*, as when he records that Johnson 'laughed immoderately' when Bennet Langton proudly announced that William Chamber drew up his will. For Boswell, this 'playful manner' and consequent 'peals of laughter' were 'not such as might be expected from the author of "The Rambler"' and 'the aweful, melancholy, and venerable Johnson' (*Life* II.260–1). Burney's frequent allusions to the jolly Johnson thus are the more impressive because less burdened by Boswell's image of Johnson the epic hero. When Johnson and Burney are at Streatham, we see him laughing, droll, facetious, comical, mirthful, sporting, and in good humor. He induces these responses in others as well. Burney delights in his tale 'of the *celebrated Ladies* of his Acquaintance: an account of which, had you heard from *himself,* would have made you die with *Laughing.*' Then, 'Oh how we all hollow'd,' we hear. This Johnson 'has more fun, and comical humour, and love of nonsense about him than almost anybody I ever saw.'[10] David Garrick added that 'Rabelais and all other wits are nothing compared with him. You may be diverted by them; but Johnson gives you a forcible hug, and shakes laughter out of you, whether you will or no' (*Life* II.231).

Jollity even took place among presumed enemies, as with the famous event in which Boswell maneuvers Johnson into a meeting with John Wilkes. Boswell deftly compresses time and words in narrating Wilkes's effort to please Johnson. The veal appears at table:

'Pray give me leave, Sir:—It is better here—A little of the brown—Some fat, Sir—A little of the stuffing—Some gravy—Let me have the pleasure of giving you some butter—Allow me to recommend a squeeze of this orange;—or the lemon, perhaps, may have more zest.' 'Sir, Sir, I am obliged to you, Sir', cried Johnson, bowing, and turning his head to him with a look for some time of 'surly virtue', but, in a short while, of complacency. (*Life* III.69)

Boswell has evoked 'Indignant Thales' from line 34 of Johnson's *London* (1738). His 'surly virtue' could not 'fix a friend' in the city corrupted by English politicians and French immigrants (*Yale* VI.49, 55). That is not the case for the mature Johnson in 1776. Immediately after Wilkes's compliant role, Johnson begins to speak about the actor, playwright, and manager Samuel Foote, of whom he at first thought little, but who soon raises his humor and almost friendship. Johnson met Foote at William Fitzherbert's and was determined not to be pleased. 'I went on eating my dinner pretty sullenly, affecting not to mind him. But the dog was so very comical, that I was obliged to lay down my knife and fork, throw myself back upon my chair, and fairly laugh it out. No, Sir, he was irresistible' (*Life* III.69–70). The Foote episode parallels the image of Johnson's 'surly virtue' in the initial part of the Wilkes episode. Each man then attempts to ingratiate himself with Johnson. Each succeeds and, at least for the evening, becomes an amiable companion. Wilkes does this by respectful attention to Johnson's meal. Foote does this by being 'so very comical' that grumpy Johnson stops eating and starts laughing.

These examples of Johnsonian merriment are social and induce sociability, whether he is sharing tea, stories, a meal, or laughter. The scenes give us Smiling Sam, not Sad Sam, and they are urgent aspects of his life. They also embody the continuing process of getting on with that life, of changing one's mind because one is open to change in the movement from sullen to complacent, from dark enclosure to communal delight. Irresistible social laughter counters isolating gloom.

Much of Johnson's spoken and written word also is social in its creation. Witness his extensive correspondence, his conversation with streams of visitors, his evenings at inns or clubs, the dictionary garret with amanuenses at hand, or much of the *Lives of the Poets* (1779–81) which was written with the Thrales near at hand. These social qualities indeed typify Johnson's literary as well as human modes of proceeding and judging. Witness again the exchange with his reader at the end of *The Vanity of Human Wishes* ('Enquirer, cease, petitions yet remain'), or the 'Drury-Lane Prologue' (1747) in which he brings the audience into the stage experience when he asks it to 'prompt no more the follies you decry' (*Yale* VI.108, 89). For Johnson, Gray's *Elegy Written in a Country Churchyard* (1751) includes images and 'sentiments to which every bosom returns an echo' (*Lives* IV.183–4). In contrast, the metaphysical poets (*Lives* I.200–1), Milton's prelapsarian Adam and Eve (*Lives* I.286, 288–9), and Gray's historically bound pindarics (*Lives* IV.181–3) can inhibit or alienate human response. Johnson deeply felt the deprivation of his own human community. In 1754 he used words that suggest the uncivilized wilderness prior to the *Dictionary*'s socialization of the English language. As he told Thomas Warton, since Tetty's death he felt 'broken off from mankind' and was a 'solitary wanderer in the wild of life, without any certain direction' (*Letters* I.90). The flurry of letters regarding the *Dictionary* about this time suggests Johnson's need for connection as well as for recognition. He adds: 'I would endeavour by the help of you and your brother to supply the want of closer union by friendship' (*Letters* I.90).

Johnson's 'gloom of solitude' reappears when the *Dictionary* has been completed; he recalls the wife who has 'sunk into the grave' and with whom he cannot share joy, pride, and company (*Yale* XVIII.113).

Social acts and their sad loss suggest reasons why Johnson's prose includes so many domestic metaphors and the necessary pleasures and pains of life at home. These images are as typical of his style as are general statements, Latinate diction, and expansive sentences. Johnson was exquisitely sensitive to family destruction and to its consequent grief. We see this in his periodical essays, his insights regarding human nature, and his charity sermons concerned with family anguish. Sermon 4 seeks to alleviate 'the groans of the aged...and the cries of infants languishing with hunger' (*Yale* XIV.45). Sermon 17 urges comfort for widows and support for orphans (*Yale* XIV.297–8). Sermon 19 sees that virtue put in practice 'by which the orphan may be supplied with a father, and the widow with a defender' (*Yale* XIV.207). His Sermon 26 is especially indignant regarding the 'villany heightened by perfidy and cruelty' of an orphan's abusive guardian (*Yale* XIV.278–9).

Johnson makes similar points in other genres. He is angered by Lady Macclesfield's apparent denial of maternal responsibility in the *Life of Savage* (1744). She has left him as 'a Child *exposed*' (*Life of Savage*, 75). In *Idler* 38, written in 1759, he deplores the penal system that brutally incarcerates debtors and extends the punishment to the debtor's family, for 'every man languishing in prison' bereaves 'others who love or need him.' In such a family we see 'the wife bewailing her husband, or the children begging the bread which their father would have earned' (*Yale* XIV.118, 121). Johnson here puts in secular terms the reciprocity he puts in religious terms in his sermons: such incarceration ignores 'the effects of consanguinity and friendship, and the general reciprocation of wants and benefits, which make one man dear or necessary to another' (*Yale* XIV.118). The 'Preface' to Shakespeare observes how the human mind invents potential grief. We feel the threat to a character in a play 'as a mother weeps over her babe, when she remembers that death may take it from her' (*Yale* VII.78). Cordelia's death so troubled Johnson that he could not reread it until he edited *King Lear* in 1765. He found Othello's murder of Desdemona so 'dreadful' that 'it is not to be endured' (*Yale* VIII.1045). These violations of the family's protective role connote Johnson's deep and utterly normal need for connection at so intimate a level.

It is all the more understandable, then, that Johnson so often emphasized continuity within his immediate family. This could be as mourning for his parents, brother, and wife whom he hoped ultimately to join hereafter, as in the funeral sermon for his wife Tetty in March of 1752: with proper Christian faith, one calmly looks upon the grave of the departed 'with the hope of that state in which there shall be no more grief or separation' (*Yale* XIV.267). He is most moving in the tender final moments with his Lichfield servant Catherine Chambers. On 18 October 1767 he said that she was 'my dear old Friend...who came to live with my Mother about 1724, and has been but little parted from us since. She buried my Father, my Brother, and my Mother' (*Yale* I.116–17). Johnson obliterates class distinctions, space, and time. The servant is a friend. The 'us' from whom she has rarely parted includes Johnson as if he had never left home some forty years ago. The familial burial rites in which she engaged require the reciprocity that tearful Johnson is now privileged to perform in his final social act with her. He becomes priestly intercessor, paternal comforter, and vehicle of compassion and faith for Catherine on her deathbed. The scene is both wrenching and pleasing in its simple style, emotional depth, and repeated physical contact. It consists of a frame of private and personal exchange before and after a formal prayer and its evocation of the protective father:[11]

> I desired all to withdraw, then told her that we were to part for ever, that as Christians we should part with prayer, and that I would, if she was willing, say a short prayer beside her. She expressed great desire to hear me, and held up her poor hands, as she lay in bed, with great fervour, while I prayed, kneeling by her, nearly in the following words.
>
> Almighty and most merciful Father, whose loving kindness is over all thy works, behold, visit, and relieve this thy Servant who is grieved with sickness. Grant that the sense of her weakness may add strength to her faith, and seriousness to her Repentance. And grant that by the help of thy Holy Spirit after the pains and labours of this short life, we may all obtain everlasting happiness through Jesus Christ, our Lord, for whose sake hear our Prayers. Amen.
>
> Our Father.    (*Yale* I.117)

The prayer soon becomes an intense human exchange of loss, love, and hope:

> I then kissed her. She told me that to part was the greatest pain that she had ever felt, and that she hoped we should meet again in a better place. I expressed with swelled eyes and great emotion of tenderness the same hopes. We kissed and parted, I humbly hope, to meet again, and to part no more. (*Yale* I.117)

Johnson thus needed, received, and gave spiritual and emotional support through various kinds of family connections. It therefore is puzzling that so many of his—and our—contemporaries regard his invited London family as a form of self-flagellation. Sir John Hawkins characterized Johnson's London home-life as a near-criminal activity on behalf of the vulgar and undeserving who 'elbowed' their way through the world. Johnson encouraged and housed these indigents whom he recommended to credit, and whom he knew would never pay their debts (*Hawkins*, 245). Hawkins's Johnson is guilty of conspiracy, fraud, abuse of contracts and of credit. He had 'a natural imbecility...arising from humanity and pity' to such 'creatures, that was prejudicial to his interests' (*Hawkins*, 248). No wonder, Hawkins states, that he was 'driven from his own home' by these noisy 'enemies to his peace' (*Hawkins*, 246).

Hester Piozzi's Johnson houses a full 'nest' of 'odd inhabitants.' It was 'vexatious and comical' to see him deal with these ungrateful, uncomprehending squabbling brats (*Shaw-Piozzi*, 89, 131). He would spend the week at Streatham but return to London on the weekends to feed, accompany, and thereby respect his housemates. They so pestered and harangued one another and Johnson that he was afraid to go home. Yet worse, he scolded Hester Thrale when she tried to put them in their place on his behalf. She was too grand, he implied, to sympathize with the needs and tribulations of poverty (*Shaw-Piozzi*, 131).

Boswell paints a gentler picture, in which Johnson's benevolence is part of his larger kindness to the wealthy as to the poor. Boswell also respects Johnson's housemates by naming them, as neither Hawkins nor Piozzi generally does. Boswell as Boswell, however, regards the women as sexual conveniences, whom oddly chaste Johnson nevertheless controls: 'He has sometimes suffered me to talk jocularly of his group of females, and call them his *Seraglio*' (*Life* III.368). Boswell quotes Johnson's letter to Hester Thrale in which he writes that 'Williams hates every body; Levet hates Desmoulins, and does not love Williams; Desmoulins hates them both; Poll loves none of them' (*Life* III.368). Here is a collection of crooks, upstarts, ingrates, noisy birds, creatures, and poorly ruled women.

Johnson himself, however, knew that his boarders were friends and protections from silence and the night. The restless crew filled the house with its noise and provided otherwise absent life and energy. Johnson's charity sermon, No. 27, for Henry Hervey Aston in 1745 states the benevolent obvious: 'private friendship...is necessary, not to the enjoyment only, but to the support of life' (*Yale* XIV.289).[12] Almost all of Johnson's relevant letters refer to such friends as necessary supports. For example, on 5 July 1783 the aged and ill Johnson laments the loss of his created family. His 'old Friend Mr Levet is dead...Mrs Desmoulins is gone away, and Mrs Williams is so much decayed, that she can add little to anothers gratifications' (*Letters* IV.167–8). On 20 September he laments to Charles Burney that, after Anna Williams's death, he had come home 'to a very desolate house....My domestick companion is taken from me. She is much missed, for her acquisitions were many, and her curiosity universal; so that she partook of every conversation' (*Letters* IV.199). On 10 November he praised Anna Williams and lamented the death of the friend who 'has been to me for thirty years in the place of a sister' (*Letters* IV.236). Johnson well may have had his own home in mind when in 1781 he said of the often troubled relationship between Pope and Martha Blount: their conversation 'was endearing, for when they met, there was an immediate coalition of congenial notions' (*Lives* IV.52*)*. The death or departure of these surrogate family members evokes grief for them and for himself. In Levet's case, Johnson writes a great elegy that both hides and reveals his pain and perhaps presumptuously decides that God will love Levet as much as Johnson himself did. 'And sure th' Eternal Master found/The single talent well employ'd,' Johnson says of his humble housemate in a generous inversion of the Parable of the Talents (*Yale* VI.315).

Johnson's most important surrogate family was the Thrales at whose center was Henry rather than Hester, who complained that Johnson was 'a yoke my husband first put upon me' (*Shaw-Piozzi*, 101). Henry brought Johnson into the world of practical politics and politicking; into the world of commerce in liquid goods like beer; and into the world of children, heirs, loss, and Henry's obvious infidelity and fatal dining appetites. Johnson knew that Henry's death in 1782 ended his time with the Thrales. Upon his last departure, Johnson thanks God the merciful father for his years there; he asks for the ability to leave 'with holy submission'; and he twice asks for mercy upon himself (*Yale* I.337–8). Johnson typically uses a divine family image to extend that prayer to the human group in which he had such sustained and sustaining pleasure: 'To thy fatherly protection, O Lord, I commend this family. Bless, guide, and defend them. That they may pass through this world as finally to enjoy in thy presence everlasting happiness for Jesus Christ's sake. Amen' (*Yale* I.337–8). He also pays a last visit to the Streatham church: 'Templo valedixi cum osculo' ('I bade the church farewell with a kiss,' *Yale* I.337). Church is part of the family, and tears are appropriate for parting from each. His morning devotions seek paternal guidance and mercy for himself and for the Thrales he must leave.

I have argued that such rebalancing extends to other familiar orthodoxies, another of which is Johnson's religion, often assumed to be narrow and intolerant High Church Anglican. I suggest, instead, that his religion is enriched by his needs for healthy social connections and the ways in which they enhance virtue in our difficult and dangerous world. These connections scarcely limit themselves to Anglican High Church or to persistently harsh views of man's fate. The devoutly Christian *Vanity of Human Wishes* ends with heavenly knowledge transmuted to comforting secular knowledge: 'celestial wisdom calms the mind,/And makes the happiness she does not find' (*Yale* VI.107). Johnson's sermons and religious principles often are pervaded with hope and confidence in God's mercy. Boswell had it about right when, on 25 June, he recorded Johnson's 'liberal sentiment' that 'all Christians, whether Papists or Protestants, agree on the essential articles, and that their differences are trivial, and rather political than religious' (*Life* I.405). Johnson does not discriminate among the Established Church, the dissenting English Protestant, or the Roman churches, all of whom share belief. Boswell also had it right in 1769 when he corrected William Robertson's claim that Johnson would 'strenuously defend the most minute circumstance connected with the Church of England.' 'You are much mistaken as to this,' Boswell responds, 'for when you talk with him calmly in private, he is very liberal in his way of thinking' (*Life* III.331). Thomas Tyers, another of Johnson's early biographers, shared Boswell's view. Johnson was a devoted friend to the Church of England but would not persecute any one for 'speculative notions.' He opposes only those who oppose revelation and the existence of a future state (Johnsonian Miscellanies II.369–70).

Johnson's need for supportive social and family contact included his own role as steward of God's gifts in order to pass them to others. Johnson's religion thus regularly concerned him with the fate of those he loved, as with his final recorded prayer on 5 December 1784. He there humbly asks for a merciful God's blessing on Jesus's behalf. He hopes that his 'imperfect repentance' will be accepted and that his prayer will confirm his faith, establish his hope, and enlarge his charity. Even in these nearly deathbed words, however, Johnson seeks to extend God's gifts. 'Have mercy upon me and pardon the multitude of my offences. Bless my Friends, have mercy upon all men' (*Yale* I.418).

He also was liberal and scarcely a Church of England zealot when on his deathbed and making his will. John Hoole (whose biographical *Narrative* about Johnson was published in 1789) was present when Hawkins asked Johnson whether he 'would choose to make any introductory declaration respecting his faith.' Johnson agrees. 'Sir John further asked if he would make any declaration of his being of the church of England: to which the Doctor said "*No!*" '[13] Instead, Johnson gives Hawkins a note summarizing much of the spiritual progress in his prayers. He acknowledges his polluted soul, but trusts that his own repentance and Jesus's sacrifice will have cleansed it before an infinitely merciful God. Johnson regularly stresses broad Christian principles rather than tribal affiliation.

Johnson exemplified those broad principles in his sermons, which often are moving and practical documents in the arts of living in social units. Such arts include pleas for toleration and resistance to the rigors of clerical formalism. For Johnson, our benevolent God cares for the quotidian social as well as the spiritual world and requires an irenic pastoral voice. Johnson disagrees both with Roman Catholics and with Dissenters; but he generally does so with respect and without what he calls 'uncharitable censure' (*Yale* XIV.33). He well knows that 'Every sect may find, in its own followers' those who replace true piety with mere form (*Yale* XIV.143). Johnson also laments the calamitous 'wars kindled by differences of opinions' and deplores 'the sword of persecution' (*Yale* XIV.240). His 1745 charity sermon rejects the 'fatal confidence, that all other sects are to be considered, as the enemies of God' and are to be 'persecuted as beasts of prey, and swept away, as too prophane to enjoy the same sun, or to tread the same earth, with the favourites of their maker' (*Yale* XIV.290). At an indeterminate time he comparably laments the 'rancour and hatred, the rage and persecution with which religious disputes have filled the world' (*Yale* XIV.11).

Johnson's sermons regularly seek to avoid such rage by encouraging community. He reminds us that God has designed connection and consequent dependence upon one another in what he calls 'the natural system of the universe' (*Yale* XIV.13). The Apostles taught 'an amicable reciprocation of...civility' and a 'system of domestick virtue...to fill the greater part of the circle of life' (*Yale* XIV.126). God's 'assistance may be extended equally to all parts of his creation' (*Yale* XIV.154). Human beings and families 'are to be made happy by the same means,' by virtue as 'the parent of felicity' (*Yale* XIV.13). Such virtue depends upon 'the reciprocity of kindness' (*Yale* XIV.267)—necessary because a man's 'own happiness is connected with that of every other man.' Since millions partake 'of one common nature' (*Yale* XIV.238), we are necessary for one another (*Yale* XIV.194–5). We deserve respect in part to the degree of our 'usefulness to mankind' (*Yale* XIV.220–1). By so behaving, we join 'the great community of relation to the universal Father' (*Yale* XIV.146 and see also *Yale* XIV.208).

One contrast and one illustration should yet further clarify Johnson's social and communal religion. In 1752 Lord Orrery writes long *Remarks* concerning Jonathan Swift. After lamenting the fourth book of *Gulliver's Travels* (1726) of which, he says, 'I am heartily tired,' Orrery turns to Swift's religious pamphlets and their anger toward Dissenters, whom he held 'in the utmost degree of ridicule and detestation.'[14] Indeed the 'dislike was mutual on both sides. Dr SWIFT hated all fanatics: All fanatics hated Dr SWIFT.'[15]

Now contrast this with Johnson's 'Life' of the Dissenter Isaac Watts, to whom Johnson immediately applies the honorific Doctor (*Lives* IV.105), and whom he himself chose to be included in the *Lives of the Poets*. Johnson has mixed feelings regarding Watts's poetry, but none regarding his personal life. As often is the case in the *Lives*, Johnson praises tender family connections and here places them in a religious context. Watts's father 'had the happiness, indulged to few parents, of living to see his son eminent for literature and venerable for piety' (*Lives* IV.106). Johnson admires that piety irrespective of Watts's dissent. The specifics of religion are less important than the practice of its benign values: 'Such he was as every Christian Church would rejoice to have adopted' (*Lives* IV.105). He delivered his sermons extemporaneously, without gesticulation, and with 'gravity and propriety [that] made his discourses very efficacious' (*Lives* IV.108). His 'incessant solicitude for souls' subordinated philosophy 'to evangelical instruction' and perpetually encouraged one to wish 'to be better' (*Lives* IV.109). Johnson regrets that Watts was not of the Established Church, but that regret is scarcely more than a throwaway line at the end of the 'Life' and is insignificant in comparison with Watts's other virtues in a biography that concludes with 'God.' Youths 'may be safely pleased' when reading Watts and adults may 'imitate him in all but his non-conformity.' The fortunate reader should 'copy his benevolence to man and his veneration to God' (*Lives* IV.110). Here indeed are some of the 'essential articles' of religion to which Johnson referred (*Life* I.405).

Johnson, then, was neither the perpetual melancholic nor the incompetent master of his destructive home. Nor was he a religious exclusionist for whom only his own Church was the Church of salvation. He enjoyed what Birkbeck Hill called 'no small share of that happiness which here on earth can fall to the lot of man.'[16] That happiness often was part of a shared social life, whether through written or spoken words, through visits to or from others, in his own home, at the Thrales's house in Streatham or elsewhere, and certainly in his relationship with God and with Christians in general. Boswell and others characterized Johnson as he characterized himself, as religiously liberal and, of course, as humble before omnipotence whose mercy he sought. Such rebalancings may, I hope, begin to suggest the complexity and breadth of vision in Johnson's character, context, and achievement. They also may help to illumine Arthur Murphy's affectionate remark that Johnson both awakens a 'principle of gratitude...in every generous mind' and allows us 'to form a posthumous friendship' with him (Johnsonian Miscellanies I.355).

## NOTES

1. See e.g. Donald J. Greene, *The Politics of Samuel Johnson*, 2nd edn (Athens: University of Georgia Press, 1990), the Introduction of which excoriated Howard Erskine-Hill and J. C. D. Clark for claiming that Johnson was a

Jacobite; see also the dedicated volume of *ELH* on *Jacobitism and Eighteenth-Century English Literature*, 64 (1997). For an overview (and several relevant articles), see Howard D. Weinbrot, *Aspects of Samuel Johnson: Essays on his Arts, Mind, Afterlife, and Politics* (Newark: University of Delaware Press, 2005).

2.  Jeffrey Meyers, *Samuel Johnson: The Struggle* (New York: Basic Books, 2008).

3.  See, respectively, Katherine C. Balderston, 'Johnson's Vile Melancholy,' *The Age of Johnson: Essays Presented to Chauncey Brewster Tinker*, ed. Frederick W. Hilles (New Haven: Yale University Press, 1949), 3–14 (on Johnson as chained masochist); Walter Jackson Bate, *Samuel Johnson* (New York: Harcourt Brace Jovanovich, 1977), 3 (on Johnson's long and desperate struggle); Roy Porter, *Flesh in the Age of Reason: The Modern Foundation of Body and Soul* (New York: W. W. Norton & Co., 2003), 182, 175 (Johnson as haunted, oppressed); Meyers, *Samuel Johnson*, 49 (Johnson at war); and Peter Martin, *Samuel Johnson: A Biography* (London: Weidenfeld and Nicolson, 2008), xiii (Johnson as lacerated, poised). This list easily is expandable.

4.  See John Wiltshire, *Samuel Johnson in the Medical World: The Doctor and the Patient* (Cambridge: Cambridge University Press, 1991). For Tourette's syndrome and tics, see, among other sources, Lawrence C. McHenry, 'Samuel Johnson's Tics and Gesticulations,' *Journal of the History of Medicine* 22 (1967), 152–68; and J. M. Pearce, 'Doctor Samuel Johnson: "The Great Convulsionary:" a Victim of Gilles de la Tourette's Syndrome,' *Journal of the Royal Society of Medicine* 87 (1994), 396–9.

5.  Beryl Bainbridge, *According to Queeney* (London: Little Brown, 2003), 17. See also Goldsmith's more perceptive comment, quoted by Boswell, regarding the bear image: Johnson indeed had 'a roughness in his manner; but no man alive has a more tender heart. He has nothing of the bear but his skin' (*Life* II.66).

6.  See *The Odes and Epodes of Horace*, trans. Charles E. Bennett (London and Cambridge, MA: William Heinemann Ltd. and Harvard University Press, 1952), 365.

7.  George Birkbeck Hill, 'Lord Macaulay and Johnson,' in *Dr Johnson, his Friends and his Critics* (London: Smith, Elder, & Co., 1878), 123–45.

8.  Richard Cumberland, *Memoirs of Richard Cumberland. Written by Himself* (London: Lackington, Allen and Co., 1806), 270.

9.  Ibid., 262–3.

10. See *The Early Journals and Letters of Fanny Burney* III. *The Streatham Years*, eds. Lars Troide and Stewart J. Cooke (Kingston and Montreal: McGill-Queen's University Press, 1994), III.99, 151, 255.

11. See Chester Chapin, 'Johnson's Prayer for Kitty Chambers,' *Modern Language Notes* 76 (1961), 216–18. Johnson here is adapting *The Book of Common Prayer*'s 'Service for the Visitation of the Sick.'

12. See also Sermon 27 (*Yale* XIV.297) and Sermon 28 (*Yale* XIV.304).

13. 'Narrative by John Hoole,' *Johnsonian Miscellanies* II.355.

14. John Boyle, Earl of Orrery, *Remarks on the Life and Writings of Dr Jonathan Swift…In a Series of Letters…To his Son, the Honourable Hamilton Boyle*, 2nd edn (London: A. Millar; Dublin: George Faulkner, 1752), 190, 192.

15. Ibid., 193–4.

16. Hill, *Dr Johnson, his Friends and his Critics*, 145.

# References

## PRIMARY SOURCES

Akenside, Mark, *The Pleasures of Imagination* (London: R. Dodsley, 1744).

Allen, Francis, *A Complete English Dictionary* (London: J. Wilson and J. Fell, 1765).

*The Amours of Carlo Khan* (London: John Lever, [1789]).

Anderson, Robert, *The Life of Samuel Johnson LL.D. with Critical Observations on his Works* (London: J. and A. Arch; Edinburgh: Bell & Bradfute, J. Mundell, 1795).

Aristotle, *Nicomachean Ethics*, trans. Terence Irwin (Indianapolis, IN: Hackett, 1985).

Auden, W. H., *Collected Shorter Poems 1927–1957* (London: Faber and Faber, 1966).

Augustine, *Augustine: De Bono Coniugali; de Sancta Uirginate*, ed. and trans. Patrick Walsh (Oxford: Clarendon Press, 2001).

——, *Confessions,* ed. and trans. Henry Chadwick (Oxford and New York: Oxford University Press, 1991).

Austen, Jane, *The Cambridge Edition of the Works of Jane Austen*, ed. Janet Todd, 9 vols. (Cambridge: Cambridge University Press, 2005–9), *Juvenilia*, ed. Peter Sabor (2006).

Bailey, Nathan, *A New Universal Etymological English Dictionary: containing not only Explanations of the Words in the English Language*, revised and corrected by Joseph Nicol Scott (London: T. Osborne and J. Shipton, 1755).

——, *An Universal Etymological English Dictionary* (London: E. Bell, J. Darby, A. Bettesworth et al., 1721).

Bainbridge, Beryl, *According to Queeney* (London: Little Brown, 2003).

[Baskerville, John], *A Vocabulary, or Pocket Dictionary* (Birmingham: Dod, Rivington, 1765).

Beattie, James, *Dissertations Moral and Critical*, 2 vols. (Dublin: Exshaw, Walker, 1783).

——, *Essays. On Poetry and Music, as they affect the Mind. On Laughter, and Ludicrous Composition. On the Utility of Classical Learning* (Edinburgh: William Creech; London: for Edward and Charles Dilly, 1776).

Bellow, Saul, *Herzog* (Harmondsworth: Penguin, 1965).

Bergson, Henri, *Henri Bergson: Key Writings*, eds. Keith Ansell Pearson and John Mullarkey (London: Continuum, 2002).

Blake, William, *The Complete Writings of William Blake: With Variant Readings*, ed. Geoffrey Keynes (London, New York, and Toronto: Oxford University Press, 1966).

Bond, Donald F., ed., *The Spectator*, 5 vols. (Oxford: Clarendon Press, 1965).

——, ed., *The Tatler*, 3 vols. (Oxford: Clarendon Press, 1987).

*The Book of Common Prayer* (Edinburgh: James Watson, 1720).

Boswell, James, *Boswell's Column*, ed. Margaret Bailey (London: William Kimber, 1951).

——, *Boswell's Life of Johnson; Together with Boswell's Journal of a Tour to the Hebrides and Johnson's Diary of a Journey into North Wales*, 6 vols., ed. George Birkbeck Hill, revised and enlarged by L. F. Powell, 2nd edn (Oxford: Clarendon Press, 1971).

Boyle, John, *Remarks on the Life and Writings of Dr. Jonathan Swift…In a Series of Letters…To his Son, the Honourable Hamilton Boyle* (London: A Millar; Dublin: George Faulkner, 1752).

Browne, Arthur*, Miscellaneous Sketches: or, Hints for Essays*, 2 vols. (London: G. G. and J. Robinson, J. Johnson, and R. Faulder, 1798).

Buchanan, James, *Linguæ Britannicæ vera Pronunciatio: or, a New English Dictionary* (London: A. Millar, 1757).

Burke, Edmund, *Reflections on the Revolution in France*, ed. C. C. O'Brien (Harmondsworth: Penguin, 1968).

Burney, Frances, *Diary & Letters of Madame D'Arblay*, eds. Charlotte Barrett and Austin Dobson, 6 vols. (London: Macmillan, 1904–5).

——, *The Early Journals and Letters of Fanny Burney*, gen. ed. Lars E. Troide (Kingston and Montreal: McGill-Queen's University Press, 1988–), III: *The Streatham Years: Part 1, 1778–1779*, eds. Lars E. Troide and Stewart J. Cooke (1994).

Burton, Robert, *The Anatomy of Melancholy*, eds. Thomas C. Faulkner, Nicolas K. Kiesling et al., 6 vols., corrected (Oxford: Oxford University Press, 1992–2000).

Byron, George Gordon, Lord, *Selected Poetry of Lord Byron*, ed. Leslie A March and (New York: Modern Library, 2001).

Callender, James Thomson, *A Critical Review of the Works of Dr Samuel Johnson* (London: T. Cadell, 1783).

——, *Deformities of Dr. Samuel Johnson. Selected from his Works* (Edinburgh: W. Creech, T. Longman, 1782).

Carlyle, Thomas, *Works of Thomas Carlyle* (*Centenary Edition*), ed. H. D. Traill, 30 vols. (London: Chapman and Hall, 1897–1904).

Coleridge, Samuel Taylor, *Coleridge's Miscellaneous Criticism*, ed. Thomas Middleton Raysor (London: Constable & Co., 1936).

——, *Coleridge's Shakespearean Criticism*, ed. Thomas Middleton Raysor, 2 vols. (London: Dent, 1960).

Cumberland, Richard, *Memoirs of Richard Cumberland. Written by Himself*, 2 vols. (London: Lackington Allen, 1806–7).

Dennis, John, *The Critical Works of John Dennis*, ed. Edward Niles Hooker, 2 vols. (Baltimore, MD: Johns Hopkins University Press, 1939–43).

Dodsley, Robert, *A Collection of Poems. By Several Hands*. 3 vols. (London: R. Dodsley, 1748; 4th edn, 4 vols, 1755).

——, *A Collection of Poems. By Several Hands*, ed. Michael Suarez (London: Routledge/Thoemmes Press, 1997).

[Drake, Judith], *An Essay in Defence of the Female Sex* (London: A. Roper, E. Wilkinson, and R. Clavel, 1696; 3rd edn, 1697).

Dryden, John, *The Works of John Dryden*, eds. H. T. Swedenberg, Jr. et al., 20 vols. (Berkeley and Los Angeles, CA, and London: University of California Press, 1956–2002).

[Duncombe, John], 'Impartial and Critical Review of New Publications,' *The Gentleman's Magazine* 51 (1781), 271–82.

Elstob, Elizabeth, *The Rudiments of Grammar for the English-Saxon Tongue* (London: W. Bowyer, 1715).

Empson, William, *Collected Poems*, ed. John Haffenden (London: Allen Lane, 2000).

Fenning, Daniel, *The Royal English Dictionary: or, a Treasury of the English Language* (London: S. Crowder, 1761).

Fisher, Anne, *An Accurate New Spelling Dictionary, and Expositor of the English Language*, 2nd edn (London: Hawes, Clarke, and Collins, 1773).

Freud, Sigmund, *The Standard Edition of the Complete Works of Sigmund Freud*, eds. James Strachey et al., 24 vols. (London: Hogarth Press and the Institute of Psychoanalysis, 1953–74).

Garrick, David, 'Upon Johnson's Dictionary,' *The Gentleman's Magazine* 25 (1755), 190.

Goldsmith, Oliver, *Collected Works of Oliver Goldsmith*, ed. Arthur Friedman, 5 vols. (Oxford: Clarendon Press, 1966).

Gould, Robert, *A Satyrical Epistle to the Female Author of a Poem, call'd Silvia's Revenge* (London: R. Bentley, 1691).

Gray, Thomas, William Collins, and Oliver Goldsmith, *The Poems of Thomas Gray, William Collins, Oliver Goldsmith*, ed. Roger Lonsdale (London and Harlow: Longmans, Green, and Co., 1969).

Halley, Edmond, *Correspondence and Papers of Edmond Halley*, ed. Eugene Fairfield MacPike (Oxford: Clarendon Press, 1932).

Hammond, A., ed., *A New Miscellany of Original Poems* (London: T. Jauncy, 1720).

[Hawkesworth, John], 'Some Account of a Dictionary of the ENGLISH LANGUAGE,' *The Gentleman's Magazine* 25 (1755), 147–51.

Hawkins, John, *The Life of Samuel Johnson, LL.D.*, ed. O M Brack, Jr. (Athens, GA: University of Georgia Press, 2009).

Hazlitt, William, *The Complete Works of William Hazlitt in Twenty-One Volumes: Centenary Edition*, ed. P. P. Howe (London: J. M. Dent, 1930–4).

Heidegger, Martin, *Being and Time*, trans. John Macquarrie and Edward Robinson (Oxford: Blackwell, 1962).

Herbert, George, *The Works of George Herbert*, ed. F. E. Hutchinson (Oxford: Clarendon Press, 1941).

[Heyrick, Elizabeth], *Observations on the Offensive and Injurious Effect of Corporal Punishment* (London: Hatchard and Son; Hurst, Chance, 1827).

Hill, George Birkbeck, ed., *Johnsonian Miscellanies*, 2 vols. (Oxford: Clarendon Press, 1897).

*The Holy Bible, containing the Old and New Testaments translated out of the Original Tongues*, 4 vols., trans. Benjamin Blayney (Oxford: T. Wright and W. Gill, 1769).

Hooker, Richard, *The Folger Library Edition of the Works of Richard Hooker*, general ed. W. Speed Hill, 5 vols. (Cambridge, MA, and London: Harvard University Press, 1977–90).

Horace, *The Odes and Epodes of Horace*, trans. Charles E. Bennett (London and Cambridge, MA: William Heinemann and Harvard University Press, 1952).

Iliffe, Rob, Milo Keynes, and Rebekah Higgitt, eds., *Early Biographies of Isaac Newton, 1660–1885*, 2 vols. (London: Pickering & Chatto, 2006).

James, Henry, *The Art of the Novel: Critical Prefaces*, ed. Richard P. Blackmur (New York: Scribner's, 1962).

James, P. D., *Time to Be in Earnest: A Fragment of Autobiography* (London: Faber and Faber, 1999).

James, William, *The Principles of Psychology*, 2 vols. (New York: Dover, 1950).

Johnson, Samuel, *The Yale Edition of the Works of Samuel Johnson*, eds. John Middendorf et al. (New Haven, CT, and London: Yale University Press, 1958–).

I: *Diaries, Prayers, and Annals*, ed. E. L. McAdam, Jr., with Donald and Mary Hyde (1958).

II: *The Idler and The Adventurer*, eds. W. J. Bate, John M. Bullit, and L. F. Powell, 2nd edn (1970).

III–V: *The Rambler*, eds. W. J. Bate and Albrecht B. Strauss (1969).

VI: *Poems*, ed. E. L. McAdam, Jr., with George Milne (1964; repr. 1975).

VII–VIII: *Johnson on Shakespeare*, ed. Arthur Sherbo (1969).

IX: *A Journey to the Western Islands of Scotland*, ed. Mary Lascelles (1971).

X: *Political Writings*, ed. Donald J. Greene (1977).

XIV: *Sermons*, eds. Jean Hagstrum and James Gray (1978).

XVI: *Rasselas and Other Tales*, ed. Gwin J. Kolb (1990).

XVII: *A Commentary on Mr. Pope's Principles of Morality, or Essay on Man (A Translation from the French)*, ed. O M Brack, Jr. (2004).

XVIII: *Johnson on the English Language*, eds. Gwin J. Kolb and Robert DeMaria, Jr. (2005).

XXI–III: *The Lives of the Poets*, ed. John H. Middendorf (2010).

——, *A Dictionary of the English Language; in which the words are deduced from their originals and illustrated in their different significations by examples from the best writers* (London: J. and P. Knapton, T. and T. Longman, C. Hitch and L. Hawes, A. Millar, and R. and J. Dodsley, 1755).

——, *A Dictionary of the English Language . . . Abstracted from the Folio Edition*, 2 vols. (London: J. Knapton, 1756).

——, *A Dictionary of the English Language*, 2 vols, 4th edn (London: William Strahan et al., 1773).

——, *A Dictionary of the English Language on CD.ROM, the First and Fourth Editions*, ed. Anne McDermott (Cambridge: Cambridge University Press, 1996).

——, *An Account of an Attempt to Ascertain the Longitude at Sea . . . by Zachariah Williams* (London: R. Dodsley, 1755).

——, 'Dissertation on the Epitaphs Written by Pope,' *The Universal Visiter, and Monthly Memorialist* V (1756), 207–19.

——, *Early Biographical Writings of Dr. Johnson*, ed. J. D. Fleeman (Farnborough: Gregg International, 1973).

——, *The Letters of Samuel Johnson: The Hyde Edition*, ed. Bruce Redford, 5 vols. (Princeton, NJ: Princeton University Press, 1992–4).

——, 'The Life of Dr. Herman Boerhaave, late Professor of Physic in the University of Leyden in Holland,' *The Gentleman's Magazine* 9 (1739), 37–8, 72–3, 114–16, 172–6.

——, *Life of Savage*, ed. Clarence Tracy (Oxford: Clarendon Press, 1971).

——, *The Lives of the Most Eminent English Poets; with Critical Observations on their Works*, ed. Roger Lonsdale, 4 vols. (Oxford: Clarendon Press, 2006).

——, *The Poems of Samuel Johnson*, eds. David Nichol Smith and Edward L. McAdam, 2nd edn, rev. J. D. Fleeman (Oxford: Clarendon Press, 1974).

——, *The Poetical Works of Samuel Johnson, LL.D.*, ed. George Kearsley (London: George Kearsley, 1785).

——, *Samuel Johnson: The Complete English Poems*, ed. J. D. Fleeman (Harmondsworth: Penguin, 1971).

——, *Samuel Johnson's Prefaces and Dedications*, ed. Allen T. Hazen (New Haven, CT, and London: Yale University Press, 1937).

Kant, Immanuel, *Critique of Judgment*, trans. Werner S. Pluhar (Indianapolis, IN: Hackett, 1987).

Kelty, Mary Ann, *Loneliness and Leisure: A Record of the Thoughts and Feelings of Advanced Life* (London: Hamilton, Adams, 1866).

Kipling, Rudyard, *The Oxford Authors: Rudyard Kipling*, ed. Daniel Karlin (Oxford: Oxford University Press, 1999).

Leclerc, George-Louis [Comte de Buffon], *Discours sur le style* (1753), in *Oeuvres Complètes de Buffon*, ed. F. D. Pillot, 28 vols. (Paris: Salmon, 1829).

Lennox, Charlotte, *The Female Quixote*, ed. Margaret Anne Doody (Oxford: Oxford World's Classics, 1989).

'List of Books, — with Remarks', *The Gentleman's Magazine* 45 (1775), 81–93.

Marchant, John, *A New Complete, English Dictionary, Peculiarly Adapted to the Instruction and Improvement of those who have not had the Benefit of a Learned or Liberal Education* (London: J. Fuller, 1760).

Martin, Benjamin, *Lingua Britannica Reformata: or, a New English Dictionary* (London: J. Hodges, 1749).

Marvell, Andrew. *The Oxford Authors: Andrew Marvell*, eds. Frank Kermode and Keith Walker (Oxford: Oxford University Press, 1990).

Maxwell, John, *A Letter from a Friend in England To Mr. Maxwell, Complaining of his Dilatoriness in the Publication of his So-Long-Promised Work* (Dublin: S. Powell, 1755).

Miłosz, Czesław, *The Land of Ulro*, trans. Louis Iribarne (New York: Farrar, Straus, and Giroux, 1984).

Newton, Isaac, *Observations upon the Prophecies of Daniel, and the Apocalypse of St. John*, ed. Benjamin Smith (London: J. Roberts, J. Tonson et al., 1733).

Ogilvie, John, *Philosophical and Critical Observations on the Nature, Characters, and Various Species of Composition*, 2 vols. (London: for G. Robinson, 1774).

Philips, Katherine, *Poems* (London: R. Marriott, 1664).

Pope, Alexander, *The Twickenham Edition of the Poems of Alexander Pope*, ed. John Butt, 11 vols. (London: Methuen, 1939–69).

I: *Pastoral Poetry and An Essay on Criticism*, eds. E. Audra and Aubrey Williams (1961).

III.i: *An Essay on Man* (1733–4), ed. Maynard Mack (1950).

VII: *The Iliad of Homer*, ed. Maynard Mack (1967).

Roberts, David, ed., *Lord Chesterfield's Letters* (Oxford: Oxford University Press, 1992).

Rolt, Richard, *A New Dictionary of Trade and Commerce* (London: T. Osborne and J. Shipton, 1756).

Rowe, Elizabeth Singer, *The Miscellaneous Works in Prose and Verse of Mrs Elizabeth Rowe... To which are added, Poems on Several Occasions, by Mr. Thomas Rowe*, 2 vols. (London: R. Hett and R. Dodsley, 1739).

Shakespeare, William, *The Plays of William Shakespeare*, ed. Samuel Johnson, 8 vols. (London: Jacob and Richard Tonson et al., 1765).

Shaw, William, and Hester Lynch Piozzi, *William Shaw, Memoirs of the Life and Writings of the Late Dr. Samuel Johnson; Hester Lynch Piozzi, Anecdotes of the Late Samuel Johnson, LL.D.*, ed. Arthur Sherbo (London: Oxford University Press, 1974).

Smart, Christopher, *The Poetical Works of Christopher Smart*, 6 vols. (Oxford: Clarendon Press, 1980–96), I: *Jubilate Agno*, ed. Karina Williamson (1980).

Smith, Adam, 'A Dictionary of the English Language,' *The Edinburgh Review* 1 (1755), 61–73.

Spence, Joseph, *Observations, Anecdotes, and Characters of Books and Men*, ed. James M. Osborn, 2 vols. (Oxford: Clarendon Press, 1996).

[S, W.] (1749), 'The Signification of Words now Varied,' *The Gentleman's Magazine* 19 (1749), 65–6.

Swift, Jonathan, *The Cambridge Edition of the Works of Jonathan Swift*, general eds. Claude Rawson, Ian Higgins, and David Womersley, I: *Tale of a Tub and Other Works*, ed. Marcus Walsh (Cambridge: Cambridge University Press, 2010).

Thrale, Hester Lynch, *Thraliana: The Diary of Mrs. Hester Lynch Thrale, Later Mrs. Piozzi, 1776–1809*, ed. Katherine C. Balderston, 2 vols., 2nd edn (Oxford: Clarendon Press, 1951).

Trimmer, Sarah, *Some Account of the Life and Writings of Mrs. Trimmer, with Original Letters, and Meditations and Prayers, Selected from Her Journal* (London: F. C. and J. Rivington and J. Johnson, and J. Hatchard, 1814).

Warton, Joseph, *An Essay on the Genius and Writings of Pope... The Fourth Edition, Corrected*, 2 vols. (London: J. Dodsley, 1782).

Warton, Thomas, *The Enthusiast: Or, The Lover of Nature. A Poem* (London: R. Dodsley, 1744).

——, *Observations on the Faerie Queene of Spenser* (London: R. and J. Dodsley, 1754).

——, *The Pleasures of Melancholy. A Poem* (London: R. Dodsley, 1747).

——, ed., *Poems upon Several Occasions... by John Milton* (London: J. Dodsley, 1785).

[Wesley, John], *The Complete English Dictionary*, 2nd edn (Bristol: William Pine, 1764).

Williams, Anna, *Miscellanies in Prose and Verse* (London: T. Davies, 1766).

[Wollstonecraft, Mary], ed., *The Female Reader, or Miscellaneous Pieces in Prose and Verse, selected from the best writers and disposed under proper heads, for the improvement of young women* (London: Joseph Johnson, 1789).

Wooll, John, *Biographical Memoirs of the Late Revd. Joseph Warton, D.D.* (London: Cadell and Davies, 1806).

Yeats, W. B., *W. B. Yeats: The Poems*, ed. Richard J. Finneran (London: Macmillan, 1983).

Young, Edward, *Conjectures on Original Composition. In a Letter to the Author of Sir Charles Grandison*, 2nd edn (London: A. Millar and R. and J. Dodsley, 1759).

## SECONDARY SOURCES

Alkon, Paul, 'Johnson and Time Criticism,' *Modern Philology* 85 (1988), 543–57.

Balderston, Katherine C., 'Johnson's Vile Melancholy,' in Frederick W. Hilles, ed., *The Age of Johnson: Essays Presented to Chauncey Brewster Tinker* (New Haven, CT: Yale University Press, 1949), 3–14.

Barnbrook, Geoffrey, 'Johnson the Prescriptivist?' in Jack Lynch and Anne McDermott, eds., *Anniversary Essays on Johnson's Dictionary* (Cambridge: Cambridge University Press, 2005), 92–112.

Basker, James, 'Myth upon Myth: Johnson, Gender, and the Misogyny Question,' *Age of Johnson* 8 (1997), 175–87.

——, 'Radical Affinities: Mary Wollstonecraft and Samuel Johnson,' in Alvaro Ribeiro and James Basker, eds., *Tradition in Transition: Women Writers, Marginal Texts, and the Eighteenth-Century Canon* (Oxford: Clarendon, 1996), 41–55.

Bate, Walter Jackson, *The Achievement of Samuel Johnson* (New York: Oxford University Press, 1955).

——, *The Burden of the Past and the English Poet* (London: Chatto & Windus, 1971).

——, *Samuel Johnson* (New York: Harcourt Brace Jovanovich, 1977).

Boulton, James T. ed., *Samuel Johnson: The Critical Heritage* (London: Routledge, 1971).

Bowers, Fredson, 'The Text of Johnson,' *Modern Philology* 61 (1964), 298–309.

Brewer, Charlotte, ' "Happy Copiousness"? *OED*'s Recording of Female Authors of the Eighteenth Century,' *Review of English Studies* (forthcoming).

——, 'The *OED*'s Treatment of Female-Authored Sources of the Eighteenth Century,' in *Current Issues in Late Modern English*, eds. Ingrid Tieken Boone van Ostade and Wim van der Wurff (Bern: Peter Lang, 2009), 209–38.

——, 'The Use of Literary Quotations in the *OED*,' *Review of English Studies* 61 (2010), 93–125.

Bronson, Bertrand H., 'The Double Tradition of Johnson,' *ELH* 18 (1951), 90–106.

——, 'Johnson Agonistes,' in *Johnson Agonistes and Other Essays* (Cambridge: Cambridge University Press, 1946), 1–52.

——, 'Personification Reconsidered,' in *New Light on Dr. Johnson: Essays on the Occasion of his 250th Birthday*, ed. Frederick W. Hilles (New Haven, CT: Yale University Press, 1959), 189–231.

Chapin, Chester, 'Johnson's Prayer for Kitty Chambers,' *Modern Language Notes* 76 (1961), 16–18.

Clifford, James L., *Dictionary Johnson* (London: Heinemann, 1980).

Clingham, Greg, ed., *The Cambridge Companion to Samuel Johnson* (Cambridge: Cambridge University Press, 1997).

Coates, Jennifer, *Women, Men and Language* (Harlow: Longman, 2004).

Collis, Maurice, *Somerville and Ross: A Biography* (London: Faber and Faber, 1968).

Davie, Donald, *The Late Augustans: Longer Poems of the Later Eighteenth Century* (London: Heineman, 1958).

Davis, Philip, 'The Future in the Instant: Hazlitt's Essay and Shakespeare,' in *Metaphysical Hazlitt: Bicentenary Essays*, eds. Upendra Natarajan, Tom Paulin, and Duncan Wu (London: Routledge, 2005).

——, *In Mind of Johnson* (London: Athlone, 1989).

——, 'Johnson's Cosmology: Vacuity and Ramification,' in *English Literature, Theology and the Curriculum*, ed. Liam Gearon (London: Cassell, 1999), 173–89.

Deelman, Christian, *The Great Shakespeare Jubilee* (London: Michael Joseph, 1964).

DeMaria, Robert, Jr., *The Life of Samuel Johnson: A Critical Biography* (Blackwell: Oxford, 1993).

——, 'Plutarch, Johnson, and Boswell: The Classical Tradition of Biography at the End of the Eighteenth Century,' in *The Eighteenth-Century Novel*, eds. Albert J. Rivero and George Justice, 6–7 [double volume] (2009), 79–102.

——, *Samuel Johnson and the Life of Reading* (Baltimore, MD; London: Johns Hopkins University Press, 1997).

Doherty, Frank, *Samuel Beckett* (London: Hutchinson, 1971).

Eliot, T. S., *On Poetry and Poets* (New York: Farrar, Straus, and Giroux, 1969).

Engell, James, *The Creative Imagination: Enlightenment to Romanticism* (Cambridge, MA: Harvard University Press, 1981).

England, Martha Winburn, *Garrick's Jubilee* (Columbus, OH: Ohio State University Press, 1964).

Fairer, David, ' "Fishes in His Water": Shenstone, Sensibility, and the Ethics of Looking,' *The Age of Johnson* 19 (2009), 129–48.

Fleeman, J. D., *A Bibliography of the Works of Samuel Johnson*, 2 vols. (Oxford: Clarendon Press, 2000).

Gardner, Howard, *Frames of Mind: The Theory of Multiple Intelligences* (New York: Basic Books, 1983).

Gove, Philip, 'Notes on Serialization and Competitive Publishing: Johnson and Bailey's Dictionaries, 1755,' *Proceedings of the Oxford Bibliographical Society* 5 (1938), 305–22.

Gray, James, *Johnson's Sermons: A Study* (Oxford: Clarendon Press, 1972).

Greene, Donald J., ' "Pictures to the Mind": Johnson and Imagery,' in *Johnson, Boswell, and their Circle: Essays Presented to Lawrence Fitzroy Powell, in Honour of his Eighty-Fourth Birthday* (Oxford: Clarendon Press, 1965), 137–58.

Greene, Donald J., *The Politics of Samuel Johnson*, 2nd edn (Athens, GA: University of Georgia Press, 1990).

Griffin, Dustin, *Literary Patronage in England* (Cambridge: Cambridge University Press, 1996).

——, 'The Rise of the Professional Author?' in *The Cambridge History of the Book in Britain*, eds. John Barnard, D. F. McKenzie, David McKitterick and I. R. Wilson, V: 1695–1830, eds. Michael F. Suarez and Michael L. Turner (Cambridge: Cambridge University Press, 2009), 132–45.

Grundy, Isobel, 'Johnson: Man of Maxims?' in *Samuel Johnson: New Critical Essays*, ed. Isobel Grundy (London: Vision; Totowa, NJ: Barnes & Noble, 1984), 13–30.

——, *Lady Mary Wortley Montagu* (Oxford: Oxford University Press, 1999).

——, 'Samuel Johnson as Patron of Women,' *Age of Johnson* 1 (1987), 59–77.

——, 'Samuel Johnson: A Writer of Lives Looks at Death,' *Modern Language Review* 79 (1984), 257–65.

Guest, Harriet, *A Form of Sound Words: The Religious Poetry of Christopher Smart* (Oxford: Clarendon Press, 1989).

Hagstrum, Jean, 'Johnson and the *Concordia Discors* of Human Relationships,' in *The Unknown Samuel Johnson*, eds. John J. Burke, Jr. and Donald Kay (Madison, WI: University of Wisconsin Press, 1983), 39–53.

Hanks, Patrick, 'Johnson and Modern Lexicography,' *International Journal of Lexicography* 18 (2005), 243–66.

Hayley, William, *The Life of Milton, in Three Parts* (London: Cadell and Davies, 1796).

Hazen, Arthur T., 'The Beauties of Johnson,' *Modern Philology* 35 (1938), 289–95.

Hill, George Birkbeck, *Dr. Johnson, His Friends and His Critics* (London: Smith, Elder, 1878).

Hopkins, David, *Conversing with Antiquity: English Poets and the Classics, from Shakespeare to Pope* (Oxford: Oxford University Press, 2010).

Iammartino, Giovanni, 'Words by Women, Words on Women in Samuel Johnson's *Dictionary of the English Language*,' in *Adventuring in Dictionaries: New Studies in the History of Lexicography*, ed. John Considine (Newcastle upon Tyne: Cambridge Scholars Publishing, 2010), 94–125.

Isles, Duncan, 'The Lennox Collection,' *Harvard Library Bulletin* 18 (1970), 317–44.

——, 'The Lennox Collection (*Continued*),' *Harvard Library Bulletin* 19 (1971), 36–60, 165–86.

——, 'The Lennox Collection (*Concluded*),' *Harvard Library Bulletin* 19 (1971), 416–35.

Johnston, Freya, *Samuel Johnson and the Art of Sinking 1709–1791* (Oxford and New York: Oxford University Press, 2005).

——, 'Savage, Richard (1697/8–1743),' *Oxford Dictionary of National Biography* (Oxford: Oxford University Press, 2004; online edn, Jan 2008).

Kinney, Arthur F., 'Continental Poetics,' in *A Companion to Rhetoric and Rhetorical Criticism*, eds. Walter Jost and Wendy Olmsted (Oxford: Blackwell, 2004), 80–95.

Knox, Vicesimus, *Essays Moral and Literary*, 2 vols. (London: Charles Dilly, 1782).

Kolb, Gwin and James Sledd, 'Johnson's "Dictionary" and Lexicographical Tradition,' *Modern Philology* 50 (1953), 171–94.

Korshin, Paul, ed., *Jacobitism and Eighteenth-Century English Literature*, ELH 64 (1997).

——, 'Johnson and the Renaissance Dictionary,' *Journal of the History of Ideas* 35 (1974), 300–12.

Kuist, James M., *The Nichols File of the Gentleman's Magazine: Attributions of Authorship and Other Documentation in Editorial Papers at the Folger Library* (Madison, WI: University of Wisconsin Press, 1982).

Lipking, Lawrence, *Samuel Johnson: The Life of an Author* (Cambridge, MA: Harvard University Press, 1998).

Lovejoy, A. O., *The Great Chain of Being: A Study of the History of an Idea* (Cambridge, MA: Harvard University Press, 1936).

Martin, Peter, *Samuel Johnson: A Biography* (London: Weidenfeld and Nicolson, 2008).

McDermott, Anne, 'Johnson's "Dictionary" and the Canon: Authors and Authority,' *The Yearbook of English Studies* 28 (1998), 44–65.

McGilchrist, Iain, *Against Criticism* (London: Faber and Faber, 1982).

——, *The Master and his Emissary: The Divided Brain and the Making of the Western World* (New Haven, CT, and London: Yale University Press, 2009).

McHenry, Lawrence C., 'Samuel Johnson's Tics and Gesticulations,' *Journal of the History of Medicine* 22 (1967), 152–68.

Meyers, Jeffrey, *Samuel Johnson: The Struggle* (New York: Basic Books, 2008).

Moody, A. D., 'Johnson's Poems: Textual Problems and Critical Readings,' *The Library*, 5th ser., 26 (1971), 22–38.

Mugglestone, Lynda, 'The Dictionary as Watch,' *The New Rambler*, (2007–8), 70–7.

——, 'Registering the Language—Dictionaries, Diction, and the Art of Elocution,' in *Eighteenth-Century English: Ideology and Change*, ed. Raymond Hickey (Cambridge: Cambridge University Press, 2010), 309–38.

Murray, James A. H., *The Evolution of Lexicography* (Oxford: Clarendon Press, 1900).

Nussbaum, Felicity, *The Brink of All We Hate: English Satires on Women, 1660–1750* (Lexington, KY: University Press of Kentucky, 1984).

Osborn, James M., 'Johnson on the Sanctity of an Author's Text,' *PMLA* 50 (1935), 928–9.

Overholt, John, and Thomas A. Horrocks, *A Monument More Durable Than Brass: The Donald & Mary Hyde Collection of Dr. Samuel Johnson. An Exhibition* (Houghton Library, Cambridge, MA: Harvard University Press, 2009).

Parker, Fred, *Scepticism and Literature: An Essay on Pope, Hume, Sterne, and Johnson* (Oxford: Oxford University Press, 2003).

Paulin, Tom, *The Day-Star of Liberty: William Hazlitt's Radical Style* (London: Faber and Faber, 1998).

Pearce, J. M. S., 'Doctor Samuel Johnson: "The Great Convulsionary" a Victim of Gilles de la Tourette's Syndrome,' *Journal of the Royal Society of Medicine* 87 (1994), 396–9.

Phillips, Adam, *Going Sane* (London: Penguin, 2006).

Porter, Roy, *Flesh in the Age of Reason: The Modern Foundation of Body and Soul* (New York: W. W. Norton, 2003).

Potter, Robert, *The Art of Criticism; as Exemplified in Dr. Johnson's Lives of the Most Eminent English Poets* (London: T. Hookham, 1789).

Quinlan, Maurice, *Samuel Johnson: A Layman's Religion* (Madison, WI: University of Wisconsin Press, 1964).

Quinton, Anthony, 'Spaces and Times,' *Philosophy* 37 (1962), 130–47.

Read, Allen Walker, 'The Contemporary Quotations in Johnson's Dictionary,' *English Literary History* 2 (1935), 246–51.

Reddick, Allen, *The Making of Johnson's Dictionary, 1746–1773*, rev. edn (Cambridge: Cambridge University Press, 1996).

Reid, Hugh, ' "The Want of a Closer Union …:" The Friendship of Samuel Johnson and Joseph Warton,' *The Age of Johnson* 9 (1998), 133–43.

Ricks, Christopher, *Allusion to the Poets* (Oxford: Oxford University Press, 2002).

Sacks, Arieh, 'Samuel Johnson on "The Art of Forgetfulness," ' *Studies in Philology* 63 (1966), 578–88.

Schreyer, Rüdiger, 'Illustrations of Authority: Quotations in Samuel Johnson's *Dictionary of the English Language*,' *Lexicographica* 16 (2010), 58–103.

Sherman, Stuart, *Telling Time: Clocks, Diaries, and English Diurnal Form, 1660–1785* (Chicago, IL, and London: University of Chicago Press, 1996).

Shoemaker, Robert, *Gender in English Society, 1650–1850* (London: Longman, 1998).

Smith, Hannah, 'English "Feminist" Writings and Judith Drake's "An Essay in Defence of the Female Sex" (1696),' *The Historical Journal* 44 (2001), 727–47.

Sobel, Dava, *Longitude: The True Story of a Lone Genius who Solved the Greatest Scientific Problem of his Time* (London: Fourth Estate, 1995).

Steen, Jane, 'Samuel Johnson's Anglicanism and the Art of Translation,' *The New Rambler* (2007–8), 49–51.

Stochholm, Johanne Magdalene, *Garrick's Folly: The Shakespeare Jubilee of 1769 at Stratford and Drury Lane* (London: Methuen, 1964).

Tracy, Clarence, *The Artificial Bastard: A Biography of Richard Savage* (Cambridge, MA: Harvard University Press, 1953).

Vance, John, 'Samuel Johnson and Thomas Warton,' *Biography* 9 (1986), 95–111.

Vickers, Brian, ed., *Shakespeare: The Critical Heritage*, 6 vols. (London: Routledge & Kegan Paul, 1974–81).

Wasserman, Earl R., 'The Inherent Values of Eighteenth-Century Personification,' *PMLA* 65 (1950), 435–63.

Watkins, W. B. C., *Perilous Balance: The Tragic Genius of Swift, Johnson, and Sterne* (Princeton, NJ: Princeton University Press, 1939).

Weinbrot, Howard D., *Aspects of Samuel Johnson: Essays on his Arts, Mind, Afterlife, and Politics* (Newark, NJ: University of Delaware Press, 2005).

Westburg, Daniel, *Right Practical Reason: Aristotle, Action, and Prudence in Aquinas* (Oxford: Oxford University Press, 1994).

Westfall, Richard S., *Never at Rest: A Biography of Isaac Newton* (Cambridge: Cambridge University Press, 1980).

Wiltshire, John, *Samuel Johnson in the Medical World: The Doctor and the Patient* (Cambridge: Cambridge University Press, 1991).

Wimsatt, W. K., Jr., *Philosophic Words: A Study of Style and Meaning in the Rambler and Dictionary of Samuel Johnson* (New Haven, CT: Yale University Press, 1948).

——, *The Prose Style of Samuel Johnson*, 2nd edn (New Haven, CT: Yale University Press, 1963).

# Index